Also by Heather Rogers

Gone Tomorrow: The Hidden Life of Garbage

GREEN GONE WRONG

Dispatches from the Front Lines
of Eco-Capitalism

Heather Rogers

V

VERSO

First published in the UK by Verso 2010
© Heather Rogers

1 3 5 7 9 10 8 6 4 2

Verso
UK: 6 Meard Street, London W1F 0EG
US: 20 Jay Street, Suite 1010, Brooklyn, NY 11201
www.versobooks.com

Verso is the imprint of New Left Books

ISBN-13: 978-1-84467-901-0

British Library Cataloguing in Publication Data
A catalogue record for this book is available from the British Library

Typeset in Minion Pro by Hewer Text UK Ltd, Edinburgh
Printed in Sweden by Scandbook AB

To my family

Contents

GREEN GONE WRONG

INTRODUCTION

Green Dreams

The riots started in early 2007. The first country to erupt was Mexico. In just one year the price of corn, the key ingredient in tortillas, had shot up more than 80 percent. Suddenly, not just the poorest but also wage earners were unable to put food on the table. Tens of thousands of workers and peasants angrily took to the streets, marching down Mexico City's main thoroughfare to the famous Zócalo, setting off what came to be called the "tortilla riots." To quell the uproar, Mexican president Felipe Calderón was forced to announce a price freeze on corn. In the ensuing months the world convulsed with violent unrest in over thirty countries, including Egypt, Somalia, Colombia, Indonesia, Thailand, Vietnam, Cameroon, and Haiti. The sometimes deadly protests were set in motion by a global food crisis triggered in part by the diversion of food crops to refineries making plant-based transportation fuels known as biofuels. Considered ecologically sustainable, biofuels can substitute for fossil fuels, thereby cutting emissions of carbon dioxide, a major contributor to global warming. However, today's eco-friendly fuel is made from edible crops such as corn, soybeans, sugarcane, and palm oil (a vegetable oil); thanks to subsidies and the high price of oil, at that time selling crops for biofuels offered a bigger return than selling them for food, so growers and agribusiness followed the money.

By the spring of 2008 food prices peaked further still, having surged by more than 50 percent from the year before. Discontent ignited across the globe as grocery bills went through the roof. The cost of vegetable oils, wheat, rice, and other basics soared well beyond reach in developing countries, where many people spend half or more of their income to keep their families fed. As strife over rising prices intensified, more than forty people were killed in Cameroon. In Haiti, the prime minister was ousted and at least four rioters were shot and killed amid street protests

1

over the scarcity and escalating costs of food. In China, a stampede at a supermarket that had discounted its prices left three shoppers dead and another thirty-one injured. Small vendors in outdoor markets in Indonesia sold vegetable oil that appeared new but was used; the dark color from cooking was eliminated by adding household bleach, which buyers would unwittingly ingest.

As the terrible social impacts of crop-based biofuels grew more acute, questions also began arising about their supposed environmental benefits. People such as David Pimentel, professor of ecology and agriculture at Cornell University, claimed it required more energy to grow and refine corn ethanol than the alt-fuel could provide. According to assessments such as Pimentel's, corn ethanol was a net loser when it came to preventing carbon dioxide emissions. In other arenas environmental groups such as the Rainforest Action Network and Friends of the Earth were already campaigning against the supposedly eco-friendly fuels. These organizations said escalating demand for biofuels was driving deforestation as agribusiness expanded into tropical-forest zones. Detailing these knock-on effects, two reports published in early 2008 in the journal *Science* stated that more carbon dioxide was being released into the atmosphere from the production of some biofuels than if people continued filling their tanks with gasoline and diesel.

That same year deforestation rates in Brazil shot up sharply. Similarly, Indonesia had recently earned the dubious distinction of becoming the world's third-largest carbon dioxide emitter, trailing only China and the United States. Much of Indonesia's spike in CO_2 came from clear-cutting and burning trees to make room for crops that could be refined into biofuels. Imagine millions of acres of dense rain forest teeming with the world's most diverse flora and fauna. A crew armed with chain saws and bulldozers forges a narrow path through the trees. The workers begin to rip away and flatten the forest as wildlife, including endangered species such as orangutans, flee for their lives. A bulldozer shoves innumerable splintered trees into tangled piles that stretch for miles, and crews set them alight. Ferocious fires blast through what was once a dynamic web of life, leaving behind a carbon dioxide–filled haze and a silent, charred wasteland. After the forest has been erased it's almost impossible to imagine what was once there.

Such outcomes—violent social upheaval, and the further shattering of vital ecosystems—reveal some of the dangers of taking up solutions without serious critical assessment. So how do we work toward solving the profound ecological problems we face in ways that don't make matters worse?

MORE IS LESS

From today's vantage point, 2006 was a big year. That's when global warming was finally acknowledged by the last, and very powerful, holdouts: U.S. government and industry. The city of New Orleans still lay smashed from the previous year's Hurricane Katrina—a storm that was likely intensified by the effects of global warming. Commissioned by the British government, the *Stern Review* was published, the foremost study on the grim economic impacts and financial risks of climate change. Also in 2006, Al Gore's documentary film, *An Inconvenient Truth,* helped convince the mainstream that global warming was real and the result of human activity. These events were backed up by reports from the Intergovernmental Panel on Climate Change—a global body of scientists and governments created in 1988 under the auspices of the United Nations to assess the latest atmospheric science—that confirmed industrialized society plays a significant role in creating global warming.

Newfound acceptance of the dangers of unchecked greenhouse gas emissions set off a barrage of coverage in magazines and newspapers, on talk shows and websites. Major rock groups such as the Rolling Stones, KT Tunstall, and the Dave Matthews Band started planting trees to cancel out the CO_2 released from their tours and the production of their albums. Hillary Clinton, Leonardo DiCaprio, and the pop entrepreneur Richard Branson began proselytizing about the need to take action. Even George W. Bush, the notorious global warming denier, uttered the words "climate change" in his 2007 State of the Union address.

As of 2007 global warming had become a fact of life, and growing numbers of people were looking for solutions. A news broadcast from that year, a midday edition of CNN International, typified the emerging state of affairs. The lead story featured an intrepid but well-coiffed reporter exploring catastrophic ice loss at the north pole. Visually incongruous with the blank, undulating landscape, the perky newswoman explained that temperatures were climbing faster in arctic regions than elsewhere on the planet, and at a more rapid clip than previously thought. The latest projections, she reported, said summer ice may be extinct as soon as 2040, taking several animal species with it. The follow-up segment on CNN that day was what Wal-Mart—the biggest retailer on the planet—was doing to address ecological degradation. In addition to reducing energy consumption in its stores and using more fuel-efficient trucks, the company committed to push its 180 million customers to buy more commodities it deemed helpful to the environment. As this example suggests, the dire and depressing problem of climate crisis is increasingly being answered by the next phase of environmentalism: the buying and selling of ecologically responsible products.

Not so long ago wheat germ, solar panels, and electric minicars were the purview of activists, hippies, and renegade engineers. Recently, however, a rush of fashionable responses to ecological meltdown has crowded out the previous generation's reaction—often characterized as strident and blaming. The new green wave, typified by the phrase *lazy environmentalism,* is geared toward the masses that aren't willing to sacrifice. This brand of armchair activism actualizes itself most fully in the realm of consumer goods; through buying the right products we can usher our economic system into the environmental age. The new naturalists don't reject the free market for its reckless degradation of the air, water, and soil as their forebears did. Instead they aspire to turn the forces of economic growth and development away from despoliation and toward regeneration. Couched in optimism that springs from avoiding conflict, the current approach asks why taking care of ecosystems must entail a Spartan doing without when saving the planet can be fun and relatively easy.

Over the past several years *green* has gone from just a color to indicating that something possesses what's needed to protect the earth's natural systems. *Green* is now used as a modifier to differentiate products that are healthier for the planet: green cars, green architecture, green fashion, green investing, green energy. The word has also become a verb: we can now green our homes, cars, and even our lives. Indeed green goods have become all the rage. In the decade leading up to the economic crash of 2008–9, eco-products conquered the market. Whole Foods, the all-natural grocery store chain, turned into a Wall Street darling, while such food manufacturing giants as General Mills, Kraft, and Unilever began offering organic goods. And Wal-Mart set out to make itself into a top vendor of organic groceries. During that time the organic-foods industry expanded by double digits each year, far outstripping conventional food, which remained stalled at less than 3 percent annual growth. Homebuyers' and commercial developers' demand for ecologically astute architecture continues to spread even as the real estate market overall is still struggling through its grueling recovery. Often considered a badge of honor, and in some circles a status symbol, this method of design and construction using materials that promote energy efficiency, reduce polluting emissions, diminish natural-resource degradation, and encourage more eco-friendly living is now de rigueur in the industry.

In terms of automobiles, most major carmakers now offer gas-electric hybrid models, as well as vehicles that can run on biofuels. And both Toyota and General Motors are poised to mass-produce what might be the next generation of superefficient cars: plug-in gas-electric hybrids. Although it's still unclear in what form the various auto firms will survive the industry's drastic downturn, vehicles that are more ecologically sensible have become a must. On the transportation-fuels front, after three solid years of rapid expansion, biofuel production fell into disarray in 2009 with the plummeting price of oil and the collapsing economy. Nevertheless, Big Oil and Big Ag continue pushing for transportation fuels derived from plants. BP has claimed for itself the leadership position in eco-fuels even though its investment in biofuels was negligible until 2007. That year the company poured a half billion dollars into a controversial biofuels research center at the University of California, Berkeley, which works in partnership with a lab at the University of Illinois, Urbana-Champaign. Since then BP has committed over $1.5 billion to various plant-based fuel ventures. Keeping drivers on a liquid diet via biofuels is preferable to the oil industry because it can curtail the switch to electric vehicles, which are juiced up by the competition: power plants. Coupled with ongoing mandates and subsidies in the United Kingdom, the European Union, the United States, Brazil, Indonesia, and parts of China, biofuels are clearly here to stay. More broadly, government support and funding for green-collar jobs, renewable power such as solar and wind, and energy-conservation measures promise to keep ecologically oriented industries growing. Without question a greater awareness of the environmental impacts of mass consumption is changing what's for sale.

The promise implicit in these changes is that global warming can be stopped by swapping out dirty products for green ones, with little disruption to daily life. Getting behind the wheel of a gas-electric hybrid is not so different from driving a regular car. Ethanol and biodiesel come out the nozzle the same as ordinary petrol. Eating organic breakfast cereal no longer feels unfamiliar because it's coated with sugar and comes in cartoon-covered boxes. And paying a little extra for an airline ticket to cancel out CO_2 emissions from a flight takes almost no effort at all. One of the most popular current tools to counteract the mucking up of the earth is the reusable shopping bag. Nowadays more people are bringing them along to the store so they won't need new plastic bags each time. These totes—often decorated with cheerful images of trees and animals, or sporting slogans like I AM NOT A PLASTIC BAG or I AM EARTH WISE— exemplify today's popular environmentalism. There is good that comes from using them, but they are also symbols that convey responsibility while glossing over the more significant issues of what goes into those bags, how much, and how often.

MENDING OUR WAYS

For at least twenty years the captains of industry and their operatives, together with compliant politicians, have labored to cast doubt on the majority scientific opinion that global warming is under way. For over a century scientists have recognized carbon dioxide emissions from human activities as having a warming effect on the planet. Svante Arrhenius, a Swedish chemist working at the turn of the last century, was the first to argue, in an 1896 report, that CO_2 resulting from burning fossil fuels would cause global warming. Arrhenius, a prolific researcher (albeit a prominent eugenicist), and Sweden's first Nobel Prize winner, considered higher temperatures desirable to fend off another ice age. During one of his lectures he mused, "We would then have some right to indulge in the pleasant belief that our descendants, albeit after many generations, might live under a milder sky and in less barren surroundings than is our lot at present." Sixty years after the Swede's death, James Hansen, an esteemed NASA climatologist, voiced his decidedly less rosy take on global warming as potentially highly destructive. In a dramatic episode, testifying before a Senate committee on a searingly hot summer day in 1988, Hansen told lawmakers that he believed with "ninety-nine percent confidence" that climate change was real and the world was heating up.

Today a majority of Americans agree that climate change is real despite the concerted efforts of the biggest polluters and their allies to revive doubt. This book takes as its starting point that these matters are settled—

the conversation on global warming and other grave afflictions the natural world suffers must move forward. Part of the next step is a critical assessment of solutions to ecological crisis.

I started thinking about this book as I was doing talks for my last book, which was about garbage. Almost everywhere I spoke in the United States, Canada, and the United Kingdom, at least one person in the audience would say he or she thought we could cure our environmental ills by consuming the right products. I began this project because I wasn't sure the answer was so straightforward. Ultimately, I was concerned that the remedies being promoted in the marketplace may not have the power to keep biodiversity intact and the planet cool. The following pages take the reader into forests, fields, factories, and boardrooms around the world to draw out the unintended consequences, inherent obstacles, as well as successful methods, that lie beneath the surface of environmentally friendly products. I visited a different geographical location for each chapter to piece together a global picture of what's happening in the name of today's environmentalism.

As some readers will note, all this flying and driving made no small contribution to greenhouse gas emissions. I regret the resulting environmental impacts, but not the journeys themselves. In an effort to shrink my swollen carbon footprint, which became double what it normally is, I could simply pay a CO_2 offset company to "neutralize" my greenhouse gases. But after the research I've done, I don't have the confidence that this would have the intended impact. Although the average American spits out almost twice the CO_2 of a European, and five times more than the average Chinese, none of us do so simply based on our individual choices. I've come to realize that my toxic emissions are not solely mine. Instead they are linked to a larger socioeconomic system that actually depends on pollution to maintain its well-being. As we currently keep the books, stewarding the health of the biosphere costs more than dumping and endlessly extracting from nature, so our society does the latter. Environmental depredation, it turns out, better serves the bottom line. America is the world's largest economy (for now, anyway) and its most profligate consumer; with just 5 percent of the global population the United States burns through over 20 percent of the planet's energy and, along with China, is the top emitter of greenhouse gases.

As a society over the last half century we've wavered between ecological awareness and the bliss of ignorance. This back-and-forth isn't just the outcome of stretches of greediness followed by spells of guilt—although these are factors. In the late 1960s and 1970s mounting concern over the well-being of the planet culminated in the rise of the environmental movement. But political pressure and persuasive PR that said everything was fine coming from the fossil-fuel industry and the manufacturing sector helped contain the movement's force. Public awareness reemerged in the late 1980s and early 1990s, only to be outmaneuvered by vested interests once again. Today, a popular desire to find solutions to ecological devastation has slowly worked its way back to the fore despite the repressive efforts of the richest, most powerful industries in history, namely oil. But where we direct the energy of this latest awakening is the key question. Although truly remedying global warming and its attendant ecological ills can seem insurmountable, it's not. But finding solutions that work requires us to learn what to fight for.

G*reen Gone Wrong* is structured in three parts—food, shelter, and transportation—to address the basic aspects of what we need and use in daily life.

In delving into the issue of food for Part I, I made two separate trips to investigate the implications of locally grown organic food as well as produce cultivated in faraway locales for consumption in the West. My initial destination was New York State's Hudson Valley, one of the biggest farmers' market regions among Western countries. I went to find out what day-to-day existence is like for small organic farmers who raise their crops and animals without chemicals, hormones, or antibiotics on land that's managed to maximize biodiversity. Locally raised food has captured the imagination of healthy eaters and a new generation that believes alternative cultivation can undo the damage inflicted by scorched-earth industrial agriculture. The reach of this insurgent project, however, is confined by the meager income earned by farmers who practice organic methods. For even the most successful growers, costs, including manual labor, add up fast. Although they sell the highest-priced produce around—which only a wealthier clientele can afford—many of these cultivators can barely make ends meet. While a vibrant discussion has blossomed about organic and local food as an important antidote to ecological decay, the economic struggles of small organic farmers must not go overlooked.

As consumer demand for organics exploded during the last decade, natural-foods processors and retailers began sourcing ever more produce from Latin America and Asia. To further explore the implications of ditching conventional food for organic, for chapter 2 I ventured to the South American country of Paraguay, among the world's top organic sugar producers and exporters. Organic farming is seen as a solution to global warming and ecological destruction by facilitating a widespread shift to holistic cultivation practices. But as more players enter the field, major food processors such as General Mills and retailers such as Wal-Mart are making some controversial compromises. Most crucially they rely on growers who use methods that tack back toward conventional agriculture.

Seeking the lowest costs, Western food processors and retailers increasingly source from large producers in developing countries where land and labor are cheap, and environmental protections lax. This is the case in an astounding number of places, including China, many Southeast Asian nations, and parts of Latin America. In Paraguay I found an organic sugar plantation that was violating the organic standards of the U.S. Department of Agriculture and the International Federation of Organic Agriculture Movements, a group that's considered the global authority on organic standards. Among the plantation's sketchy activities was monocropping, or the cultivation of the same crop in the same fields season after season. Farming in this way can cause dramatic erosion, exhaust the soil's nutrients, and deplete groundwater. More startlingly, I discovered what appeared to be the clearing of native forests to plant organic fields, also forbidden under international organic standards. In interviewing registered Fair Trade smallholder farmers, I found that many aren't paid the higher incomes that consumers in the West believe. In distant places the real workings of operations that call themselves organic can be obscured, leaving room for manipulation of the rules and outright fraud.

In considering the question of shelter for Part II of the book, I went to three different eco-villages, one in a London suburb and two in the German city of Freiburg. The communities I visited are considered to be some of the most ecologically sustainable and successful in the world's developed countries. For chapter 3 I found out what it's like to live on almost no energy, and the circumstances that have both created and allowed green housing to flourish in these places.

Current iterations of eco-architecture have come a long way from the earthships and geodesic domes of the 1960s and 1970s. Today's environmentally sound dwellings are straightforward and modern, more closely resembling standard housing. They often incorporate features such as energy-efficient appliances, chemical-free wall paint, and solar water-heaters. Sustainably harvested wood, lumber milled from trees extracted in a manner that doesn't degrade forests or displace forest dwellers, is a popular construction material. Green roofs are also a staple of the eco-abode. Comprised of plants, grasses, and mosses, these rooftop gardens provide an earthen blanket that cuts energy use by helping the building retain heat in the winter, and cool air in the summer. Environmentally sound homes are becoming more affordable and culturally accessible for average people—not just the committed hippie or wealthy maverick. Perhaps surprisingly, buildings account for almost 40 percent of CO_2 emissions in the United States; the fossil fuels, primarily coal, used to light, heat, and cool them are the top source of greenhouse gases. The communities I visited in the UK and Germany have achieved major reductions in CO_2 levels while creating highly functional, comfortable dwellings. So how do they do it, and what's keeping this architecture from spreading to more places?

Since transportation involves fuel, vehicles, and emissions, I made three different stops for Part III of the book. As the 2007–8 riots revealed, crop-based biofuels wreck food supplies, but they also strain the earth's vital ecosystems. For chapter 4 I journeyed to Indonesia, the world's top producer of palm oil, which is an increasingly important raw material for biodiesel. Much of this oil comes from plantations established on the incinerated ruins of clear-cut tropical rain forests on the Indonesian island of Borneo. The island comprises carbon-rich forests that are the sole remaining viable habitat for the critically endangered orangutan, and home to ancient indigenous societies including Dayaks. With some of the last large rain forests on the planet, Borneo's natural systems are integral to maintaining global atmospheric carbon balance. Regardless, the clear-cutting continues apace thanks in large part to biofuel mandates and targets in the world's biggest economies.

For chapter 5 I visited Detroit, historically the nerve center of the auto industry. There I sought out why the major automakers in the United States—the world's leading vehicle market from the industry's inception until late 2009—have confined less environmentally destructive cars to the sidelines. When Toyota launched the Prius in Japan in 1997 and in the United States and Europe three years later, it was a surprise hit. Yet the vast majority of cars the big automakers continue producing run on gas and diesel, as will likely be the case for decades to come. With the

Obama administration strengthening fuel economy standards from 27.5 mpg in 2009 to 35.5 by 2016, it would appear we're on the right track. While higher efficiency is good, consider that American firms profitably make and sell fuel-frugal cars overseas—some that get over 80 mpg—and the change seems feeble at best.

We know that burning fossil fuels is the number one source of carbon dioxide, so why don't car companies give U.S. drivers a cleaner set of wheels? Many people believe the Detroit Three—Ford, General Motors, and Chrysler—bury ecologically responsible vehicle technology to ward off change. After all, General Motors, as portrayed in the documentary film *Who Killed the Electric Car?*, scotched its first viable electric-car program after only a few years. The problem of getting more green rides on the road is not simply technological. Despite what we're so often told—"the right technology is just around the corner"—highly efficient cars already exist. We're still driving gas-guzzlers because green vehicles aren't profitable enough. Another crucial piece of the story is the complicity of consumers. Given that the first Ford Model T built in 1909 got 26 mpg, why have drivers accepted, even embraced, lackluster fuel economy?

The situation looks set to shift as a new green wave washes over the struggling auto industry, bringing with it more efficient cars. At the forefront was the Prius, while the latest rising star is GM's new Chevy Volt. The car is a higher-tech gas-electric hybrid that the company says will get a staggering 230 mpg. Sounds great, but this mpg can only be achieved under specific conditions; depending on how it's driven, according to Edmunds.com, the Volt can also get a perplexingly low 38.3 mpg. Charging our vehicles from the grid presents further, and paramount, questions about just how eco-friendly automobiles can really be. In 2007 electricity generation accounted for 42 percent of the U.S.'s total carbon dioxide output. Until the grid is juiced up with renewable energy from sources such as wind and solar, we will not have solved the problem.

When all else fails, consumers can turn to a new type of service that promises to expunge their CO_2 after it has been released. Companies claiming they can balance out pollution from fossil-fuel-intensive activities such as airplane flights and road trips sell what are called carbon offsets. Consumers pay a fee based on how much CO_2 they create, and the offset firm channels that money to projects such as planting trees and constructing renewable energy facilities. To find out how and if counteracting CO_2 works, for chapter 6 I went to India, which hosts more than 25 percent of carbon-offset projects globally. I discovered that some projects don't seem to be happening at all, some are poorly implemented, and others are causing additional ecological damage. Such outcomes easily go unnoticed, however, because the voluntary industry is wholly unregulated. Critics argue that the overall offset system is flawed because it's impossible to truly rub out carbon. Even if it is, the greenhouse gas certainly won't be neutralized immediately, but only over the duration of an offset project. For example, say a consumer buys offsets for a flight and the money goes toward a reforestation project. The CO_2 balance from that person's travel will only be settled over the lifetime of the trees, which, depending on the species, can be as long as thirty, fifty, one hundred years, or more. Meanwhile, these greenhouse gases don't disappear, but linger in the atmosphere at precisely the moment we need to contain pollution. Carbon emitted today cannot be wiped out today, if at all, even though most buyers believe otherwise.

With widespread acceptance of the problem of global warming, a torrent of responses has issued forth from pent-up environmentalists, eco-entrepreneurs, and government. President Barack Obama's 2009 stimulus package, the American Recovery and Reinvestment Plan, outlines unprecedented spending on a range of more ecologically sound solutions. As a result, the emerging green marketplace, including organic food, energy-efficient homes, biofuels, green cars, and CO_2 offsetting, will only continue to grow. Crucially, these new products reflect people's irrepressible desire to know the processes that lie behind the things they use in daily life. More consumers now look for the Certified Organic label, Fair Trade seal, or any of the other myriad emblems—referred to as "trust marks" in the branding industry—guaranteeing a more ecologically and morally pure provenance. But these stamps, meant to illuminate, can often obscure ongoing destructive practices. As ecological remedies such as the ones covered in this book become mainstream, people will increasingly want and need to know more. Green Gone Wrong doesn't consider all of the potential cures, such as green jobs and weatherizing existing buildings, but the ground it does cover will hopefully provide a useful perspective that can be applied in these other spheres.

Green Gone Wrong is an appeal to the reader to take the evolving environmental crisis as an opportunity. If we can step back and honestly assess our options, we will make better decisions than we have in the past. We could take any number of approaches to investigate where to go from here, such as looking back: what choices and structural forces led us to this perilous place? While history is crucial, this book focuses primarily on the present. Investigating current remedies allows for an exploration of whether today's most popular solutions are up to the task. Some might interpret the findings of this investigation as discouraging. "If these solutions don't work, then nothing will!" But there is a difference between hope and false hope. *Green Gone Wrong* is an attempt to further the discussion so that we can broaden the possibilities and focus on remedies that bring results. Fundamentally, this book arises from the belief that we have the capacity to find solutions that are not simply products to buy, but ways of engaging with how we live and what we want our world to be.

PART I

Food

CHAPTER ONE

Close to Home:
Local Organic

Just as the summer sun rises, dozens of independent growers from the surrounding region unpack their trucks and vans and set up stalls to sell fresh vegetables, fruit, meat, fish, cheese, bread, honey, and flowers. They're at the Union Square Greenmarket in New York City, the gem in the crown of the city's more than one hundred farmers' markets, one of the biggest such networks in the United States. Some farm stands take up more space than others; some resemble lean-tos, with weathered sunshades pitched against box trucks lettered with names such as EVOLUTIONARY ORGANICS. Other stands are sleeker, sheltered by new white canopies that cast an even, dispersed light onto the piles of fruits and vegetables on tables below: frilly squash blossoms, bright radishes, wild spinach, and heirloom tomatoes with their full flesh folding in on itself. This produce bears little resemblance to the standardized, homogenous grocery store fare. The variegated farm stalls line the western edge of this bustling urban plaza—the type of place where, in the years before agribusiness and processed foods, farmers and shoppers would have come for exactly the same purpose.

Farmers' markets such as the one in Union Square seem to summon a feeling of ethical alignment, important amid today's global-warming-conscious environmentalism: buying here means doing the right thing. At the market it's possible to meet the people who grow the food, ask what methods they use, and directly support their efforts. Purchasing this produce then becomes a means of defending nature by supporting an agricultural system that's more ecologically sustainable, one that rejects toxic agrochemicals, uses less energy, is less polluting, and promotes long-term soil health. Short of growing it oneself, the greenmarket is as virtuous as it gets.

In recent years, farmers' markets have surged in popularity in the

United States, up by more than 150 percent, from just under two thousand in 1994 to well over five thousand last year. In 2005 revenues from farmers' markets topped $1 billion, while the following year overall U.S. sales of natural and organic products exceeded $17 billion. As of 2007 the global organic market was worth $48 billion. Greater public awareness of "food miles," the distance groceries travel from field to dinner plate, and the greenhouse-gas-emitting transport this requires, has triggered an urgent call to eat locally. Surging interest in healthy food grown close to home coupled with fear over ecological disaster has brought down a cascade of criticism of industrial agriculture, or what is oddly referred to as "conventional farming." Emerging from the storm are local organic growers, now cast as heroes who have the power to overturn the environmental catastrophe that is conventional agriculture.

Over the past half century the dominant food system in the West has based itself on a toxic model. Crops are grown on landscapes remade as flat expanses of biological minimalism, swept clean of most life-forms by use of petrochemical pesticides. These swaths are made to fruit at the behest not of natural cycles but synthetic fertilizers and profligate irrigation. (According to the *Economist* magazine, "Farming accounts for roughly 70% of human water consumption.") Similarly, industrial farming has transformed animal husbandry into a practice more akin to mass assembly-line production. It is saturated with chemically engineered antibiotics and growth hormones that render animals so malformed—to bulk up quickly for higher profits—that the sheer weight of their musculature can make them lame.

The fallout from conventional agriculture can be devastating. Synthetic fertilizers typically contain high levels of nitrogen and phosphorus, much of which eventually washes into coastal waters where it fuels rampant algae growth. Algal blooms colonize these aquatic systems, sapping them of oxygen, thereby suffocating fish and most other marine life. These mass underwater "dead zones" now plague large areas in the Gulf of Mexico, up and down the U.S. East Coast, the Baltic and Black seas, and are beginning to choke the waters off Australia, South America, China, and Japan.

In addition to flowing into rivers, lakes, and oceans, pesticides also linger as residues on food. A U.S. Department of Agriculture (USDA) survey found that out of eight fruit and twelve vegetable crops assessed, 73–90 percent were contaminated by pesticides. And almost half of the items tested had residues from multiple chemicals, compounding toxicity. A 2009 study on whether organic food is more nutritious, and therefore healthier, than conventional edibles showed no significant difference between the two. However, according to a report in the *Guardian* (UK), the researchers perplexingly did not factor fertilizer and pesticide residues that persist on conventionally grown food into their calculations. The most commonly used agricultural pesticides wreak havoc on human health, affecting the nervous system, harming the skin, eyes, and lungs, causing a variety of cancers as well as genetic damage, and impairing reproductive organs and normal hormone functions. Rejecting the food establishment that aims to conquer ecosystems, today's small farmers are building an agriculture that's fundamentally compatible with nature.

But this change doesn't come cheap. It's no mystery that food raised locally and without chemicals, hormones, or antibiotics costs more, sometimes a lot more. Among the chemical-free growers at Union Square, one sells milk for $20 a gallon and eggs for $14 a dozen; another offers tomatoes for $5 a pound, and still another marks leafy greens at almost $20 per pound (in winter, the same vegetables raised in greenhouses can ring in at over double that). As for meat, one Union Square farm sells its naturally raised Italian pork sausage for $12.50 per pound. Compared to meat and vegetables at the conventional grocery store, the difference is staggering. A recent circular from the supermarket near my house advertises twelve eggs for $1.50, vine-ripened tomatoes at $1.99 per pound, and Italian pork sausage for just $1.99 a pound. The organic premium can start at 10 percent above conventional prices, but, as the comparison above demonstrates, the discrepancy can easily hit 500 percent or higher. While advocates and shoppers often believe that a revolution in food will be led by local farmers, many of these revered husbandmen and women don't earn a living wage. Because their prices can be exorbitant, it's easy to assume that unconventional farmers have healthy incomes; in reality, many of them couldn't afford to buy the very food they grow.

Part of why organically raised goods are so expensive is that caretaking natural systems is more labor-intensive than industrial agriculture, which engineers its way to productivity. Richard Pirog, associate director at the Leopold Center for Sustainable Agriculture, an Iowa State University research institution, explains, "Conventional farming is cheaper because it externalizes its true costs onto the environment and public health. Unconventional cultivation internalizes those costs so it carries a higher price tag." Many organic farmers must rely on hand labor to bring in crops and keep fields free of weeds and bugs instead of using sprays; more workers and the time needed to manage them drive up costs. In raising meat, pastured animals can take considerably longer to fatten than those finished on grain. The average grass-fed head achieves its "kill weight" at around thirty months, whereas conventionally raised cattle can be slaughtered as young as twelve months. The more time it takes until slaughter, the more expensive each cut of meat becomes. On top of that, meat processing is substantially more expensive for the small farmer sending through a few head a week than it is for the big industrial packers, who kill hundreds or thousands a day.

Once the produce is ready to go, unconventional farmers must cope with a marketing and distribution system that's woefully inadequate, creating inefficiencies that drive up costs. What's more, these growers are typically located in areas near urban markets, where real estate values are higher, and so are mortgages and property taxes, thus contributing to heftier prices. All of this on top of the normal risks farmers endure: bad weather, pests, disease, and the more general vagaries of the market. So, despite the steep premium their products can garner, many small unconventional farmers face a myriad of economic pressures that can make for a seriously unstable situation.

Local, seasonal agriculture is firing up a new generation of food activists amid a flurry of enthusiastic press coverage from the *New Yorker* to *Mother Jones,* the *New York Times,* and an expanding slate of books. But what isn't being talked about is that many of the small organic producers who are expected to lead the reinvention of the food system can barely make ends meet. How able are these frontline farmers to withstand, indeed transform, the industrial food juggernaut? Why would small organic family farms be able to hold their own against the agribusiness establishment when their conventional forebears could not? Even though it's clear that alternative, organic farming is environmentally sustainable, it's not certain that this type of cultivation is economically sustainable. While local organic growers are hailed as leaders of ecological salvation, they face a plethora of difficulties that make their existence startlingly precarious.

WINDFALL

I meet Morse Pitts at Union Square on Wednesday, July 4, 2007, around 7 p.m. His farm stand is whittled down to just four card tables, each piled high with baby greens, arugula, squash, purple carrots, and Sungold tomatoes. Unusually, the market feels deserted—it's a holiday and a gloomy rain has been falling all afternoon. Pitts stayed late because he's hoping to make up for the day's slow traffic, one of the risks of doing direct sales. His workers have been at it for almost thirteen hours, and now they're ready to deal. "Buy one, get one free!" Kevin shouts, smiling. "That's two for five dollars," booms Tim, his coworker. "No pesticides!" announces Kevin. "No herbicides!" says Tim. "No homicides!" they chime together. They've done this routine before.

Some people approach the produce-laden stall with caution, or a tinge of suspicion. "How do I cook these? What *are* they?" one man asks holding a bag of snap peas tentatively aloft. Another woman wants to know what to do with the delicate nasturtium blossoms. The different types of leafy greens are more trustworthy, but many potential buyers still aren't sure just what they're looking at. I quickly realize that much of the work at the farm stand involves rather extensive public education.

A woman in office garb holds up a bag of young dandelion greens and asks Tim if they're organic.

"It's better than organic," he quips.

"If they're not certified organic, then I'm not buying them," she says.

"*Organic* doesn't mean anything anymore," Tim says as he embarks on another series of lines he's recited before. "There are no chemicals whatsoever used to grow these vegetables. But they're not organic." He begins to lay out the somewhat complex argument that, ever since the U.S. Department of Agriculture took over certification, organic standards have been watered down to such an extent they've become meaningless. Pitts is not officially certified as organic and has chosen not to be, as have between two thousand and thirty-five hundred other organic farms in New York State alone. But, as I will find out at his farm, he grows food in a way that is markedly more ecologically responsible and sustainable than is required by current USDA regulations.

Before Tim can finish his rap the woman's attention falters and she walks away.

Eventually, Pitts and his helpers pack up the truck and we drive north out of town. As we cross the Hudson River, distant Independence Day fireworks decorate the gray night sky.

Windfall Farms is located on the edge of the small town of Montgomery in Orange County, New York, sixty-five miles from the city. Pitts has been planting its soil for twenty-seven years, all of it as an organic farmer. His family inherited the property unexpectedly when Pitts was a child. An uncle who'd passed away willed a neighbor the right to use this farm until he died, at which point ownership reverted back to the family. Pitts's father, an engineer, hadn't thought about the place in decades, so did not anticipate the turn of events and was surprised again when his son wanted to become a farmer. "Ever since I was little, I wanted to grow things," Pitts tells me. "I transplanted mint in an empty lot when I was three years old, and it took!"

Pitts is in his fifties, isn't married, and has no kids, but constantly surrounds himself with friends. He's tall with gray hair and eyes that remain serious even when everyone's joking around; although Pitts rarely acts silly himself, he deftly draws that quality out in others. Well respected in farming and culinary circles, Pitts has received a stream of good press over the years and is praised by the likes of Alice Waters, the Bay Area, California, chef who is widely regarded as the doyenne of the locally grown organic movement.

The bedroom I've been assigned is on the second floor of the rambling farmhouse. In the morning I wander down to the basement, where there's a second kitchen, an office, and the refrigerated storage and processing facilities for the produce. It's 9:30 a.m. and Pitts appears just as I walk outside to see what he and the workers are up to. We go back in for breakfast. I ask what they're doing in the fields, and he says they haven't started yet. The place is nonstop on Tuesdays and Fridays when they're preparing for market the following morning. But it's Thursday so things are relatively quiet.

Over the years Pitts has cleared a path for his business, one that would be hard to duplicate. Before he got into the farmers' market, he sold produce to restaurants. At first it seemed like a good idea because it meant guaranteed customers. But, as he explains over eggs from his henhouse and toast made with bread and butter he swaps for vegetables at the market, this was not tenable. "Selling to restaurants is basically like making an unsecured loan to a shaky business—no interest—that maybe will be paid someday," he tells me. After several years Pitts was owed $40,000 by twenty-five different establishments, so he decided to get out. He then managed, after years of wrangling, to secure one of the highly coveted spots at the Union Square market. Centrally located and at a major subway hub in Manhattan, it is the busiest, most profitable farmers' market in the region. Now Pitts only sells at Union Square, and mostly to regular shoppers; he maintains just a few commercial clients, including the New York Museum of Modern Art (for its restaurants), and chefs who buy from his farm stand. No one ever gets more than a week to pay up.

To grow Windfall's produce Pitts cultivates only 15 of the 140 acres he inherited. Just after breakfast he takes me to see the 12 acres planted across the road from the house. The air is heavy, sunlight still burning off the morning haze. The field is luxuriant with snap peas, fennel, basil, and Swiss chard. The vegetables grow in distinct parallels at some points, then in other parts of the field they interlace and overlap. Weeds are here, too, blurring the lines between rows; a reminder that the order cultivation asserts is only temporary.

As we walk deeper into the field, green gives way to rich brown-black soil. Here the activity is mostly taking place underground. Short stalks of corn are embarking on their ascent, but won't be ready until next month. More carrots are planted beyond the corn, and under the dark blanket of earth are kale and a variety of mustard greens that will push their way up for the late summer and early fall. These leafy vegetables are best when it starts getting cold at night; the plants produce sugar as a protective measure, so their taste sweetens. "Just after the first frost is the best time to eat them," I hear Pitts say one day at the greenmarket. The more distant edge of the large field was recently "disked" (plowed) and will get covered with manure from a nearby horse farm in the coming days. Pitts will then seed the area with a cover crop of buckwheat, which keeps weeds from sprouting, minimizes erosion, and can be turned into the soil to add nutrients, before the next seeds are sown. The horse dung is the only substance Pitts adds to his crops from off the farm, meaning he uses no chemical fertilizers, herbicides, or insecticides.

After walking the big field we head back toward the house to check out the farm's other three acres, stopping at the potato patch. Here Pitts is conducting an experiment with black plastic fabric that he wants to use to keep the weeds down. He's planted a couple different varieties of potatoes along the edge of the sheeting to ascertain which will grow around the cover, and which will get stuck beneath it. The tubers that are reaching out, finding the sunlight on their own, are the ones he'll cultivate next year.

This is how Pitts does things. "Trial and error. I farm through trial and error," he tells me more than once. To build soil health, avoid using pesticides, and make the labor easier, he does complicated rotations and diverse plantings. He's deciphered how to outsmart the bugs by growing crops in different places each year. He mixes seeds and tosses them into the path of the rototiller to see what will come up, like rolling dice. (While it may sound haphazard, the method, known as broadcasting, was forged by the Japanese natural-farming pioneer Masanobu Fukuoka over a half century ago.) By broadcasting one year Pitts discovered he could grow turnips sooner in the season than he'd realized, and by doing that, the harvest would come before a troublesome turnip-eating pest arrived. As with any type of farming, timing is key. Pitts races the weeds, planting certain vegetables so they grow taller faster, then he simply harvests from the upper areas. Planting more than he needs means the workers can pick what is easiest to reach without having to painstakingly search through dense leaves and pull weeds to clear the way. "We plant tons of stuff," Pitts explains. "Growing it is not that expensive, picking it is. So we try to make that part as easy as possible."

It's midday and the laborers have arrived, about ten of them. They've eaten lunch but are out behind the house knocking around a soccer ball instead of working because a heavy rain is on the way. Many of these farmhands are from Mexico and have come to Windfall through Hector Gonzalez, who has worked here since 1993. As Pitts tells the story, Gonzalez approached him because he wanted a job at a place that didn't use pesticides. For years he'd been working on another farm, also in Orange County, that gave him, as part of his wages, a house on the edge of its land. However, when the crops were sprayed, so was his home. Not only did he have to labor in the chemical-laden fields, but he and his family had to live in them as well. A few years after Gonzalez had begun working for Pitts, his sixteen-year-old son was diagnosed with cancer. Two years later he died.

Gonzalez oversees the field labor at Windfall. They do the harvesting, then wash and pack all the vegetables for market. The produce goes from the field to the customer's hands in less than twenty-four hours. The converted school bus Pitts loads with vegetables and takes to market runs on biodiesel made from waste oil he collects at restaurants in Manhattan when he goes in each week. The biodiesel also powers and heats the farm's greenhouses. Pitts is not a numbers guy—he doesn't keep tabs on how much fossil fuel he isn't using, how much CO_2 he's not emitting, or how much water he's not polluting by farming and distributing the way he does. But he's righteous about it.

Pitts is opinionated about official USDA organic because, in his estimation, it's simply not good enough. "It's just a list of things you can and can't add to your crops. I take a whole approach to farming. It's not some checklist I tick off," he says irritably. Since the USDA fully implemented organic standards in 2002—a process that began a dozen years earlier and went through several contentious rounds—many farmers, precisely the type that consumers imagine when they see the organic label, reject certification outright. Growers who practice organic methods—chemical-free farming and grazing, complex crop rotation to build and maintain soil health, fertilizing with green manure (cover crops that allow soil to regenerate), low or no fossil-fuel consumption, and labor practices that are more socially just—now call themselves "beyond organic," "unconventional," "real."

Many of these farmers are also critical of the process of earning USDA certification because it's costly and time-consuming. They must keep detailed records on the planting and tending of each individual crop—the chard, the snap peas, the carrots, the kale—something that's clearly inappropriate for a farmer such as Pitts, but highly doable for a large-scale operation. "If you have five thousand workers and one million acres, you can allocate one worker to spend all day doing paperwork," Pitts tells me hyperbolically. "But on a small farm you can't spend your day filling out paperwork, because then you're not growing the food." He is loath to do the complicated documentation of all his various plantings, such as the frequent rotations and broadcasting. It also costs hundreds and sometimes thousands of dollars to ensure the paperwork is in order and to pay the certifier, a sum many small producers can't afford.

Another Hudson Valley grower, Ron Khosla of Huguenot Farms, further elucidates problems with USDA certification. Earning and keeping the seal is supposed to work like this: The farmer maintains detailed logs of planting, fertilizing, and pest, weed, and disease management. Once each year a third-party certifying agency hired by the farmer and licensed by the USDA dispatches an inspector to assess the farm and review its records. Then the inspector submits the report for evaluation by the certifier, and if everything is up to snuff, the organic seal is granted.

But, as Khosla explains, inspectors are only required to do what's called a "visual inspection" of the farm. Khosla—who founded a peer-based certification program called Certified Naturally Grown and formerly served as a consultant to the United Nations Food and Agriculture Organization—tells me of instances of inspectors visiting farms, yet never setting foot in a field. He knows farmers who've had auditors conduct visual inspections by peering at crops through living-room windows. Astonishingly, official USDA rules require no soil samples or chemical-residue tests on produce. That means any such tests are entirely at the discretion of the certifier. Because certification companies must bear the cost of running these tests, plus time for the added paperwork, they have an incentive to avoid it. Consequently, visual inspections are all consumers can rely on.

Because inspectors typically have such heavy workloads, Khosla explains, they may not always make it to some of the farms that bear the organic seal. Khosla also tells me how a certification company he contacted brainstormed with him on how to cheat. "It was incredible!" The bottom line: "Certification companies don't want to pressure farmers because they don't want to lose the business," Khosla imparts. "The for-profit certifiers and the nonprofits, too, they don't want to lose their jobs." Being too strict could increase the risk of farmers switching to the competition. This capacity for fraud is another reason growers such as Pitts dismiss official organic.

Back at the Pitts farm, perched in front of the main house is a hand-painted sign that reads WINDFALL FARMS. Underneath the name are letters that used to say ORGANICALLY GROWN VEGETABLES. Pitts tells me that while he was away at a conference in California in 2000, the USDA announced the first phase of implementing federal organics standards. As soon as he heard, he called Gonzalez to repaint the sign immediately. With a few tight insertions and alterations, it now reads UNCONVENTIONALLY GROWN VEGETABLES.

Pitts doesn't have a mortgage because he inherited the place, as the farm's name suggests. So, unlike many of his fellow small-scale cultivators, he doesn't have the burden of debt. Yet he is still facing circumstances that are driving him off his land.

Most significant is Pitts's hefty property-tax bill. He tells me the Montgomery Town Council rezoned a large area as commercial about fifteen years ago, including Windfall and several other farms. The council realized they could shift to a more lucrative commercial tax base by taking advantage of the transportation infrastructure, which includes a major freeway, railway lines, and a small airport. But by encouraging a change in land use away from agriculture, the town officials have created an impossible situation for most local small farmers. Among the new neighbors is a manufacturer of medical and surgical supplies called Cardinal Health, which, Pitts tells me, built a single warehouse covering twenty-three acres. These operations generate considerably more income from their fertile Hudson Valley land than does farming, yet Pitts must fork over as much in taxes as his corporate neighbors. "It's like you're renting your own farm forever and the rent just keeps going up," he says. "The tax system is thwarting people who want to preserve farmland." Consequently, he laments, "Farms are just gone from here."

To beat the precipitous taxes Pitts, too, must leave. For the past several years he's been looking for a new farm, and while some prospects have been exciting, they've all fallen through. Finding the right spot is a tall order. Pitts has spent a generation building up his soil, and accumulating local knowledge of such things as weeds and bugs and weather patterns. Now he must go and begin again somewhere else, hopefully not too far away. At this point he could stop or be stopped by circumstance. No meaningful subsidies or supports exist for farmers such as Pitts, even though the environmental value of what they're doing is indisputable. If he used industrial methods and doused his fields with chemicals to grow commodities such as corn and soy, he'd be better able to tap into the U.S. Department of Agriculture's knowledge base and resources. But as it is, he's pretty much on his own.

As Pitts is showing me the squat, narrow greenhouses where he raises baby lettuces and tomatoes, the sky opens up, dropping long, full lines of summer rain. He joins several workers outside to secure things around the farm from the storm. A few of us shelter inside the sloping walls of one of the greenhouses. No one talks over the beating of the midafternoon rain. Looking up, I can see through the clear plastic roof as the drops hit, fleetingly puddle, then slip down the side.

The next morning the place is abuzz with activity; it's Friday and a lot must get done before market tomorrow. I eat a breakfast of dandelion and mustard greens, Sungold tomatoes, and eggs we gathered yesterday while Pitts sits at the table wiping down the handwritten, laminated signs he uses to label his produce at the stand. Meanwhile workers bag lettuce in the basement's refrigerated room. Gonzalez, who grew up tending his family's orchard in Mexico, walks into the kitchen. "It's too wet to hoe, and too wet to plant, but it's good weeding weather, so perhaps we'll do that," Pitts says out loud. Gonzalez cuts Pitts off by gently casting his eyes down. It's a subtle no. Gonzalez has other plans for the workers today, which he doesn't actually articulate. It's the nonverbal exchange of brothers or an old couple. Without discussion, Pitts consents.

The farm has six full-time workers whose starting pay is $7.50 an hour. A few of Pitts's additional laborers, such as Kevin, who minds the farm stand, are volunteers. Pitts's employee situation has gone through several configurations: early on he used interns, then local high school kids, then his sister Kathy brought in disabled people to work—"It wasn't the right setting for them," he tells me—then he went on to college kids from the nearby town of New Paltz, then Gonzalez arrived. Gonzalez, his brother and sister-in-law, and their relatives now fill many of the jobs on the farm.

At one point Windfall employed twenty-eight people, but the payroll taxes and workers' compensation fees got to be too much. The only company in the area that offers workers' compensation insurance once recommended to Pitts that he should stop farming organically because then he'd need fewer employees and that would lower his costs. Pitts sees the problem as being deeply embedded in current economic policy. "If you're going to employ people here, the government will tax the hell out of you," he says. "But if you employ slaves in China, they'll reward you." He also thinks agricultural policy is to blame: "Lots of little farms could meet the needs of the market. Why doesn't this happen? Because the USDA thinks it's good to stop farming, get people off the farm. This made sense during the Dust Bowl, but not anymore."

Pitts tells me it can get tricky managing his employees—Gonzalez and his field hands are prone to working too hard, picking more than will sell at the farmers' market. The extra labor drove his earnings down considerably last year. When I ask, Pitts tells me that in 2006, he earned about $7 an hour. That's fifteen cents below New York State's minimum wage. "It's not a living, it's a life," he tells me. "You're not gonna get rich, but you get to do what you love all day. And if you're working on the farm, you're not spending much money, so the money you make you can just put back into the farm. And believe me, the farm will gulp it all down." Before leaving Windfall I ask Pitts how economically sustainable his farm is. "It's basically not," he says. "Anything can knock it over, it's always hanging in the balance."

STONE BROKE AND SWEET TREE

The bus is crowded for 6 a.m. on a Monday, headed *out* of town. In the row behind me a teenage girl sleeps; the jacket she'd pulled over her head has slouched down around her shoulders. I disembark after two hours traveling north through the Hudson Valley to the town of Kingston, New York. Here I meet Joshua and Jessica Applestone, owners of Fleisher's Grass-Fed and Organic Meats, a butcher store located on the main shopping street. They have invited me to come with some of their employees to visit the farm of their main beef supplier, David Huse.

Fleisher's sells meat only from animals grazed on pasture and raised without hormones or antibiotics. It's a relatively young business and like farmers' markets it's part of the burgeoning network for nonfactory food. Fleisher's buys carcasses from small farmers, cuts them into steaks and chops, grinds them into burgers and sausages, and makes soap with the leftover fat. The Applestones, both in their thirties, revived Joshua's family butcher shop, also called Fleisher's. Started by his great-grandfather in Brooklyn, New York, over a century ago, the original went out of business around the time industrial meat processing took off. By working with farmers such as David Huse, the Applestones aim to help build a lasting market for humanely raised, ecologically sustainable meat.

From Kingston we drive an additional ninety miles north in two separate cars. I ride with Joshua and his main butcher, Aaron. Jessica is in the SUV behind us with two employees and two interns (the unpaid labor of idealistic youngsters seems to be a key feature in the emergent clean-food movement). Joshua and Aaron, who exchange a jocular banter like old college friends, tell me about the trials of being butchers selling strictly grass-fed, nonhormone, free-range meat. One of the most difficult aspects of the trade is getting and keeping access to slaughterhouses. Because USDA guidelines are tailored to industrial meatpacking plants, Joshua and Aaron explain, it's disproportionately more expensive for local abattoirs to stay in business, and far costlier for small farmers to process animals. Federal food-safety laws are written for—and often de facto by—big corporations such as ConAgra and Tyson, not producers such as Huse and Fleisher's.

Joshua and Aaron also talk about how the art of butchering is being lost. What gets taught in agriculture schools these days is referred to as meat cutting. When animals are slaughtered and packed at large-scale, mechanized facilities, where most meat in the United States is processed, they get broken down into bulk parts, sealed in thick plastic, boxed, and sent to retail stores. Here, the meat cutter comes in. Unlike a butcher, a cutter only has to know which way to position the block of beef when running it through the band saw to shear off, say, a T-bone steak. Eric Shelley, who runs the Meat Lab at the State University of New York, Cobleskill, a schoolroom slaughterhouse, explains, "If people are under forty years old, they don't know where the meat comes from on the animal. Traditional butchers know how to bring something walking in on its feet to something that leaves in a package that can go straight onto the grill."

According to Joshua and Aaron, losing the skill of butchering reinforces our reliance on dirty factory-farm production. This is exactly what's happened; as of 2000, the top four companies slaughtered more than 80 percent of U.S. beef, leaving few choices for processing meat outside the industrial oligopoly. By not knowing how to take apart an animal, we're forced to get meat from producers that confine their cows, pigs, and birds, stuff them full of feed they can't digest, and inundate their systems with chemicals including hormones and antibiotics. Fleisher's aim is to fuel a transformation of the food system that's crucial for the survival of ecological health, animals included.

We crest a quiet hilltop. "It's right around here somewhere," Joshua says from behind the wheel as Aaron inspects the cryptic directions written in black marker on butcher paper. Joshua and Jessica visited the farm this time last year, not long after they first started working with David Huse. Today's outing is part of how they stay connected to the growers that raise the meat they sell. "That's the whole point, to know exactly where your food comes from," Joshua says. We head up the driveway past a small wooden sign that reads STONE BROKE FARMS.

The Huse farm consists of seven hundred acres of mostly hilltop land just south of New York State's Adirondack Mountains. Tall elms, oaks, and cedars rustle and shimmer when the summer breeze breaks through.

The pastures are full of tall, pale grasses. Only a few houses dot the landscape. David Huse and his father have raised five hundred or so Angus and Hereford cattle here each year for the last four decades. Over that time they perfected their livestock, breeding solid blacks, white-faced blacks, and white-faced reds to achieve a specific musculature. Joshua, who was a vegan for seventeen years, effusively describes these animals as "walking blocks of steak."

David and his father work their cattle farm themselves, occasionally hiring kids from the town down the hill to help with repairing equipment and other menial tasks. The elder Huse is from Kansas, and, according to David, "He was the first in his family who wasn't a farmer, a preacher, or a schoolteacher." David's father left the family wheat farm to eventually become a vice president at Bell Telephone. In 1966 he bought this acreage for his retirement; that way he could be a small farmer with his own economic safety net. When the Huses moved here, David was still in high school. After earning his associate's degree in animal husbandry in 1972, he joined his father raising cattle full-time.

The family house is a sprawling, two-story ranch-style homestead, built in the 1940s. Inside, the place more closely resembles a suburban dwelling than a farmhouse. Its decor is of a different time, like a Technicolor film from the 1960s that has faded but retains its elegance. The living-room furniture is arranged around a massive, spotless picture window that frames the view down onto the undulating Cobleskill Valley majestic with cumulus clouds of green trees.

It's early July, the height of killing season. "We start slaughtering in June and continue through October. We do about three or four head a week," David says as we pile into his truck to go see the "breeders" a few fields away. David Huse is of medium build, about six feet tall, and is at once grizzled and boyish. He has on muddy cowboy boots, coveralls, and a baseball cap that says NASCAR and has yellow lightning bolts that shoot from his temples. When I ask why he's a cattle farmer, he comes back with "Everybody wants to be a farmer, now don't they?"

We've driven the short distance to where the breeders and calves are chomping away in what used to be the front yard of a farmhouse. The white, two-story Victorian is burned out, just barely standing. The animals seem not to notice our arrival. Calves, all born about two months ago, stand close to their mothers, who graze in one big group. As they bite and pull on the grass, the brown and black lines of their backs move like the lapping of waves in a pond. Their hides are slick against the curves of their stomachs. Digested grass shit lands in clumps at their feet. Tails swoosh and swat at flies. Knees crook and hooves kick out, then drop back heavily upon the ground. Deep eyes stare not at us, but languorously through us.

What happens on a grass-based livestock farm is relatively straightforward: the animals graze. As for what the cattle eat at Stone Broke, fifty different types of grasses carpet the Huse acreage including brome, rye, timothy, bird's-foot trefoil, and white and red clovers. "Whatever naturally grows up here is what's best," David says. "I haven't used fertilizer in ten years." As for *how* the animals eat, the Huses have adopted a system called management-intensive grazing, popular among all-natural grassfed meat farmers. Put simply, management-intensive grazing entails herding the cows to a new field each day and using portable electric fencing to keep them out of the previously munched area so the grass can regenerate. This method safeguards against overgrazing, which is what happens when ruminants—mammals such as cows that chew their cud—are left to their own devices. Since new shoots of many grasses are sweet and tender, cattle will return to nibble at the same spots, preventing the emerging leaves from fully growing. Fresh blades are what nourishes the root systems, so if they can't form because of too much grazing (and the continuous traffic that compacts the soil), the grasses will suffer. Overgrazing has multiple ecological effects: It destroys ruminants' primary source of food, forcing farmers to resort to feed, the most affordable of which is grown using polluting, irrigation-intensive industrial methods. And, as grasses die off, a cycle of degradation sets in. Opportunistic weeds begin to take over, and runoff and erosion increase, all of which lead to further loss of the soil's ability to support life. In the most extreme cases, this process can result in desertification.

By contrast, management-intensive grazing fosters a nutritive cycle whereby ruminants and their forage feed each other—with some gentle encouragement from the farmer. As cows eat, they move across the land distributing and planting grass seeds while fertilizing the soil with their poop. As the writer Michael Pollan puts it, "The coevolutionary relationship between cows and grass is one of nature's underappreciated wonders." The management-intensive husbandry comes in at this point to safeguard against overgrazing. Every day the Huses corral their beeves into a renewed paddock and pull up, then reinstall, the lightweight electric fencing. At Stone Broke it takes about three to four weeks for a field to rebound, then the cows are brought back for another feast.

When raised this way, cows become an impressively efficient way of turning grass into protein; the only energy source that's needed is the sun. However, the situation isn't so cut-and-dried. Even when they're grass-fed, cows belch and fart a lot of methane, a potent greenhouse gas. Methane is over twenty times more heat-trapping than carbon dioxide, and livestock including cattle account for about 18 percent of global methane emissions. While raising animals as the Huses do eliminates many of the fossil fuels, chemical fertilizers, soil erosion, and toxic runoff that result from industrially grown cattle and the feed they rely on, it is not a panacea.

Later that afternoon, David's father appears along the road. He wades a short distance into a parcel of land a few hundred feet from where the breeders and their calves are still drinking water. He summons them. I can't hear his call, but from behind I see his torso moving from the effort. First one, then another of the animals looks up and begins to lumber over. The dark bodies now head toward him in a flock, V-shaped and slow. In the restored field the tips of summer grass feather up almost to the elder Huse's shoulders.

The Huses didn't always farm this way. Although they've used management-intensive grazing since the early 1980s, it wasn't until about three years ago that they stopped relying as much on grain to feed and finish their livestock. And it wasn't until then that the Huses ceased sending their animals for standard processing. Stone Broke used to sell its cattle to Moyer Packing Company, an old-school conventional plant in Pennsylvania. David tells me he liked working with Moyer, but things got rough after Smithfield Foods Company, now the fifth-largest beef processor in the United States, bought out the regional slaughterhouse in 2001. Almost immediately, the new corporate owner started lowering the prices it paid for cattle. Because of the rampant consolidation in the industry, the Huses were virtually held captive. By 2002 the family's revenue from selling its beeves had dropped to 1972 levels. "When you let that concentration happen, you get put in a place where you take what they offer or you go somewhere else, but there's nowhere else to go," David tells me. He says part of why they decided to switch to organic methods was to access a more lucrative market. The Huses now earn more per pound; however, they rely strictly on Fleisher's. "I'm shipping to one little butcher shop, and if he closes, I don't know what I'd do," David says. This year Stone Broke is hoping to break even. I ask what will happen if they don't and he replies, "I could never do this if we had a mortgage payment." He goes on, "My father's retired and he has a pension. . . . I'm not crying poverty, it just hasn't worked out the way I thought it would."

Ironically, a major obstacle unconventional farms such as Windfall and Stone Broke face is the outcome of the very success of organic. As demand for all-natural food has expanded beyond a niche market, to keep costs down and stay competitive, most higher-volume retailers and processors have stopped buying inputs in small quantities. At Whole Foods' first store in Austin, Texas, opened in 1980, much of the organic fruit and vegetables on offer were from local farmers. But as the organic industry has ventured into bigger markets, it's become much more expensive to manage accounts with, say, twenty growers than it is with one large farm.

A 2007 study of small organic farmers in California illustrates the point. Some growers said they struggled to attract and keep middlemen because their volumes were too low. Whole Foods showed interest in the berries of one cultivator, but because he couldn't provide two hundred cases a week, he lost the deal. Unable to find an organic buyer to work with, more than one grower ended up having to off-load organic crops as conventional at a considerable loss. Each of those surveyed eventually gave up organic production. Some stopped farming altogether, and others went back to conventional because it was easier to sell and therefore more profitable.

Building an appropriate distribution network isn't the problem; the barriers lie in keeping it open to small producers. Alternative farmers and retailers from the first wave of the organic food movement in the United States created such a system. Established in the 1970s and 1980s, it consisted of small regional circuits that ran throughout New England and many other parts of the United States. Among the early dealers was Norman A. Cloutier, a health-food-store owner in Rhode Island. In the late 1970s, he started a distribution company, Cornucopia Natural Foods, Inc., and a few years later bought two key regional distributors in the Northeast. Over the ensuing decades Cornucopia aggressively pursued growth through a flurry of mergers and acquisitions of regional cooperatives and distribution outfits built up by small health food retailers and buyers' groups. Today the company, now incorporated under the name United Natural Foods, Inc. (UNFI), is the leading handler of natural products nationwide. UNFI boasts over twenty thousand customers including Whole Foods and Sodexo U.S.A., a major food-service corporation that supplies hotels, restaurants, and institutions such as universities. According to Samuel Fromartz in *Organic, Inc.,* UNFI's "purchase of the last two natural-food-distribution cooperatives, Blooming Prairie in the Midwest, and Northeast Cooperatives in New England [in the early 2000s], marked the end of any alternative distribution network." The need to stay competitive in the marketplace compelled UNFI to buy out smaller firms and shutter any regional distribution facilities it deemed redundant, whether or not these lines were crucial to small organic farmers.

I sit shotgun with Huse in a John Deere four-wheel, all-terrain buggy. The jerky ride takes us downhill through a field to where a few dozen one-year-old heifers are grazing. They are perched on a slope bordered by trees, the lower branches of which have been pruned by deer into a perfect line hovering just above the darkness of the grove.

Even though he raises his cattle strictly on grass, infrequently supplemented in small quantities with organic feed, Huse hasn't bothered getting certified organic—none of the meat Fleisher's sells carries the official seal. As with vegetable farms, the certification can cost hundreds and sometimes thousands of dollars each year and involves piles of paperwork that eat up valuable work time. Also, like Morse Pitts and many other nonchemical, holistic farmers, the Huses and Applestones believe that as organic has gone mainstream, it's been stripped of any real substance.

As we mingle with the cattle, Huse and Applestone talk shop, that is, about killing and butchering. (Huse imparts to me that some people believe this shouldn't be done in front of animals destined for "harvesting.") "Around here there's a real bottleneck when it comes to slaughtering," the farmer says. Stone Broke uses an abattoir that's one of just two remaining regional facilities. There used to be eleven small houses around here, Huse explains, but in the last few years nine have shut their doors. This means it's harder to get a slot for his animals, and processing costs are higher than ever.

Before the biggest firms consolidated the industry, Huse would pay twenty cents per pound to process a beeve, and, he says, "You'd give 'em the hide for the kill fee." That would have meant a $160 outlay for an eight-hundred-pound animal. Now, for the same service, he must fork over about $500. By contrast, Huse tells me, it costs the commercial companies just $50 to kill and pack a head of beef at one of their industrial facilities. Processing fees are so much more at the local operations because there aren't enough of them to meet demand, and each one handles far fewer animals than the mega-slaughterhouses. Compounding this, small slaughterhouses must pay disproportionately more to keep a shop that meets USDA specs.

According to Eric Shelley of the Meat Lab, "All the costs of running a slaughterhouse are basically the same whether you're a small plant or a large plant. But if you're a large plant, those costs get diffused, spread out." Shelley tells me that small operators have to buy the same gear that the big places do, such as stainless steel equipment, and specific high-end stun guns, saws, and knives. He mentions one required knife that goes for $3,000. While it makes sense that anyone handling food should have the most professional tools, these industrial accoutrements may well exceed what a small facility will ever need. They also typically drive the cost of opening a USDA-approved plant well over a million dollars.

Not long after visiting Stone Broke, in a regional newspaper I come across a profile of a farmer named John Wing, who'd built a new slaughterhouse in Benson, Vermont, five years before. Because of the area's lack of capacity he decided to start processing his own animals. State inspectors convinced him to construct his place to comply with federal standards. That way he could help alleviate the region's slaughterhouse bottleneck that stretched south into New York and Massachusetts. Although it would cost much more, Wing decided to take their advice. The facility is still running today, handling about one hundred animals a week, but the $1.75 million he spent to outfit the small plant put Wing through Chapter 13 bankruptcy.

Also contributing to these higher costs are meatpacking regulations adopted by the USDA in 1996. The first meaningful revision since the Meat Inspection Act was originally passed in 1906 amid public outcry stirred by Upton Sinclair's book *The Jungle,* the updated rules ironically seem to work in favor of the largest corporations. Central to the USDA's new specifications is what's called Hazard Analysis and Critical Control Point, or HACCP (pronounced "hassup"). All meat processors regardless of size are now required to write a HACCP plan—"basically a book, it's *that* detailed," Eric Shelley tells me—which can be particularly onerous for small operators. The document covers a range of issues related to potential exposure of meat to unwanted contaminants, such as chemicals, pathogens, hair, and bits of metal, at all points throughout the slaughtering and processing chain. While such a plan is undoubtedly a good idea, the document requires specialized knowledge in engineering and science that most small-time butchers don't have. So they must hire outside consultants to write their HACCP plan; this can cost thousands of dollars for the initial document, and even more for revisions, which are common. But that's not all—HACCP requires constant documentation. Huse tells me it takes his butcher an hour and a half every day to fill out the paperwork. "USDA makes it so hard to operate, many slaughterhouses are guys who are sixty to sixty-five years old, and they just get tired and quit and no one takes their place," Huse says. "Why would they?"

That HACCP better suits the bigger facilities isn't surprising. Before being taken up by the USDA, HACCP was adopted and refined by the fast-food chain Jack in the Box. The company revamped its system in an effort to salvage its reputation after a 1993 *E. coli* 0157:H7 outbreak was traced back to the company's food. The dangerous bacteria sickened seven hundred people across the United States and killed four, including children, and were linked to meat processed in large industrial facilities. According to Marion Nestle's book *Safe Food*, the spread of *E. coli* coincides with the rise of factory farming. "The earliest case [of *E. coli*] seems to have occurred in 1975, but the first reported outbreak occurred in 1982. . . . Outbreaks are increasing in frequency; there were 6 in 1997 but 17 in 1998." As for why, she writes, "The most reasonable explanation involves the profound changes in society and food production that have taken place." The changes have been dramatic indeed; in 2007 over half the cattle slaughtered went through just fourteen meatpacking facilities. Although HACCP introduces procedures that, when carried out well, could improve food safety, the regulations were shaped by and for industrial-scale processors to the detriment of their small-scale competitors, not to mention public health.

Frank Johnson's farm is decidedly unassuming compared to Huse's. It's tucked in the valley on a much smaller two-hundred-acre parcel just outside the small town of Carlisle. The place is well-worn, unadorned. Off the main road, a dirt drive leads past a modest one-story, white house, where Johnson lives with his family. The main barn is across the drive from the house, and behind it are Johnson's pastures. We walk to a field where the forty-five or so cattle Fleisher's will be carving in the coming weeks are grazing on grass that's a fluorescent green. Upon seeing the animals' black bodies bulging with muscle, Applestone punches the air in excitement.

Johnson has salt-and-pepper hair and, unlike Huse, doesn't look the part of a farmer. He's wearing faded denim shorts, a T-shirt, and sneakers. He looks like a suburban dad on a Sunday afternoon. He tells me he farms holistically "because you should leave the earth in better shape than when you got here." Johnson is neither an eco-evangelizer nor a hippie who went back to the land. Huse shares these qualities. These men are straight-up farmers.

Johnson has known this is the life for him since he was a kid on his family's dairy farm. However, when he was married to his first wife, he earned a living doing construction, he says, because she didn't want him to work the land. But the desire to raise animals persisted. After Johnson divorced and then married a second time, he and his new wife, Judy Pangman—who wrote an authoritative book on chicken-coop construction—went into farming. About ten years ago they bought the "land base" of his family's dairy farm, where the crops were grown. (The milking facilities are on the half that they didn't buy.) They named their new place Sweet Tree Farm and have been paying the sizable mortgage ever since.

"Joel Salatin"—a grass-fed beef–farming guru—"says you shouldn't have money tied up in land, but we have a mortgage. We had to," Johnson tells me. "If you inherit the land, you're in a really different situation." So, to help service the debt, Johnson maintained an "off-farm job," as they're called, until just three years ago. And Pangman works full-time for an engineering company. "If it wasn't for her income, we wouldn't be farming," Johnson says.

There is a tinge of shame in this admission, as is true with other farmers I talk to who must rely on external income to stay afloat. But, in reality, there's nothing abnormal about it. According to the USDA Economic Research Service, the average small farm earns 85–95 percent of its income from "off-farm sources" such as the wages of a spouse. Medium-size farms, ones that earn between $250,000 and $499,999 in annual sales, rely on off-farm resources for almost 50 percent of their income. This means that most small growers don't even come close to earning a living from being farmers. Old news in many respects, but with an increasing emphasis on organic and local, the struggle of the small farmer is cast in a new light.

Needless to say, Johnson works hard. He raises his own animals, finishes the Huse cattle, does his own butchering, and brings Sweet Tree's products to farmers' markets twice a week, selling the goods himself. Before our group leaves, Johnson shows me a smokehouse he built last year. The idea was he could make smoked cuts, adding value to his meat, boosting his earning potential. But he hasn't yet been able to use it because he can't get USDA approval. Thanks to convoluted regulations, which he said Cornell University's trusted extension workers couldn't help him figure out, Johnson's smoker sits idle.

As Johnson traces his efforts to make Sweet Tree more profitable, all the things he's done to cut costs and be more self-sufficient, he says he's getting worn-out. "That's the point I'm at. I'm raising the beef, I'm doing the butchering, I'm smoking my own meat, I'm doing inventory, and the markets. If I try to do more, it becomes a snowball. I can't say it can't be done, I just don't have the ambition to do it. I was always ambitious, but these last eight years, doing both the farming and the markets have really taken it out of me." Throughout the visit Johnson tells me several times that he's afraid he's going to have to stop farming and go back to wage labor.

LOGIC OF THE LOCAL

In the summer of 2007 I place a call to the USDA's National Organic Program, or NOP, in Washington, D.C. Established in 2002, the NOP is the top body in charge of overseeing the organic system in the United States. A man picks up without identifying the office. I ask to speak to someone in communications. He tells me to hold on, then puts the receiver down and continues a conversation that I can hear and that my call has obviously interrupted. Several minutes later he picks the phone back up. I ask how many people are currently in the office. He says six. I ask what he knows about organic farming. "Nothing," he tells me. I ask how long he's been at the job. "A couple of weeks." He's a temp.

From its inception in 2002 through 2008, the NOP staff fluctuated between five and eight people even though the program has a heavy workload. Its duties include interpreting and amending the constantly evolving regulations and enforcing organic rules. The NOP is also charged with training, accrediting, and monitoring the independent third-party bodies that issue organic seals. Approximately one hundred third-party certifiers are registered with the NOP, which might sound like a manageable number. But those companies are in turn responsible for keeping tabs on thousands of domestic as well as foreign farmers and processors that sell in the American market. From early 2008 through the end of 2009 the NOP lacked a director, operating instead under an acting director, Barbara Robinson, who held another full-time job at the USDA. Meantime, the key post of head of Compliance and Enforcement sat vacant until late 2008. Among Compliance and Enforcement's stated goals for 2009 was to "establish an internal management system" because, for the first time, the division had a staff.

The NOP's funding is allocated with each new farm bill. Congress writes and passes the legislation every five years and has never set aside mandatory financing for the USDA's National Organic Program. Instead, each year the NOP must slog through the appropriations process in the House of Representatives and the Senate, justifying its costs to politicians who hold its fate. Each successive farm bill sets a ceiling on how much the NOP can receive, but no floor—Congress is under no obligation to give the program any funds. Although lawmakers have never outright denied resources, there's no guarantee the money will come.

The most recent farm bill, passed in 2008, raises the NOP budget from about $1.5 million annually to $3 million for 2009, and $3.8 million for 2010. This represents the first significant increase since the agency opened despite that organics have seen annual growth rates in the double digits for over a decade. Thanks to the added funds, and President Obama's apparent support, the NOP is undertaking a reorganization to better carry out its tasks. Most significantly the new plan involves hiring additional employees—by summer 2009 the office's numbers surged to an all-time high of fourteen—and at last a full-time head, Miles McEvoy. While some changes will doubtless result, the NOP nevertheless remains starved of the resources it would need to become a vital tool for promoting and supporting truly ecological agriculture.

Other facets of the most recent farm bill offer support for organic farmers, but the scales are tipped well in favor of agribusiness. The document tenders billions toward marketing, distribution, research, extension, and education for growers using conventional factory methods. The law also shells out tens of billions more dollars to subsidize industrial farms. The 2008 farm bill rings in at about $300 billion. From such largesse the plan sets aside a meager $78 million for organic research and extension over five years. A fivefold increase from the previous farm bill's spending on organic research and extension, the sum nevertheless reveals that more biologically destructive farming practices still rank high on the USDA and Congress's list of priorities.

What has come of the first wave of organic agriculture from the 1970s demonstrates just how hard it can be to survive while keeping a green commitment intact. Some holistic growers have stayed in business yet remain cloistered in the confines of "boutique farming." Here they serve a limited consumer base that can pay prices prohibitive to most shoppers. Morse Pitts is a prime example; what he's doing shows that alternatives are possible, but its reach remains confined. Another outcome is that a great many organic and natural food endeavors have simply gone bust. Innumerable small cultivators who hung on by a thread, not unlike Frank Johnson, couldn't ultimately make it. Finally, some farmers decided to play by the rules of the market and go up against the big guys. As is true in conventional agriculture, with more competition comes greater pressure to streamline production to lower prices and create a more uniform, and shippable, product. Case in point is the Washington State–based Cascadian Farm, started three decades ago by back-to-the-landers looking for alternatives to the mainstream. One of its founders ended up taking the farm in a more commercial direction and, in the 1990s, sold out to General Mills. Some now criticize Cascadian Farm's practices as following a less rigorous version of organic, having surrendered more holistic methods to tap bigger markets. Jeff Moyer, current chair of the National Organic Standards Board, the official body that recommends standards changes, spoke to this when he told the *Washington Post,* "As the organic industry matures, it is becoming increasingly more difficult to find a balance between the integrity of the word *organic* and the desire for the industry to grow."

Many Big Organic proponents argue that working on such a large scale pays off because it means a lot of synthetic chemicals that would have been used in conventional farming are avoided. Peter LeCompte, once a worker on a small organic farm who is now head of organic buying for General Mills, is a prime example. When I interview him, he tells me that even though he knows working for the establishment compromises him, it's the best, and most realistic, option for widespread change he can see. Agriculture went toxic and industrial largely because doing so was most effective at beating rivals and fattening the bottom line. When producers try to achieve greater economies with organic, they often do so by swerving back toward less sustainable cultivation methods—that's why LeCompte and his ilk must compromise. Ultimately, however, this incarnation of organic stifles biologically sound farming because it helps the major food producers maintain their dominant position; small growers can't compete with firms such as General Mills in lobbying Congress for incentives and regulations to bolster their market position. Big Organic reinforces the political, economic, and regulatory apparatus currently in place that favors the most powerful food processors as well as the agribusiness elite. Meanwhile life remains rough for growers such as Pitts, Huse, and Johnson, and processors such as Fleisher's. To get by, the unconventional operator must instead rely on the subsidies of inherited land, free and low-cost labor, and off-farm income. If alternative farmers and processors are too beaten down by the lack of resources for cultivation and distribution, inappropriate food safety rules, insurmountable debt, and inadequate pay, then, no matter how much we as consumers want local, ecologically responsible food, the people who make it may well go extinct.

CHAPTER TWO

All the World's a Garden: Global Organic

Most of Paraguay remains unmapped. The landlocked country lies in the heart of South America, surrounded by Brazil, Argentina, and Bolivia. In the nineteenth century Paraguay was among the first countries on the continent to build a railroad; its extensive tracks reached far into the countryside and were still in use until recent decades. But the military dictatorship of Alfredo Stroessner, who ruled from 1954 until 1989, left the railways in tatters. Paraguay's eastern expanse is interlaced with uncharted dirt roads built to access villages and fields, and as an initial step in deforestation. The subtropical Upper Paraná Atlantic Forest, said to be among the most biodiverse in the world, is home to a wealth of plants and rich with fauna including jaguars, tapirs, a plethora of reptiles and amphibians, and over five hundred species of birds. However, it is continuously being transformed into cattle pasture and immense stretches of commodity crops such as soy, wheat, and, increasingly, sugarcane.

The native Atlantic Forest once carpeted about 100 million acres, an area comprising eastern Paraguay and crossing over into Brazil and Argentina. Perhaps surprisingly, and until only recently, Paraguay had one of the highest deforestation rates in Latin America. Today just 8 percent of the primary Upper Paraná ecosystem remains. The destruction began to decelerate in late 2004 when the government enacted law no. 2524/4, the so-called Zero Deforestation Law, for the Atlantic Forest region. Although the World Wildlife Fund reports the measure has dramatically slowed the felling of trees, the casual observer can't help but see that clearing nevertheless continues.

In the state of Guairá, the country's primary sugar-growing region, only a few main arteries are paved; everything else is dirt, and it's easy to get lost. There may be small hand-painted signs, which should sometimes be followed, other times not. A driver might unexpectedly hit a makeshift roadblock of felled trees piled high, or an unmarked, sudden drop-off. Few private automobiles travel these rural roads, but bicycles are everywhere, and so are pedestrians—in the remotest spots and along the biggest thoroughfares, all day and late into the night. The motorized vehicles I see most often are cheap, domestically assembled motorcycles and lumbering eighteen-wheelers piled high with freshly cut sugarcane. The bikes buzz through thick dust past knots of traffic, dodging the heavy trucks that dominate the roads during the spring and summer harvest season. The long, spindly stalks of cane are chained together into thousand-pound bundles that bounce, as if in slow motion, precariously on the backs of the open-bed lorries.

Great plantations and networks of smallholder plots advance across Guairá's lowlands and inch up its lush hillsides. Peasant farmers have cultivated the area for generations, living mostly off the abundance of food that sprouts from the region's productive soils, and selling modest yields of sugarcane for income. Increasingly, smallholders and large plantations alike are growing organic to meet booming demand for natural foods from big organic processors and retailers in the West.

Paraguay is an epicenter of organic sugar production and exemplifies how the globally grown, ever more corporate organic food system works. The country is among the leading organic sugar producers and exporters in the world, sending most of its granules to the United States and Europe. Paraguay's top organic sugar makers include a company called Azucarera Paraguaya (AZPA), which, according to its importer, provides a third of all organic sugar consumed in the United States. AZPA's crystals course through the American food system, selling in stores such as Whole Foods under the brand name Wholesome Sweeteners, the Paraguayan firm's Sugarland, Texas–based importer, which is a subsidiary of Imperial Sugar, the largest sugar company in the United States. AZPA's sugar is also used by top processors including General Mills for its Cascadian Farm and Muir Glen products, and Dean Foods, the biggest dairy concern in the United States, in its Silk soymilk goods. Even in the era of healthy eating, the fraught and mysterious commodity of sugar continues to play a major role; as producers and retailers take organic mainstream, they are remaking natural food as processed, packaged, and sugar-rich.

Runaway sales of organic in the United States, the United Kingdom, and Europe and double-digit overall growth rates for the industry marked the 1990s and much of the first decade of the 2000s. Although consumption of all-natural goods has slowed somewhat due to the economic recession, the sector nevertheless continues its ongoing expansion. As a result, regional farms, even big ones, are not always able to keep pace, leaving existing local and national supplies stretched thin. In 2004, organic milk producer Organic Valley ended its lucrative deal with Wal-Mart because the dairy couldn't turn out enough product. Unable to find sufficient alternatives nearby and year-round, processors and retailers are going farther—sometimes very far—afield. Consequently, food from around the world is appearing in supermarkets stamped with the word *organic,* a moniker that doesn't reveal all the resources required to get that chemical-free morsel to the grocery aisle.

The notion of "food miles"—the distance an item travels to make it to the consumer—became a hot issue in the early 2000s. A debate flared in the United States and the UK about what made more sense, buying locally produced organic that was raised in energy-sucking greenhouses, or organic imports from warmer climates. Were the fossil fuels used to keep the vegetables and fruits from freezing contributing more to global warming than those used to transport them from overseas? The UK's Soil Association, the country's top organic-certification entity, considered pulling its seal for imported products. After conducting a study into the matter, however, the organization decided on a compromise. As of 2009 it began extending organic certification to airfreighted food that also meets ethical trade standards. The Soil Association reasoned that not buying organic crops from developing countries would inadvertently punish small farmers who've become reliant on the income.

While the discussion of food miles has died down somewhat in the United States, it has only deepened in the UK. British processors and retailers are beginning to focus on the overall carbon footprint of food (and other goods)—not just emissions from transport, but also those created from farming, storing, and packaging, and even from consumer trips to the store. To address this the UK-based Carbon Trust, a government-established independent company, created the Carbon Reduction Label, which divulges the total greenhouse gases embodied in an item, from every stage of production and disposal. Participants in the program include PepsiCo, Heinz, Kellogg's, Coca-Cola, Cadbury, and the major

British supermarket chain Tesco. Versions of the Carbon Reduction Label are being adopted across Europe, the United States, Canada, and Australia. Disclosing CO_2 releases, coupled with official organic certification, which, in some countries such as the UK, includes the Fair Trade component, sounds like a foolproof system.

Nevertheless, thorough as they may seem, these metrics can fail to capture the realities of how organic crops are grown in distant lands. Even as supermarkets brim with produce from such places as China, Chile, and Paraguay stamped with seals pledging higher standards, questions inevitably persist: What are the realities of unconventional farming in developing countries with notoriously exploitative labor practices and where environmental controls are often insufficient and go unchecked? How holistic can "certified organic" on a global scale truly be?

The spread of organic cultivation internationally is not always as beneficial as it might sound; in daily dealings, the reality of organic can diverge from its ideal in ways that are difficult to see from a distance. To understand these issues more fully, I traveled to South America in the fall of 2007 and, at an organic food conference, met a representative from Wholesome Sweeteners. I subsequently visited AZPA's plantation, and some of the peasant farmers who supply the company. There, I found a system riddled with inconsistencies, loose interpretations of established organic rules, and what seems to be outright fraud. Such transgressions are facilitated in part by surprisingly inadequate official organic standards. While ignoring and breaking regulations can and does happen in the United States and Europe, when an operation is, say, in a remote, impoverished country in an unmapped rural area and run by a powerful company, checks and balances can more easily fall away.

TEBICUARY

AZPA's mill and sprawling plantation are situated in the state of Guairá, about three hours' drive east of the country's capital, Asunción. AZPA was started a century ago by a partnership of families, "pioneers" according to the company's website, "who planted a dream in Paraguay's wilderness." I've come here by way of Dario Zaldivar, who is Wholesome Sweeteners' point man in Paraguay. Zaldivar deals exclusively with AZPA, which supplies much of Wholesome's product. AZPA's compound on the banks of the Tebicuary River is a classic setup: an orderly, tree-lined entrance leading to narrow streets of whitewashed worker housing, a school, church, health clinic, commissary, hotel for official guests, the house of the owners, and, of course, the mill. The buildings and grounds are meticulously maintained, an outpost of civility in the undeveloped countryside. The company's ever-expanding crew of workers—Zaldivar says it's now at about seven hundred full-time and half as many seasonal—has erected, just across the Tebicuary, a shantytown that looks like a movie-set version of itself. Zaldivar calls it "the Wild West."

In addition to organic, AZPA makes ethanol and conventional sugar— one of its biggest Paraguayan customers is Coca-Cola. Since organic is the most profitable of AZPA's products, the company is rapidly expanding its operations to increase output. In 2007, the firm tripled the mill's sugarcane grinding capacity from five thousand to fifteen thousand metric tons per day. AZPA's organic acreage is also on the rise. I'm told that the sugar maker isn't converting any of its conventional land, but is instead establishing new organic fields.

Rubén Darío Ayala oversees AZPA's agricultural land as the company's head of crop care. I first meet him when he arrives on the small, rain-soaked, unpaved road where the car I'm riding in is lodged deep in the mud. My guide, after several fruitless attempts at extracting the vehicle himself, finally places a cell-phone call for help. He dials AZPA. They quickly dispatch Ayala with three others in a company-issued 4x4, a technology few here can afford. Ayala has a solid build, and a baggy, sun-tanned face, and looks completely at ease as he and the others go about the messy job of extricating our car. Several people had stopped to offer help before Ayala's crew arrived. My guide offhandedly declined, telling each of them that someone from AZPA was on the way. The company has a powerful presence in the region, and not just as an employer and buyer of cane. It helps maintain roads and funds area schools and medical clinics. Most people who live here, from the wealthy to the poor, have some connection to the company.

After our car is on solid ground, Ayala, who's in his midthirties, drives us out to the company's older organic fields in an area called Tebicuary. He tells me his responsibilities are increasing because the company has embarked on an expansion of its organic cropland; he has no formal training so he's learning as he goes. Out the window I see pools of water that have collected after last night's heavy downpour that now reflect a silvery blue sky. From the wet soil rise phosphorescent new shoots of three-month-old organic cane. The precise rows form lines that converge at a distant vanishing point somewhere on the horizon. We get out of the truck and stand amid thousands of acres of cane.

As is true with domestically raised organic crops, those grown outside the United States and the European Union must meet binding organic standards set by those governments and verified by a third party. To qualify a farm must abide by rules including bans on certain chemical fertilizers, pesticides, and fungicides, and it must avoid monocropping. Monocropping is a factory-farming method that entails transforming existing ecosystems or traditional farmland into large fields planted with the same crop year after year, a method designed to reduce costs. Organic methods are intended to counteract the deleterious effects of conventional industrial cultivation, which destroys biodiversity, wipes out soil health, contributes to erosion, and helps deplete groundwater due to increased runoff. The organic seal is meant to signal that a farm abides by nature-supporting practices, which are typically more expensive to implement. (With organic certification, farmers can not only advertise their more sustainable methods, but also charge higher prices to help recoup their costs.)

I ask if Ayala considers organic monoculture a contradiction. "I understand it's a monocrop," he says, but "because it's a perennial, we can't avoid doing monocropping." He recounts a trial his team did a few years ago with just over six hundred acres of organic soy as a rotation. "It almost killed me. Lots of expenses, weeds took over, we had a drought that year, it didn't grow, caterpillars and other bugs . . . we had a lot of problems."

As its certifier AZPA employs California-based Quality Assurance International (QAI), established in 1989 and owned by NSF International, an American nongovernmental organization that develops public-health standards. QAI is a for-profit firm that is a major player in the global organic trade; its stamp of approval adorns the labels of two-thirds of all certified organic food on U.S. grocery store shelves. Ayala says QAI has issued minor warnings about AZPA's monocropping, citing the need to maintain greater biodiversity. So, he explains, despite the earlier fiasco, currently his workers plant some fields with regenerative crops. When I ask how much land is currently under rotation, however, he says he's not sure.

E ven though AZPA is clearly failing to adequately cycle in various plants to repair its soil, not all crops need to be rotated at the same rate. Compared to other perennials, sugar is less taxing on the soil and less disease-prone. So in relative terms growing cane nonstop isn't as destructive as growing more nutrient-hungry crops such as tobacco and bananas. But, according to Richard P. Tucker, a professor of natural resources at the University of Michigan, "Sustainability depends on far more than the biological potential of a single crop." While it may fare well in the short run, over longer periods of time this stripping away of biological complexity has a more profound impact. Just because sugarcane is typically tougher against infestation and more forgiving to the soil doesn't mean it's immune from harm. This becomes apparent as soon as Ayala directs my attention to the plants in the field where we're standing.

The head of crop care digs up one of the young organic cane plants by its roots. "Here, this is the mark of a driller," he says as he points to a brown borehole in the base of the stalk. He cuts into the plant's green and white flesh with his pocketknife searching for the culprit, but the pest has already moved on. Drillers are a serious problem because they suck the sweet liquid from the plant, leaving it unable to mature. Every stalk Ayala pulls up carries the telltale mark. The bugs also plague some of AZPA's vast conventional fields, Ayala tells me. But he doesn't bring up the connection between the pest infestation and monoculture farming, nor does he mention that unhealthy soil conditions created by single-crop farming also increase runoff that would otherwise recharge groundwater sources. This is a serious issue on AZPA's plantation since it sits atop the massive Guaraní Aquifer, one of the biggest underground stores of freshwater in the world, and a major source of drinking water in South America.

An outsider might conclude that these results are at odds with official USDA National Organic Program (NOP) regulations, but the devil is in the details. The legal text that delineates NOP standards doesn't explicitly ban monocropping—in fact the word is never mentioned. Further, the rule sheet uses the term *biodiversity* just once, in the definition of organic farming: "A production system that is managed in accordance with the Act and regulations in this [document] to respond to site-specific conditions by integrating cultural, biological, and mechanical practices that foster cycling of resources, promote ecological balance, and conserve biodiversity." The text does call for crop rotation, which all organic farms must engage in—save for farms that cultivate perennials such as sugar-cane. "Perennial cropping systems [must] employ means such as alley cropping, intercropping, and hedgerows to introduce biological diversity in lieu of crop rotation." So, technically speaking, AZPA doesn't have to tear up its sugarcane every year and plant soy or some other nitrogen-fixing legume. But the company is required to grow other types of crops amid the cane. While AZPA might employ these practices, Ayala never says so, and I don't see such efforts at biodiversity in the organic fields I visit.

QAI seems more forgiving of the sugar maker, however. Each year the certifier dispatches a freelance inspector to AZPA; for the past several years they've sent Luis Brenes from Costa Rica. When we talk over the phone, Brenes won't speak specifically about AZPA, but claims that NOP standards on biodiversity are too vague for a certifier such as QAI to impose restrictions on farms that monocrop. "If you have a requirement that is not concrete enough to be measured or in some way evaluated, you cannot audit it," Brenes asserts. "And that's something that happens with biodiversity."

"That sounds like a bit of a cop-out to me," says Jim Riddle, former chair of the National Organic Standards Board, the body that wrote and administers NOP regulations. As Riddle explains, while the language in the official code doesn't itemize specifics for every bioregion, organic inspectors aren't meant to use any lack of detail as a loophole, adding, "There are some certifiers that are much more attuned to biodiversity, and QAI is not one of them."

Adhering to more straightforward NOP organic rules, AZPA plows without turning the soil, weeds by hand, and forgoes chemical fertil-izers, herbicides, and insecticides (for example, Ayala and his crew are releasing wasps to try to drive out the drillers). But as a soil amendment AZPA relies heavily on chicken manure from industrial poultry farms—the type that administers antibiotics and uses feed laced with arsenic to speed growth (not to mention breeding birds to bulk up so quickly their legs snap beneath the weight, and packing the animals tightly into indoor pens). Again, counter to common sense, this practice is entirely acceptable under the current law. NOP regs make no distinction between manure from an organic animal farm and that from a chemically reli-ant industrial operation. Further, although substances including arsenic are banned from organic production, the way NOP rules are currently interpreted, manure from animals fed such substances doesn't have to be treated before being applied to organic fields.

On the afternoon Zaldivar drives me through AZPA's plantation, we pass a storage area piled with grayish mounds of chicken dung. A suffocating ammonia odor infiltrates the car. "What kind of organic farm can this really be if it relies on chicken manure generated by a factory farm?" he snipes. He rails against the inadequate certification system that allows an organic operation to be dependent on an environmentally unsustainable, polluting enterprise. At another point Zaldivar tells me, "Organic is becoming exactly the same as conventional. The revolution organic once was doesn't exist anymore, it's gone." While observations such as this could be construed as hypocritical, they're not entirely uncommon in the corporate organic trade. Among the industry's key players are people with a background in progressive politics and environmentalism. I imagine this is what predisposes Zaldivar to admit that organic hasn't turned out the way he once thought it could.

Zaldivar is a former militant leftist and founding member of Paraguay's Workers Party. In his late forties, he's got a compact build, keeps his thinning hair buzzed short, and persistently tries to conceal his chronic edginess. Zaldivar tells me he started protesting the military dictatorship of Stroessner when he was a university student in the 1970s. But when police brutally killed some of his comrades, and Stroessner retained power despite the resistance, Zaldivar called it quits. "I don't do politics anymore," he says. "I decided to get a job instead." Zaldivar calculated that if he tried to save society, he could pay a dear price, but if he tried to save himself, he could prosper. And that's what's happened. He is now among the upper class who live in gated compounds and drive imported cars. I ask why he continues to work with companies such as Wholesome Sweeteners and General Mills if he doesn't believe in what they produce. "Because of the money," he replies. "In organic you can make a *lot* of money."

ISLA ALTA

Rubén Ayala didn't take me to where many of AZPA's newer organic fields are located, in an area called Isla Alta, in the state of Paraguarí, which borders Guairá to the west. AZPA's unconventional cropland traces the silhouette of the Ybytymi, a low string of hills that surround a river studded with a series of dramatic waterfalls. On the ridges above the falls gnarled succulents intertwine with mango trees, and the bulbous tops of spindly palms glimmer in the scorching sun. Sparse grasses and the red flames of flowering ginger plants dot the ground as Brazilian walnut trees—some can reach as high as one hundred feet—elegantly stretch skyward. A portion of the Ybytymi range is protected from development, having been granted national park status by the federal government several years ago. But AZPA's land is just beyond the geographical reach of the restrictions. The longtime environmental secretary for the state of Paraguarí, Flor Fretes, helped in a recent effort to extend the boundary of the park, but it failed.

Zaldivar drives me through the plantation at Isla Alta, which is just a short distance from Salto Cristal, one of the area's unprotected waterfalls. Across these hillsides span thousands of acres of both conventional and organic fields. This year's organic cane has already been harvested, but workers are still bringing in the nonorganic crops. In one field, men and machines cut and load; the heat and dust persist as ceaselessly as the desolate drone of the engines. The organic acreage is bordered by forest and pasture, which is dotted with white cows that graze under a cloudless sky heavy with humidity.

Irritable again, Zaldivar shoves his hand toward the windshield and points at the fields. He tells me he's witnessed the number of trees dwindle dramatically, "mostly in the last five years, that's when you can really see it. That's when demand for organic really picked up." Along many stretches I can see that the thick tangle of forest abruptly halts at the tidy edge of AZPA's fields. Although the company grows some conventional cane out here, this is the designated area where AZPA is expanding its organic acreage; it stands to reason that the forest in Isla Alta is being taken out for organic. As we're leaving, we come to a spot where two dirt roads intersect. At three corners sugarcane bristles up from the earth; the fourth is still dense with trees. "Totally new," Zaldivar says, pointing to the cropland.

I return to Isla Alta a few days later with Flor Fretes, and she brings her husband, Avelino Vega, who is a local lawmaker and farm extension worker. They grew up in the area, know the terrain well, and are both members of the right-wing Colorado Party. The conversation quickly turns to the clearing of trees. "Ten years ago there were no roads, it was totally forested. I've watched it change, everyone around here has," Vega says. Fretes agrees, adding, "It's very difficult to fight against. . . . Because AZPA's a big business in the area, everything is just forgotten."

As we drive the anonymous dirt roads that delineate AZPA's fields, Vega brings up another impact of the company's enterprise. Small farmers in the area used to grow a wide range of food and cash crops, such as pineapple, within the existing forest. But now, with the promise of higher incomes from organic, they have a major incentive to switch to sugarcane. The result is an overall homogenization of what used to be a far more diverse ecological gene pool, not to mention the loss of knowledge on how to raise a variety of edible plants without felling trees.

It's challenging to figure out exactly what is happening on AZPA's land. Rubén Ayala tells me the farm is fifteen thousand acres. An article from a Paraguayan government website says that AZPA cultivates twenty-seven thousand acres of a farm that spans a total of fifty thousand acres. And Raúl Hoeckle, then president of AZPA, tells me they have twenty-five thousand acres in cultivation but won't say how much additional land the company owns.

Hoeckle is about a year away from retiring and expects his son to come on at AZPA sometime soon. Before the senior Hoeckle assumed his post at the firm, he worked in the plastics industry doing manufacturing and trading, and for a company that sold snack foods from Arcor, a large Argentinean corporation that makes cookies, candy, and crackers. When I ask about the deforestation in Isla Alta, Hoeckle gets cross. "Why did you ask? We don't do it *anywhere*. The organic law doesn't permit any of the planters to deforest. We don't do it!"

Over the phone from his office in Asunción he goes on, in a still agitated tone, to explain that as a child he used to go to Isla Alta all the time because his family raised cattle there. The Hoeckle clan sold their land and later bought it back, and he says, when they did, trees had been cleared. "I can tell you that the owner from whom we bought it . . . they cut down trees before they sold it to us to make money from timber. But *they* did that, not AZPA." Hoeckle, who also serves at the Network on Investment and Export, a division of the Ministry of Industry and Commerce, wavers back and forth between asserting that the land has always been without trees and conceding that parts of the forest have been felled. "I can't tell you who cut trees before, but when we sell or buy, our responsibility starts when we buy the land. Only then is it important that we don't make something against nature—and we *don't* do it!"

Fretes tells me it's hard to believe AZPA didn't deforest the area. "Who else would?" she asks. "Even if it's not them doing it directly, even if it's other companies or small farmers, AZPA knows the land is cleared for them to grow sugarcane. Either way, AZPA is ultimately responsible." While AZPA itself may not clear land at Isla Alta, according to the people I talked to, forest that once stood is now gone and has been replaced at least in part by the company's organic crops.

Clearing trees, or transforming any native biome, to create cropland undeniably wrecks diverse ecosystems, yet NOP standards don't ban it. The official document outlining the rules never even addresses the practice. "This is the problem of how the farmers interpret the rules," explains Salvador Garibay, a researcher at the Swiss-based Research Institute for Organic Agriculture, who works extensively with organic growers in Latin America. "If the farmers and certifying agencies and buyers take into account biodiversity then this wouldn't happen." Laura Raynolds, codirector of the Center for Fair and Alternative Trade at Colorado State University, frames the issue in terms of the market. "What incentive do organic producers have to not clear land? If they are involved in commercial organic circuits, where price premiums for producers are often quite low, they are caught in the same market dynamics as conventional producers and many may disregard rules that are not enforced." If powerful farms and certifiers can bend and interpret the standards to get away with avoiding more expensive organic methods, then why wouldn't they?

Although official NOP certification rules do not forbid the destruction of native environments, QAI is also supposed to inspect AZPA's organic fields according to International Federation of Organic Agriculture Movements guidelines, a set of global rules that prohibit "opportunistic ecosystem removal." However, due to AZPA's obfuscation, when QAI asks how the land was previously used, the company can simply say it sat fallow, was cattle pasture, or has been shifted from conventional production. Since apparently no inspectors have sought to confirm this, AZPA need not mention deforestation at all, and QAI can continue rubber-stamping AZPA's organic seal. When I ask QAI about the situation at AZPA, its general manager, Jaclyn Bowen, says the company "has been an advocate for the organic industry and the biodiversity, improved soil quality, and water quality that it represents."

ITURBE

The Asociación Agrícola Cañera del Sur (Agricultural Association of Southern Cane Growers) is a half-century-old farmers' cooperative head-quartered in Iturbe, a dusty town several kilometers down the Tebicuary River from AZPA. Each year AZPA augments its supply of cane by pur-chasing the harvest of local smallholder farmers. I've come here to meet some of the growers who supply the sugar maker. We sit in the Cañera del Sur office with the windows open; a ceiling fan whirs overhead, and a few of us pass a cup of cold yerba maté, a traditional tea. Francisco Ferriera, president of Cañera del Sur, says the co-op has 220 members, most of whom grow sugarcane on farms that vary in size but can be as small as two and a half acres. Wholesome Sweeteners has been working with Cañera del Sur for the last five years, brokering their deal with AZPA, and helping them get both organic and Fair Trade certification.

Cañera del Sur farmers earn their organic status as part of what's called "group certification," which is permitted by both the USDA National Organic Program and the European Union's organic EU-Eco Regula-tion. The idea behind group certification—praised by many who promote small-scale organic agriculture in developing countries, and criticized by those who believe it can't guarantee all growers employ organic methods—is that it allows larger numbers of family farmers to earn the organic seal while minimizing costs. Under this setup, a group of farmers pool their money to pay the certifier, a fraction of the farms are physically inspected, and if they're approved, all the group members get the seal.

In the case of Cañera del Sur, AZPA—not the farmers themselves—orga-nizes the group and pays for certification. (This is a common arrangement in developing countries with impoverished farmers seeking verification seals.) That means the organic distinction doesn't belong to the farmers, but instead is the property of AZPA. Consequently, Cañera del Sur mem-bers can't vend their produce as organic on their own. If the campesinos want to get the price premium, they are obliged to sell to AZPA. Accord-ing to Zaldivar and Francisco Ferriera, if the small growers had to carry this fee, it would be their single largest fixed cost. On their own—without AZPA picking up the tab, and without group certification—most of these small farmers could never afford to get certified organic.

As for Cañera del Sur's Fair Trade certification, Wholesome Sweeteners foots the bill, again because it's too costly for the growers to fund themselves. As is true with organic, Fair Trade, or FT, is accredited by a third-party organization, which then grants the producer the right to stamp the official seal on its product packaging; for goods sold in the United States this label is issued exclusively by the nonprofit certifier TransFair U.S.A.; it is a black-and-white graphic of a person holding a bowl in each hand. FT-certified goods cost more for Western consumers because the items are grown using sound environmental practices, and, most centrally, because small farmers garner a higher—"fair"—price for their produce. The idea is to boost the income and therefore standard of living of peasant growers such as those in rural Paraguay. Zaldivar tells me that in the case of Cañera del Sur, FT status increases their earnings by about a third.

Wholesome lets the farmers keep the entire FT premium without requiring any repayment of the certification fees. I ask why his company doesn't try to recover the thousand or more dollars a year it spends to renew Cañera del Sur's license. "First, it's good marketing for Wholesome, it makes us look good," Zaldivar says. "Second, last year the market for Fair Trade in the U.S. grew by thirty-seven percent—that's a lot more than the organic market." In other words, the FT logo on Wholesome's packaging is good PR and gives the company greater access to the burgeoning mass of socially conscious shoppers. Since Wholesome pays to maintain Cañera del Sur's FT certification, however, the license belongs to the trader and not the campesinos. As with their organic-certification deal, the small farmers can't sell cane as Fair Trade to anybody but AZPA, which in turn sells that sugar only to Wholesome.

A Cañera del Sur member whom I will call Eber Ibarra is thirty-five years old and has been farming since he was a child. His parents, grandparents, and great-grandparents were farmers; as far back as he knows, his family has worked the land in Guairá. His fields are some distance from where he, his wife, and their two young daughters now live. They moved from their old house near their acreage because the road was too rough. About twenty kilometers from the nearest town, their current home is still remote but more accessible; for most of the year, the unpredictable dirt roads are navigable on the cheap motorcycle the family recently bought on an installment plan.

Out here the landscape is cloaked in rich grasses and trees, and the soil is either bright red or ocher; in every direction giant termite mounds rise like earthen stalagmites. In the distance round hills rise abruptly from the flat earth. Ibarra's small, weathered house is washed in chipping blue paint, has a rudimentary kitchen, one bedroom, and a storage room, no bathroom, and no running water. The family spends most of its time out of doors, which can get difficult in the peak of summer. We sit outside under a tree in the molded-plastic lawn chairs now ubiquitous the world over. During the time that we talk, we all periodically adjust our seats seeking shade to block the sapping, extreme gaze of the sun. Chickens and ducks flap and squawk in the dirt yard near a white horse that's tied to a tree.

Ibarra grows five acres of sugarcane on his farm. His annual crop of cane generally earns him just under $3,000 per year. Out of that he must pay workers to help harvest. He can't do it alone; when it's time to bring in the cane, it must be done quickly. When the mill issues the word that it's accepting tonnage, small producers such as Ibarra must get theirs in before other growers do, lest the company stops buying. The rapid pace is also due to the need for income; by the time harvest rolls around, most growers have earned little if any money for a full year. Out of his pay, Ibarra also has to cover the cost of transporting his stalks to AZPA's gate.

This year the harvest was difficult. After dealing with cut cane languishing on the ground uncollected for weeks, Ibarra finally got it delivered to the mill and got paid. But once he subtracted his costs for labor and hauling, he ended up well below the Paraguayan minimum wage. So, as often happens, the family will have to rely on the income of his wife, who works at the local health clinic. There she earns less than the national minimum of about $265 per month; but that, along with their subsistence crops, is what keeps the family of four fed, clothed, and able to make the payments on their motorbike. She tells me the health clinic has no medicine, and almost no supplies, so area residents most often end up relying on traditional cures using roots and herbs.

Ibarra's good friend, neighbor, and fellow Cañera del Sur member, whom I will refer to as Luis Gonzalez, has also had a rough season. Early on, Cañera del Sur encountered troubles with transport. The co-op had a contract with a hauling company called El Corre Caminos, which belongs to one of the owners of AZPA. (Cañera del Sur owns three trucks, which Wholesome helped it buy, but these are not enough for its more than two hundred members.) According to the farmers, El Corre said it could handle eight loads a day, but sometimes collected just two loads all week. Because of this Gonzalez was hesitant to cut—if the stalks sit too long they lose their juice and with it their value. Being cautious, he waited until he knew there would be a truck, but none ever came. Out of his twenty-five acres Gonzalez cut only seven; most of the stalks still lie scattered in the field. "I feel like I've been ripped off," he says, exasperated. And he wasn't alone, according to Francisco Ferriera of Cañera del Sur, about 70 percent of its members couldn't deliver their cane this season.

Gonzalez wasn't able to harvest last year either because of a shortage of field workers. This type of low-paying, hard, manual labor is failing to attract a new generation. If cane goes uncut for more than two years, it is virtually worthless; farmers might try to sell it to another mill as conventional or offer it at a pittance as cattle feed to one of the area's ranches. Gonzalez doesn't sell any other crops; everything else he raises, including a few cows and chickens, is for subsistence. His wife works the farm so when they don't move their cane, neither have an income. In years when there is little or no revenue from sugarcane, Gonzalez, his wife, and their daughter survive on money he earns as a laborer on a nearby estancia owned by a powerful senator.

When I ask Ibarra and Gonzalez why the collection trucks didn't come, they say it's because AZPA grows a lot itself, an increasing amount of which is organic. "I think this happened because AZPA has too much sugarcane to harvest," Gonzalez assesses. "We are basically competing with them now." Ibarra agrees, "AZPA is growing more organic than in the past, and they give priority to their own fields." To remedy this, Ibarra and Gonzalez tell me the co-op wants to start its own mill, where they figure they would earn 60 percent more money. And, Ibarra says, their daughters could become managers there. But when I mention this to Zaldivar, he is skeptical: "AZPA would drop them for another co-op and they would lose what they've got." He adds that AZPA intends to start its own Fair Trade co-op "with farmers it can control."

Even though Ibarra and Gonzalez are registered organic and Fair Trade, it's no guarantee they'll make a living wage. If the company's harvest was sufficient or they procure it from other growers, these campesinos won't take home the income that certification promises. According to the international body that oversees FT, the Fairtrade Labelling Organization, farmers on its rolls sell no more than 20 percent of their crops at the premium price. The rest either rots in the field or is off-loaded at far lower conventional rates. Regardless, AZPA and Wholesome get to stamp their quota of packages with the seals. This is obviously not what consumers have in mind when they purchase organic and Fair Trade items. Part of what's made Fair Trade so popular in the Global North is the notion that it will help small farmers such as Ibarra and Gonzalez earn more to improve their quality of life. In this case, however, Fair Trade status binds these growers to a single processor and trader because the cost of certification is so high. Despite how it may look from afar, the system meant to ensure ethical standards and ecological well-being can deal small farmers out from the start.

Something else Western consumers might find surprising is that although Gonzalez has been certified organic for over ten years, his farm has never been visited by an organic inspector. The cane he grows carries the seal of QAI, which has also never sent anyone to Ibarra's farm (although he was once visited by the Swiss body Institute for Marketecology, which certifies for the European market). Instead, as is allowed under NOP rules, AZPA performs the inspections itself. That means when QAI's man shows up for annual assessments, he first reviews AZPA's in-house records on its suppliers. Then the inspector randomly selects a group of farms to make the trek to. The proportion of farms he visits isn't something laid out in official organic rules, however; it's entirely at the discretion of the certification body. The more farms the inspector checks up on, the more money it costs the certifier. This can, of course, create the temptation to keep the number of visits low. One thing external inspectors might not see is that some of these farmers fail to rotate crops. Because sugarcane is a perennial and the area has rich clay-based soil, the campesinos can and do leave the roots in the ground as long as they continue to produce; these peasants can't afford to lose the income from planting a different crop to revitalize the soil. In his field Gonzalez has grown cane from the same roots for thirteen continuous years. He says he's not concerned about pests and infertility from monocropping because it hasn't been a problem yet.

Regardless of whether organic certifiers review the paperwork and walk the fields of each small farm, the reality is that cultivators such as Ibarra and Gonzalez will most likely grow without chemicals because that's what they know and can afford. Chances are low that they'll cheat by using pesticides or synthetic fertilizers, even if they don't rotate crops or maintain good diversity in their fields. But, by not visiting the farms of each grower, and relying on AZPA's audits, certifiers can miss other damaging practices.

YBYTYRUZÚ

Paraguay is comprised of two main ecosystems. In the country's north and west is the less populated, more arid Great Chaco Forest, which reaches over the Argentinean border. Stretching across all of eastern Paraguay and into both Argentina and Brazil is the Atlantic Forest. This region used to be blanketed in trees, but now what remains is a devastated biome, fragments of flora and fauna cut off by cropland and cattle pasture. Today over 90 percent of the native forest has been felled, rendering the area, according to environmental researchers, "arguably the most devastated and most highly threatened ecosystem on the planet."

Driving to the top of Acati, the second-tallest point in the Ybytyruzú chain of hills, not far from AZPA's Tebicuary mill, I come across a newly cleared field. Jagged trunks mark what used to be standing; their stubble looks awkward amid the previously sheltered dirt and grass that's now exposed. A curtain of intact trees hangs behind the freshly cleared two acres of land. Much of the Ybytyruzú area is protected by a federal law that designates it a Managed Resource Reserve, meaning that trees can be cut but only with a permit. Campesino farmers are sprinkled throughout the Ybytyruzú, their croplands creeping up into some of the last remaining clusters of native forest in eastern Paraguay.

Mariano Martinez is in charge of making sure the reserve does not further disappear at the hands of loggers, farmers, and fires. In his late thirties, Martinez has been working as the lone Ybytyruzú park guard for about fifteen years. The reserve is sixty thousand acres, all of which lies on unpaved roads, many rough and steep. Even though the government created the reserve, it hasn't allocated Martinez the tools to do his job; he's been given no vehicle, no telephone, no office, no computer, and no fire-prevention equipment. When we go to survey the cleared land, to look official he adorns himself with a khaki vest, a canvas hat, a pair of binoculars, and a tote bag from an environmental conference he once attended.

"This land is owned by Luis de Jesus Escobar," Martinez states as we stand on the road facing the deforested patch. The park guard assesses that Escobar, a campesino farmer (whose name I have changed), has cut the trees so he can cultivate sugarcane. "No question, the size of the area and its location just next to the road, this will definitely be used to grow cane,"

Martinez says. Along the road lies field after field of sugarcane. I ask if we can talk to Escobar about the deforested area, and with a wince Martinez shakes his head no. "I don't want to go talk to him. It could turn violent," he says. "Besides, the bad thing is already done."

Almost everyone around here has a .38, Martinez tells me as he pulls back his vest to reveal a handgun (which he has borrowed from another government agency because the reserve did not provide one). "I've never used my gun, but people have pulled guns on me many times," he says. On one such occasion he was walking around the reserve and a man he suspected of clearing trees put a rifle to his chest and told him to leave. Martinez recounts another incident when he was home with his wife and three kids and a car drove by firing twice into the air and once at the house. The bullet hit a wall and no one was hurt. The shooters were never found. "There are many interests: there's the political, money, business interests—those are the people who are really dangerous," Martinez explains. "The demand for organic sugar in the U.S. and Europe is a big pressure on the forests here."

Escobar's land, it turns out, is not in the reserve Martinez monitors, although it lies in the middle of the Ybytyruzú chain. Even still, looking across a steep, narrow valley directly into the reserve, deforestation is obvious to the naked eye. "We have to grant the people who live here the right to support themselves off the land," Martinez explains. "As their families get bigger, they are not leaving, so they clear more and more land to grow crops to earn a living." Martinez says that although residents in and outside the reserve are required to get permits to cut, the majority of farmers ignore this rule. And, despite the supposed success of the 2004 Zero Deforestation Law, enforcement mechanisms around here are essentially nonexistent, so the clearing persists.

According to Martinez many of the farmers in and around the reserve are certified organic, and it's likely that Escobar will seek, and win, the official seal. While deforestation is nothing new to the region—most of the forest was taken out well before official organic arrived—the price premium for organic is driving cultivators to clear more land. "When we started, we thought certifying these small farmers was a good idea, that it would form a sort of greenbelt around the Ybytyruzú chain," Zaldivar tells me. "But instead the farmers now have incentive to go into the forest and clear it away to grow organic cane."

THE POWER OF ORGANIC

The laws enacted in both the United States and EU requiring organic food and farming to meet certain standards, among other outcomes, have contributed to a streamlining of commerce, greatly easing national and international trade in organics. Since U.S. regulations apply equally in all fifty states, a producer in, say, Paraguay has to meet just one set of guidelines to sell its goods throughout the entire country. Before the American standards were fully implemented in 2002, different states and various certification companies followed an array of directives in a piecemeal system. This made it exceedingly complex for a firm such as AZPA to crack the rich and voracious U.S. market. The EU's rules, which originated in the early 1990s, have also helped its organic sector become more cohesive, albeit less so than in the United States. Because these are the most developed organic markets globally, their guidelines serve as de facto international organic rules.

Although U.S. and EU laws say organic food must be regulated, how those standards are upheld is another issue. Under the American system, the government isn't directly tasked with day-to-day enforcement. Instead, it issues licenses to private certification companies for the job. Government officials can intervene when there's a serious problem, but, otherwise, the certification firms call the shots. QAI's Jaclyn Bowen refuses to answer any questions about what's happening on AZPA's land when I inquire. She does say that as of May 2009 (a year and a half after my visit to Paraguay) QAI is no longer AZPA's certifier, but she won't say why. It serves the interests of organic certification firms to keep a lid on the situation. If QAI, or whoever goes on to certify AZPA, raises questions about, say, deforestation at Isla Alta, or deems AZPA unworthy of organic status because of monocropping, the company runs the risk of losing a valuable customer. According to Zaldivar and Ferriera, the leader of Cañera del Sur, during the seven years it was certified by QAI, AZPA spent about $25,000 annually renewing its organic certification.

While it's unclear whether QAI was aware of possible noncompliance at AZPA, the company has been known to protect powerful clients in the past. The most prominent case involves Aurora Organic Dairy, one of the largest such operations in the United States. Aurora is owned and operated by the founders of Horizon Organic Dairy (now held by Dean Foods, the leading dairy producer in America), and its milk is sold in cartons bearing the in-store labels of Target, Wal-Mart, Safeway, and other major chains. These retailers typically sell their milk at a lower price than the brand-name organic stuff. In 2007 a USDA investigation identified over a dozen "willful violations" of organic provisions by Aurora, which owns large-scale farms in Colorado and Texas, and a dairy processing center in Colorado. According to the investigation, Aurora was running its dairies more like industrial feedlots, not letting its cows sufficiently graze on pasture, integrating conventionally managed animals into its organic herds, and keeping inadequate records of its activities and transactions. The Cornucopia Institute, a Wisconsin-based watchdog group that filed the initial complaint against Aurora with the USDA, reported that the dairy company's violations were so overt it's implausible that QAI could have missed them.

Throughout the investigation, the certifier stood by its client, and in the aftermath of the USDA judgment, QAI spoke in Aurora's defense. Ultimately, Aurora signed a consent agreement with the USDA admitting no wrongdoing while accepting a probationary period during which it would address the issues raised in the investigation. QAI, however, has suffered no disciplinary action for its handling of the dairy's certification.

Joe Smillie, vice president of QAI—and a current member of the National Organic Standards Board—recently told a reporter, "People are really hung up on regulations . . . I say, 'Let's find a way to bend that one, because it's not important.' . . . What are we selling? Are we selling health food? No. Consumers, they expect organic food to be growing in a greenhouse on Pluto. Hello? We live in a polluted world. It isn't pure. We are doing the best we can."

By no means do all organic farmers and processors flout the rules. A number of organic proponents I talk to stress this point. But even when certified producers do the right thing, the guidelines and enforcement are seriously flawed. Peter LeCompte, the organic-sourcing manager for General Mills, which owns Muir Glen and Cascadian Farm under its Small Planet subsidiary, is one of the biggest buyers of organic in the world, and he's a major customer of Azucarera Paraguaya's. When I interview him, he says he can't comment on land use or farming practices at AZPA. But LeCompte agrees that the current certification system is susceptible to fraud. "Sure," he says. "If somebody wants to cheat and they're smart, they can get away with it." No doubt many in the organic industry would prefer if the public remained oblivious to this. As it stands, organic rules can be manipulated without sacrificing the price premium—which can be 10, 30, 50 percent or more above the cost of conventional food—because, as LeCompte puts it, "people's faith in organic is often not founded in knowledge." The General Mills executive isn't alone in this assessment. Bruno Fischer, director of international procurement for another large organic conglomerate, Hain Celestial, sees the matter similarly. "Most consumers are simple minds," he imparts to the audience at an organic trade show I attend. "Simple minds will look at the label and nothing else."

From grocery store aisles the competing interests and layers of inter-relations are impossible to see. Small farmers can be registered Fair Trade and organic and still not earn a living wage because they're bound to a single buyer. If that deal falls through for any reason, the campesinos lose. The organic label on a bottle of ketchup signals to the green shopper that its ingredients—including the sugar—weren't harvested from monocultures raised on land where native forest used to stand, even if that's not true. It's difficult to read these complex realities through the postage-stamp-size emblems that promise biodiversity, socially just conditions, and the abandoning of toxic chemicals. Many Westerners believe organic marks a return to a cycle more aligned with the workings of nature. But what official organic really means in such places as the eastern forests of Paraguay is not so straightforward.

After a long day in AZPA's mill and rambling plantation, Zaldivar tells me there's no guarantee Wholesome and AZPA will keep their prominent place in the organic sugar business. Some producer in some other country might come in at a lower price and "it could all be gone, in one day, just like that." The short term is the enduring quality in Paraguay, and not just in the organic trade. "I can't think of the future, I can't take it for granted," Zaldivar says. "All that is certain is uncertainty, and you just learn to live with that."

A few nights later I have a final meeting with Zaldivar at an expensive restaurant. The waiter is dressed as a gaucho and serves us grilled chicken hearts and fresh steak. Our table is on a covered patio, and a group of unwashed, rag-clothed children pass by in a horse-drawn cart filled with garbage. Zaldivar is unmoved. As our conversation goes on, it becomes clear that he's grown ambivalent about what he told me in previous days.

Tonight he says he believes Big Organic can correct the looming environmental crisis. He now claims the system will save itself—pursuing social change to create ecological stability, he says, is just too dangerous. Then his cell phone rings. His oldest son, who's twenty, has been kidnapped. He slaps his phone shut and dashes to his car. I watch the red taillights trail off down the road.

On the way back to my hotel I'm suddenly more aware of the neighborhood. My eyes are drawn to a house with the kind of lights that would be used to illuminate a football field; four squares of intense white, silently streaked by bugs that momentarily reflect the electric glare. Stationed atop tall posts, maybe thirty feet up, the lights point down into the backyard. The whole place is concealed by sheer, mute walls. Many homes in the upscale district look something like this, the physical demonstration of efforts to wipe out the unknown: the risk of strangers walking up, the chance that someone might be taken, shot at, killed.

The uncertainty in a place like Paraguay, for rich and poor, is so palpable it can begin to seem like a natural aspect of life; the presence of it changes in the way the heat changes throughout the day. The early-morning coolness lingers in the shade, near trees and bushes, and gently gives way to midday rays. But before long the sun grows stifling, there is nothing merciful about it. It singes the skin. The warmth it offered just a few hours before is now transformed into a force that's unbearable. Then with nightfall, the heat recedes as if to rest. But it is replaced by darkness, hence the floodlights.

In such a situation, dismantling biodiversity, felling trees, cutting deals with certifiers, and taking advantage of small farmers can, oddly, start to seem logical. Why not get in before someone else does, or before economic and political structures splinter? Amid extreme poverty and extreme wealth the notion of organic ceases to make sense. The market for organic is clearly not here, where most of the population must endure such realities as no running water, while those with all they could want live in constant fear. The majority of people in the tattered economies of developing countries don't understand what "organic food" is, even though they grow, sell, and eat it. Today's conceptualization of organic is a specific cultural creation. It comes from developed countries that have industrialized their own agricultural systems and are now trying to remedy the consequent ill effects. Some organic farmers follow the rules, but the incentive to cheat and to erode those rules is omnipresent. The ever-expanding growth in competitive Western economies provides constant pressure for companies to push up profits by any means necessary. The quaint picture of the small farmer raising organic crops, doing the right thing for the planet by appealing to what Western consumers want—the win-win scenario that the eco-friendly marketplace promises—can easily translate into something quite different, and ephemeral, on the ground.

PART II

Shelter

CHAPTER THREE

The Greenhouse Effect: Eco-Architecture

The outer London borough of Sutton has a long history dating back hundreds of years, but the residential area known as Beddington looks like any other British post–World War II suburb. The place is gray and flat and planted with rows of semidetached houses, each with its own small patch of grass in front and in back. Cars are parked in driveways or at the curb; some have been deposited in the lot at the Hackbridge train station for the day while their owners labor in jobs such as manufacturing or behind clerk's desks in central London. A ten-minute walk from the station sits a cluster of residential and commercial buildings topped by brightly colored metal air vents, which flag the settlement of the Beddington Zero Energy Development, or BedZED. A high-profile experiment in green building, BedZED was erected in 2002 by the local architect Bill Dunster and an environmental consulting company called BioRegional—both now headquartered at BedZED—together with Peabody, a London-based nonprofit organization that provides homes to people in need.

BedZED is higher density than most of the surrounding conventional housing, with five rectangular four-story structures that contain one hundred housing units—flats and town houses—as well as a community center and offices. Its style is distinctive; each building is clad in brick with a glass facade, and wood slats covering its backside in a rounded slope evoking a ship's hull. Nearly every unit has a modest garden; some are at ground level while others sprout on upper decks. Large sections of BedZED have what are known as green roofs, areas carpeted with vegetation (typically sedum, a low, dense flowering plant), which provides insulation in the winter and helps keep interior spaces cool in summer. BedZED has outlets in its parking lot to recharge electric cars, a water-treatment facility, banks of solar panels, and an on-site electricity and heat plant. The idea behind BedZED, as its name suggests, is to have buildings that release no carbon dioxide or other greenhouse gases into the atmosphere.

When people think about green architecture, they may conjure images of off-the-grid hay-bale houses on some rutted country road, or perhaps Highgrove House, the eco-estate of Prince Charles in Cornwall, England. The prince redesigned this stately Georgian manor to accommodate the composting of food wastes, and the recycling of the building's gray water (from sinks and showers). Highgrove sits amid thirty-seven acres of gardens and an extensive farm, all tended organically. Alternately, green architecture might bring to mind more pedestrian eco-features such as recycled-denim insulation, bamboo flooring, and chemical-free wall paint. But at BedZED, and other places like it in countries such as Denmark, Sweden, and Germany, more comprehensive green architecture, meant for average people, is flourishing. In these countries, city governments, local communities, builders, and architects are focusing not just on recycling and reusing materials, but also radically reconceptualizing home energy. Some say the resources needed to construct a house account for a far smaller—although in no way insignificant—environmental footprint than is made by the energy it consumes over its lifetime. This number, however, is difficult to calculate and has become a point of debate in green building circles. Either way, buildings are energy hogs. Power burned by residential and commercial structures accounts for almost 40 percent of all carbon dioxide emissions in the United States, about 36 percent in the European Union, and half in the United Kingdom. But what is this new generation of green houses like? Are they a realistic replacement for the current standard home?

In the winter of 2009 I visit BedZED to see what the place is like. The development's model house is a two-story apartment that offers few clues that it's superefficient. Downstairs is a full bathroom and two large bedrooms that each open onto a narrow, glassed-in veranda. It's afternoon and the bedrooms are flooded with light. Upstairs is a half bath, a smaller bedroom, kitchen, dining room, and the living room, which is joined to another sunporch. John Shakespeare, who works for Dunster, is showing me around and explains that heat from the sun collects in the patios, then flows right into the house, what's known as a passive heating system.

Dunster has found a number of ways to cut energy consumption. The flat has thickly insulated walls, high-tech windows, and is virtually air-tight, employing a special ventilation system that keeps warmth from escaping indiscriminately when fresh air comes in. "The way these houses are built, they retain the heat from the sun, as well as the heat given off by people, electrical appliances, and even pets that might be inside," Shakespeare says. (Central heat is available when needed.) Another way to reduce energy use is to let the inhabitants see how much they consume. Mounted inside a kitchen cabinet are three meters, for electricity, heat, and water. "These are normally installed in the cellar somewhere," Shakespeare tells me. "But if they're here in plain sight, we've found that people will look at them and naturally use less."

In addition, the project's developers were ambitious enough to install the complex technologies of an on-site water-treatment facility, and a waste-wood-fueled, or biomass, electricity and heat plant. BedZED was designed to provide all of its energy needs—using its biomass facility along with electricity-generating solar panels (known as photovoltaics), and solar water heaters—while staying carbon neutral. (Unlike green-house-gas-spewing fossil fuels, organic matter such as wood only releases the CO_2 the tree absorbed while it was alive.) However, because the British market has been slower to go green than some, such as Dunster, would like, technologies that are more advanced in other countries remain underdeveloped here. That has meant some of BedZED's key utilities have been plagued with problems almost from the start.

The power station hasn't worked for years because incinerating wood instead of coal or natural gas clogs the generator's system. Not long after BedZED was up and running, the company that provided servicing for the station went out of business. Since the technology was (and is) so rare in the UK, no other companies in the region had the skills to repair the machine. So, BedZED residents must pull power from the grid just like everybody else. The wastewater-treatment scheme to render as reusable the development's effluent, including its sewage, known euphemistically as blackwater, also fell short. Its designers outfitted BedZED with a series of "living machines," a technology pioneered in the United States in the 1980s by Nancy Jack Todd and John Todd. The machines are really large containers filled with a mix of plants and algae that cleanse bacteria and toxins from liquid castoffs. This unorthodox, albeit visionary, approach may have worked but BedZED couldn't, or wouldn't, bring in an adequately trained maintenance crew. BedZED has constructed another treatment system using different technology that works—at least for now—by recycling wastewater for reuse in the development's toilets. With some aspects of the project having achieved its planners' goals, while others have tanked badly, BedZED is obviously a work in progress.

Bill Dunster is barrel-chested, wears a goatee, and is older than he looks. The architect emanates a vivacity that seems impetuous, yet all he talks about are consequences and responsibility—of how important it is to stop wasting as many resources as we do. He fires up a PowerPoint presentation on his work and is already well into the slides by the time I take my seat at the glass conference table. "We did a study on the capacity for renewable energy in the UK and we found that there's very little of it," he asserts. "There's this idea that you can just switch from fossil fuels to renewables. But you can't because there's not enough of a supply from renewables. That means we simply must consume less." Dunster speeds through some statistics on peak oil and the inevitability of having to live differently from how we do today. He says that each country must address its individual energy needs, relying as little as possible on outside sources.

BedZED is Dunster's answer to this predicament. By designing housing that needs far less energy to create a high standard of living, Dunster believes he can help bridge the gap between the lifestyles people want to maintain and the imperative of cutting fuel use. When I ask about the shortcomings at BedZED, he responds, "This place is not utopia. Don't make it into something that's miraculous because it isn't." The technologies aren't up to scratch, the architect says, because they haven't received adequate support from private investors or the government. When it's just a few individuals or groups such as Dunster, BioRegional, and Peabody doing the research and development, improvements will be slower than if these technologies and methods had widespread backing. "Banks are useless, governments are useless—you just have to take it all into your own hands," he tells me.

Over the last three decades people have come to think that ecologically responsible living inevitably entails the sacrifice of going without. It is the image of hippie asceticism, of eating tasteless food, of a stinky compost pile, no television or dishwashing machine, and turning off the water while sudsing up in the shower. By contrast the new environmentalism has brought eco-luxury: high-tech houses fully fitted with the coolest green gadgets. But there seems to be little in between the two extremes.

The most die-hard go for it full tilt: An article in a 2009 issue of the *Mountain View Telegraph,* a regional New Mexico paper, profiles Kathy Baur, who moved to the area and single-handedly built an "earthship" abode. "I totally cashed in all my chips and just said, 'Gulp,' because I gave up an awful lot of material things. A house, a good job, retirement setup, the whole nine yards," she told the *Telegraph.* The report describes how after reading three books on erecting earthships—the squat, earthen structures first introduced in the 1970s by Michael Reynolds, which incorporate discarded materials such as used tires and empty cans, and typically back into a hillside for insulation—she gave herself over to the practice of self-sufficiency.

On her own, Baur pounded dirt into the one thousand tires that form the curving, textured walls of her house, where in some patches the black rubber peeks through. She also made an indoor wetland system to recycle the sink and bathtub water for an indoor garden; whatever drains off from that goes to the toilet. "That means the water is getting used three times before it goes to septic," Baur told the *Telegraph.* And like many earthships, her home is entirely off the grid. Located on a swath of remote New Mexican desert (almost no other houses are in sight), her electricity comes from a bank of photovoltaic solar panels installed on the roof, which feed a set of deep cell batteries kept in a storage room. As for heat, Baur says her house stays warm enough from the sunlight that shines in; the coolest it's ever been is fifty-eight degrees Fahrenheit.

For some this is the nightmare scenario that makes them crank up the thermostat and leave all the lights on. Fear of having no choice but what many perceive as an arduous, survivalist lifestyle has damped enthusiasm for ecologically responsible dwellings—until recently, that is. In the last decade a new wave of green architecture has emerged, and it's hardly rough going. At this end of the spectrum are single-family homes with modernist glass walls, grass roofs, and garages for the Priuses; and eco-savvy luxury high-rise towers topped with glimmering solar panels.

One Los Angeles–based developer, LivingHomes, offers elegant prefabricated eco-abodes that feature recycled building materials, photovoltaic panels, solar water heating, a system that directs shower and sink water through filters and into the outdoor garden, energy-efficient lighting and appliances, and more. But, as its website reads, these features don't come cheap: "When we speak of a good value for the price, by no means do we mean that our homes are inexpensive." The company's smallest, bare-bones model, which is just over 1,000 square feet, starts at $219,000, while its top-of-the-line five-bedroom, 3,100-square-foot home rings in at just over $1.2 million (and these prices don't include land, surveys and permits, design fees, transportation for the structure's components, and the management and labor to build a foundation and install the house).

In the dense urban jungle of Manhattan is another strain of high-end environmental living. The Solaire is a tony twenty-seven-story apartment building with almost three hundred units erected in 2003. In addition to all the expected amenities—such as a twenty-four-hour doorman, concierge, and fitness center—it boasts a range of eco-features. The Solaire was built with materials low in volatile organic compounds and high in recycled content. It has photovoltaic panels to provide supplementary power, runs its heaters and air conditioners on natural gas (which emits less carbon dioxide than coal), and treats a portion of its wastewater for reuse in toilets. According to the Solaire's architects, the building systems' design has resulted in an almost 40 percent drop in potable-water usage, and overall energy consumption that's 35 percent lower than state energy code requirements. But, again, being green requires the green. Monthly rent at the Solaire starts at $3,500 and goes up to almost $10,000. For some this type of eco-chic architecture may seem hassle-free and fit more readily into their lifestyles. But when ecologically responsible options are priced well beyond the reach of most families, the fundamental barriers to widespread change are left intact.

Developments such as BedZED inhabit the ground between these two extremes; its demographic consists of people in the middle and working classes, as well as low-income residents, who receive housing subsidies. But, because BedZED is still relatively young and small, I decided that to understand how this type of architecture works I would go to a more seasoned eco-community such as that in Freiburg, Germany. Reputedly one of the world's greenest cities, Freiburg is home to two renowned eco-villages, Vauban and Rieselfeld. Both are well established, having been around for more than a decade, and together house almost fifteen thousand people. These neighborhoods use many of the same principles and methods applied at BedZED, but on a much larger scale and over a longer time, offering a deeper view into life on the green side. While in Freiburg I focused on Vauban to find out whether stringent green living is comfortable and functional, or if it's only for the indoctrinated hippie or the well-heeled professional.

That two of the world's most respected green communities are in Germany is no accident. The country has transformed itself over the last thirty years into something of an eco-architecture and renewable energy powerhouse. Germany's pursuit of conservation and homegrown alternatives to fossil fuels initially arose in response to the dramatic and sudden fuel shortages triggered by OPEC's oil embargo in 1973 (a second abrupt fall in supply came when the Iranian revolution sparked in 1979), accompanied by a popular rejection of nuclear energy. In the midst of all this, the Green Party was founded in the late 1970s in the state of Baden-Württemberg, not far from Freiburg, helping give ecologically sound policies a political voice. Today Germany's solar power industry—panel production, power stations, and research and development—ranks first globally, although the United States, Japan, and China are hot on its trail. One in every hundred German homes has solar panels on its roof. German-built wind turbines are standing in regions across the world, and the country's application of tougher codes requiring more energy-efficient buildings— by many accounts driven by the trailblazers in and around Freiburg—has led to Germany's becoming an international leader in green building.

VAUBAN

The number three tram goes straight from Freiburg's central train station to Vauban. The trip takes about fifteen minutes and first weaves through Freiburg's medieval old city, dense with intricate buildings, some of which date back to its founding in 1120. The line then passes the newer areas that reach out toward the suburbs. When the tram heads into the quarter of Vauban, I spot a billboard advertising a green business park that's been shot up with paint balls; their large, round splotches of color drip down over the photo of a fresh-faced woman sitting at a desk.

I disembark in central Vauban, a neighborhood that's home to five thousand people. Lining the small streets and pedestrian lanes are blocks of apartments—boxy, three- and four-story buildings. (I subsequently discover that the district has no freestanding single-family homes.) The structures vary in size—some have only a handful of units, while others have eight, twelve, fifteen—and are offset from each other by various design elements: clean modernist lines, or bungalow-style finishes, whimsical paint jobs, or austere facades. Rows of photovoltaic panels line several roofs; on upper floors, outdoor decks and atriums are crammed with plants. On the ground level, small back gardens beat to mud by winter boots are now slicked over with the January ice. All the houses have sheds for bicycles just outside their front doors. The velvety, snow-dusted hills of the Black Forest rise to the east.

At first I see no cars, only people riding bicycles, even though it's snowing. Children parade in groups or follow their parents along footpaths. I head to a restaurant called Süden to meet a few Vaubanites for lunch. In the five-minute walk from the tram stop I see a health-food store, bakery, ice-cream shop, and an architect's office in storefronts that line the neighborhood's main street. In my short journey I also pass two parks.

Do you know what a heat-exchanger ventilation system is?" asks Marcus Neumann as I join the table. He explains the innovative but simple technology, which I come to learn is standard in most energy-efficient abodes. It differs from a typical circulation setup because it has a honeycomb-type filter that forces cooler incoming fresh air past the warmer air that's leaving the house, thereby recovering heat and bringing it back into the house. According to estimates, these devices allow a building to retain 90 percent of its heat. The most energy-frugal buildings have banks of south-facing windows that allow in the sun's heat, rely on a tight seal of well-milled and fitted windows and doors, thoroughly insulated walls, and heat-exchanger vents to prevent warmth from escaping unchecked. Since so much energy is expended for climate control—in the United States 56 percent of all power used by households goes toward heating and cooling, in the UK it's 58 percent, while in Germany that number is closer to three-quarters—heat-retaining features are vital. Although Neumann, who's forty years old with blue eyes and a shock of light brown hair, has his own business doing research for pharmaceutical firms, the physicist sees himself as an informal emissary of Vauban. A two-year resident of the quarter, his fervor is palpable as he rattles off facts about the ecologically sustainable power the district relies on. He later confesses that, if he could, he'd put his business on hold to do a dedicated study of energy systems and ecological building.

Andreas Delleske walks in late with a bundle of cables and a switchboard under his arm. Delleske has a slight build, silver hair, and seems pensive. He's an energy consultant and one of the earliest residents of Vauban. He insists that for lunch I have the homemade spaetzle, a specialty of the region. I take his advice, and after we order, Delleske launches right in:

"I think when people are properly informed, they will choose renewable energy. It's not ideological, it's common sense."

Delleske recounts the early days of the quarter, which is a former German military base established in the 1930s and taken over by the French army after World War II. In 1992, after the fall of the Soviet Union, the French vacated and ownership reverted to the state of Baden-Württemberg. The state government then decided to sell the site to Freiburg. At the time, the city was in the midst of a severe housing shortage, and according to Delleske, the local government initially explored marketing the area to private developers. But a group calling itself the Selbstorganisierte Unabhängige Siedlungs-Initiative (SUSI), or Independent Self-Organized Settlement Initiative, came together and proposed a different option. Their vision was to make Vauban—the name the French had given the base—into an ecological settlement open to a range of people including those with lower incomes, and students. SUSI made an initial plan for how the barracks buildings could be transformed into affordable green housing, with which they lobbied the local government. Eventually, in 1994, the town council agreed, by a thin margin, and against the wishes of then mayor Rolf Böhme, to sell four barracks buildings to SUSI.

About a year later, Delleske was hired by SUSI as an electrician on its "energy group," which was tasked with rebuilding the barracks' heating system and was one of several such groups organized to remake the buildings. On heating detail were four others, including a plumber who'd studied physics and a computer programmer. In a subsequent conversation Delleske and I have, he speaks of the time with animation: "We didn't ask, 'What are we doing?' There was almost no discussion, it was just creative." The energy group devised clever ways of minimizing consumption by, for example, catching excess heat from one apartment and sending it to another that needed more. And they experimented with alternative sources of energy. One member of the group led them in adapting the furnace to run on vegetable oil.

In this atmosphere of experimentation, a new entity, the Forum Vauban Association, was founded in 1995 by some of the earliest settlers of the district. Late-night brainstorming meetings led one into the next as the machinations of a larger energy-efficient, socially oriented community began to take shape. Soon Forum Vauban won a sizable grant from the German Federal Foundation for Environment, and further funding from the city of Freiburg, and LIFE, a European Union body that funds environmental conservation efforts. Forum Vauban's main objectives were to flesh out its socioecological planning concepts and the practicalities of how to implement them. To that end, the group set up an office to conduct its own research and held weekly gatherings to exchange ideas with the public.

Out of all this came a four-hundred-page document with a wealth of proposals. Among those eventually realized: making the quarter virtually car-parking free; establishing a strong car-sharing network; creating a rainwater retention zone and requiring green roofs on certain structures; encouraging larger, more resource-efficient apartment buildings constructed with local materials and thorough insulation; promoting self-sufficient electricity with photovoltaics, and encouraging the use of solar panels to heat water; installing an ecologically enlightened "cogeneration" district power plant, as well as small cogeneration units for individual buildings. (Also known as "combined heat and power," cogeneration harnesses the creation of electricity to make not only current but also heat. Conventional power plants allow the large amounts of heat given off as a by-product of generating voltage to escape unused, often through cooling towers. This means only about 33 percent of the energy from the fuel that's burned is actually used; the rest is lost. But cogeneration captures that excess warmth and channels it to heat buildings within close proximity, taking fuel efficiency up to between 60 and 80 percent.) Forum Vauban's plans also included mapping out the streets, buildings, and public spaces to nurture social interaction. Underpinning the group's wide-ranging scheme was the philosophy that it's not enough to build a house with sustainable materials, nor is it sufficient to run renewable power through its lines; a deeper cultural normalization of ecologically sane living must also occur.

Forum Vauban's ideas about motorized traffic proved among its most controversial. The group's primary goal was to minimize automobiles to promote a kid-friendly pedestrian zone that prioritized bicycles and mass transit. To meet this aim, Forum Vauban proposed banning parking on most residential streets, instead requiring inhabitants to leave their cars in lots on the edge of the quarter. What's more, car owners would have to pay a hefty onetime fee of €16,000 (US$24,000) for each spot. The intention was to discourage residents from having automobiles and, if they did, to get them to forgo driving for short trips. Forum Vauban wagered that if cars weren't woven into the fabric of the community, then greener options would become habit.

Such an ambitious and unorthodox plan had never before been tried, and Mayor Böhme, a Social Democrat, and many members of the town council were dubious. Ultimately, dedicated lobbying by the community and progressives on the council helped push the scheme through (the liberal Green Party enjoys significant support in Freiburg). By the time the dust settled on the first phase of development at Vauban, only 50 percent of the parking spaces city bureaucrats insisted would be needed were occupied. As of 2007 car ownership in Vauban was half the national average. Many people tell me that the hard fight for Vauban's unique traffic concept, despite its success, is not over. A few weeks after I left, a group of Vauban residents went to defend the program to Freiburg officials, who continue to insist more cars must be allowed.

Back at the restaurant, I can see the public square outside the window where farmers, butchers, and cheesemongers are setting up their stands for the weekly open-air market. I later learn that the building we're in, which is the district's community center, called Haus 037, the square it sits on, and the farmers' market are all the result of residents pushing against city planners to realize their vision of Vauban. The bureaucrats had unilaterally decided Haus 037 shouldn't be the community center, and that the public square would be located elsewhere in the district. As we finish lunch, Neumann reflects, "What you see in terms of planning in Vauban is the result of social planning and a different consciousness, a self-organization of the people. Instead of just complaining about it, people have done something."

It's been about twenty degrees Fahrenheit for the last three days, and snowing for the last two. It's noon and I've arrived with my bags at Kleehauser, a pair of apartment buildings in Vauban, and find Doris Müller on the second-floor landing. She's renting me a small one-bedroom for the next five days—I want to see what it's like to live in a house that leaves a minimal ecological footprint. So far everyone I've talked to at BedZED and in Vauban tells me that these houses are a wonder. It sounds good, but I'm skeptical. Does it really work? Will I stay warm in the middle of a cold snap in one of these places? Will it have quirks and idiosyncrasies?

At first I can't help it—I don't trust that the apartment will stay warm enough, so as soon as Müller leaves, I turn on the radiator in the bedroom. Almost involuntarily my aversion to being cold takes over. When I return at the end of the day, disappointingly the radiator is only slightly warm, so I crank it up all the way and leave it on while I sleep. I wake up toasty and sure that if I hadn't blasted the heat, I would be freezing right now (as happened the previous night at a hotel). I put my hand on the radiator and nothing, it's completely cold. It appears the heat wasn't on, or at least not strongly, all night. Yet the place is comfortable; I can't walk around in my underwear, but neither must I don a scarf. (I later find out the radiator has a thermostat that overrides the manual controls, only allowing the heat to come on if the room's temperature dips below seventy-three degrees Fahrenheit.) I decide to turn off the radiator entirely and test the mettle of this superefficient apartment.

On my first morning I open the curtains in the bedroom, which faces south. Here is where the hallowed rays of sun are meant to come in. Almost the entire wall is glass—windows and a door that opens onto a terrace. When I look out at the snow-covered park below, I notice the pane isn't frosty or even cool to the touch as it would be in a conventional building. I inspect the windows and door more closely and see that they're triple-paned with superthick wood frames of about six inches.

The apartment is compact and consists of a tiny kitchen, dining room, bedroom, and bath. It looks and feels familiar, like any other recently built flat, finished walls, new fixtures, IKEA furniture. I explore some of the other features of the eco-apartment. I take a shower, leery of being forced to submit to tepid water. When I turn on the tap, it's steaming within seconds and stays that way. Under the bathroom sink are meters, such as those at BedZED, that tell me how much energy and water I'm consuming. On the wall in the kitchen is the small duct for the heat-exchanger ventilation system, which looks like any standard air vent. I cook some food and discover that the electric stove works just like any other, as do all the lights, the Internet, and the flat-screen TV. After a few days I forget I'm consuming a fraction of the energy I do when I'm at home.

For the duration of my stay the outside temperature dips below freezing and one afternoon climbs into the forties, while the nights are much colder. Aside from my first twenty-four hours I never turn the heat on, yet the apartment holds consistent at just above seventy degrees Fahrenheit.

Michael Gies, a local architect who designed the Kleehäuser as well as some of the first newly constructed buildings in Vauban, sketches two different floor plans on a sheet of white paper. One has many sides and the other only four. "Minimizing the surface area of a building allows for more efficiencies," he says. Instead of erecting smaller separate houses, it's more sensible to put up a larger structure. "Single-family homes are a waste of space and resources. I like higher-density residential housing because it's just a better way of making housing." He sits across the table from me in a meeting room in his office, a converted apartment in an elegant old building near the center of town, decidedly un-Vauban. Retrofitting existing structures to achieve energy efficiency, he explains, is another crucial aspect of green architecture. Gies is in his fifties, has mussed gray hair, disarmingly crooked teeth, and a contemplative manner.

Kleehauser was constructed by a *Baugruppe,* or building group, from Vauban that hired Gies for the job. The *Baugruppe* model is common in, although not exclusive to, Freiburg and typically entails a group of anywhere between three to fifteen or so families getting together to build a multiunit apartment house. They employ an architect whom they work with on all the details during the design and construction, thereby cutting out the costs of the developer. Each family pays their portion and gets their flat when the building is complete. This system makes it possible for those with fewer resources to become homeowners and is a good opportunity for architects such as Gies to propagate energy-efficient dwellings.

The *Baugruppe* that built the Kleehauser employed the principles of *Passivhaus,* a tricked-out version of designs like the one applied at BedZED. The passive element of *Passivhaus* is that it lays the groundwork for the structure to retain as much warmth (or coolness in the summer) as it can on its own, without the need for energy-sucking central heat and air-conditioning—what characterizes an "active" home. To control the indoor climate in the winter, the householder must simply open the curtains to let in the sunlight and, in the summer, pull the shades in the day and open the windows at night to catch a breeze.

For this type of system to work the building must be oriented to the south (or the north in the southern hemisphere), and it must have a virtually airtight "envelope," industry jargon for the structure's overall seal from the elements. To achieve this, about sixteen inches of dense wall insulation (typically rock wool, made from splintered rocks spun with resin) are needed, as well as triple-glazed windows with inert argon gas between the panes and a special heat-retention coating, and, of course, a heat-exchanger ventilation system. Eliminating gaps between walls, windows, doors, and ceilings demands painstaking specifications that are more readily achieved through prefabrication in a clean, well-lit factory than at a weather-beaten construction site. Consequently, the most efficient buildings are made from walls, doors, and windows manufactured on assembly lines installed by skilled, vigilant craftspeople.

Architects and builders around the world—although concentrated in Germany and Scandinavia—are slowly but surely adopting *Passivhaus* technology. The *Passivhaus* design was developed by Wolfgang Feist, an engineer and architect in the town of Darmstadt, just a few hundred kilometers north of Freiburg. Feist constructed the first *Passivhaus* in 1991 and subsequently established the Passivhaus Institute, a hub of green architecture today. Feist's technology improved on efforts from previous decades whose airtight, ultra-insulated, solar-heated shelters were uncomfortable, in part due to stagnant air and mold. Structures built to *Passivhaus* specifications can derive 40 percent of their heating requirements from solar rays gleaned through windows, requiring overall just one-fifteenth the power of a conventional abode. On average an existing home in Germany uses about twenty kilowatt-hours of energy per square foot of space. Astonishingly, to do the same job, the *Passivhaus* needs a scant 1.3 kilowatt-hours.

The passive approach also ratchets up the "low-energy" design that is mandated in Freiburg for all new houses constructed on land bought from the city. This requirement, enacted in 1992, says energy consumption can't surpass six kilowatt-hours per square foot per year. All houses in the neighborhoods of Vauban and its sibling Rieselfeld, the town's other eco-village, also built on formerly city-owned land, must meet this minimum standard. The low-energy requirement is helping foster an industry that, until recently, didn't exist. "Ten years ago there were a lot of craftsmen who wanted to do things the same," explains Gies. "Even small things, the craftsmen didn't want to change." Building to low-energy, not to mention *Passivhaus,* standards requires some retraining and a shift in practices. "They said, 'No, we can't do it!' right up until [Freiburg's] low-energy law passed, then the next day they did it," Gies tells me.

I probe him about costs. Kleehauser ran 7 percent more than it would have had the group not built it to *Passivhaus* specifications. Gies's office did a comparison of Kleehauser with conventionally built apartments in town and found that the *Baugruppe*'s expenses were the same and in some cases lower. "We economized on certain aspects," such as minimizing surface area, which not only saves on energy but also labor and materials. Even though it costs more to build this way, the architect says, the added investment will pay off in the long run. After about nine years the money saved from consuming dramatically less energy will have covered the initial outlay; from then on the savings accrue to the residents. Gies tells me that Kleehauser demonstrates the costs of *Passivhaus* construction can be kept in check without compromising quality. And, he explains, this formula can be applied anywhere, even in the United States.

Given that, and although it's being adopted as a standard in some new buildings in Freiburg and throughout Germany, Gies is clear-eyed about the obstacles green architecture such as *Passivhaus* faces in achieving a larger reach. This is neither because it's too expensive, which he contends it isn't, nor because the technology isn't ready, it clearly is, but rather due to a greater lack of political will. In a city as progressive as Freiburg, he says, "There were always people in the local administration interested in green architecture. But without outside movements, a place like Vauban never would have happened."

FREIBURG

Located in the far southwest of Germany, Freiburg sits on the southern edge of the Black Forest in the country's sunniest spot. The often-cloudless skies contributed to activists in the 1970s, and inhabitants and leaders in subsequent decades, envisioning the town as a solar-power hub. Home to two hundred thousand residents, Freiburg prides itself, indeed markets itself, as a solar city, a green haven, a seat of European if not global eco-living. Freiburg's green turn came well before the 1992 low-energy standard for certain houses, and Vauban and Rieselfeld aren't the only green spots in town. Beginning in the 1970s, and expanding over the years since, the city banned auto traffic from many streets to create an ever-larger pedestrian zone in the central district. Extensive networks of bicycle paths facilitate Freiburg's current residents using two-wheelers for more than a quarter of all transport. In more recent years, public officials have upped the low-energy rule by more than 20 percent and installed solar photovoltaic panels on city hall and the main railway station. Local hotels, shops, factories, office buildings, and the town's sports stadium have also gone solar. Crucially, these projects, and the developments of Vauban and Rieselfeld, were not born whole cloth, but rather are the product of a series of larger political and historical events.

More broadly, being situated in the picturesque Black Forest, Freiburg has largely based its identity on the area's natural beauty. (Never having industrialized, Freiburg is now known as a university town with over twenty thousand students, and a major tourist destination.) But by most accounts the seeds of Freiburg's current environmentally oriented living sprouted in 1975. That year government officials decided to build one of the world's biggest light-water nuclear reactors in the small town of Whyl on the river Rhine, just thirty kilometers from Freiburg. Thousands of university students from Freiburg, and residents from nearby cities and towns, began to protest, holding ongoing demonstrations and eventually occupying the plant's construction site. This dissent happened in the post-1968 era of charged political disobedience, with strikes, rebellions, student activist movements, and militant anticapitalist groups such as the Red Army Faction in Germany and the Weathermen in the United States.

The Whyl region was dense with vineyards and cropland, and its vintners and farmers were also leery of the nuclear plant. Historically a conservative lot, the growers quickly joined the protests, finding themselves shoulder to shoulder with the radical student movement in nonviolent direct action. Converging from around Germany, as well as nearby France and Switzerland, almost thirty thousand people took part in the occupation of the site, which lasted over a year and a half. The action fostered a vibrant culture where people shared communal meals, created a school to study political topics, and built shelters for each other to stay in as the protesters occupied the site in shifts. Eventually, the activists won, permanently blocking the planned nuclear station.

On the heels of this success came similar demonstrations against nearby chemical plants and atomic-power stations. When I interview Thomas Dresel, an executive at the city's Environmental Protection Agency, he recounts an event in the early 1980s when schoolkids and university students protested an existing nuclear-energy facility just across the border in France. That day six thousand youths lay down and played dead in the streets of Freiburg. Around that time forward-looking ecologists established entities such as the Öko Institute (the German Institute for Applied Ecology), a policy think-tank, as well as the Fraunhofer Institute for Solar Energy Systems, now one of the world's leading and most respected solar-research centers. Makers of renewable energy hardware such as the solar-panel producer Solar Fabric AG also started up. Fueling greater interest in alternatives, these developments attracted environmentalists, as well as the brainpower and financial resources to refine building designs and methods based on energy conservation.

In this context, the German Green Party, one of the first in Europe, was founded in the late 1970s in Karlsruhe, just a short distance north of Freiburg. The Greens went on to become this generation's most powerful third party in German politics. They served with the Social Democratic Party in the national ruling coalition from 1998 to 2005 and continue to hold sway, especially in the Black Forest region. All these shifts became self-reinforcing; as more ecologically engaged students, teachers, scientists, investors, and politicians gravitated to Freiburg, more projects got under way.

The last major push in the formation of today's Freiburg took place in 1986 when the Russian nuclear-power plant at Chernobyl catastrophically melted down. The blast, and subsequent fire that burned for ten days, created fallout that was four hundred times more radioactive than Hiroshima. Aside from the immediate injuries and deaths, and the displacement of hundreds of thousands from their homes, a radioactive plume quickly descended over Russia and many European countries, including Germany. As the toxic cloud hung over Freiburg, no one really knew what the consequences would be. "That event had such a major effect," explains Professor Eicke Weber, director of the Fraunhofer Institute for Solar Energy Systems. "Chernobyl was the moment when everyone said, 'Wait, maybe this isn't such a great technology.' This was really a triggering moment."

In Freiburg, responses included mothers forming groups to buy milk and other comestibles from outside the area to keep their families from ingesting radioactive food. Also professionals such as architects and scientists committed themselves anew to designing buildings that needed less power, and maximizing renewable energy supplies, so nuclear would no longer be necessary. The effects shot through to the highest levels of German government: just months after Chernobyl the conservative administration of Helmut Kohl established the unambiguously named Ministry for the Environment, Nature Conservation and Nuclear Safety, which has been the catalyst for the country's pathbreaking promotion of renewable energy. (Current chancellor Angela Merkel, leader of the conservative Christian Democratic Union, served as environment minister from 1994 to 1998.) The Social Democratic–Green Party coalition government enacted the Nuclear Exit Law in 2000, which mandated a shutdown of all

German nuclear power plants within twenty years. By the beginning of 2008, nearly 14 percent of the country's electricity came from renewable energy thanks in part to vigorous support from the Ministry for the Environment. The office claims the country is on course to meet 25–30 percent of its electricity needs with green power by 2020. The events of the 1970s up through today, combined with Germany's dearth of oil and natural gas—and therefore slightly less powerful fossil-fuel interests—continue to foster a citizenry and government supportive of energy conservation and renewables.

SOLAR SETTLEMENT

"The real cost is the psychological cost of changing," Elsa Gheziel tells me as we sit in her living room discussing the higher price of green architecture. For about two years she and Marcus Neumann, the physicist, have lived in a flat in what's called the Solar Settlement, on the northeastern edge of Vauban. Gheziel thinks construction, utilities, and maintenance over the lifetime of a house have no absolute costs. "It's all relative." We have grown accustomed to assigning a certain price for a house based on the initial capital outlay, but the cheaper that is, the lower the quality and the higher the maintenance and the energy fees are over time. If somehow these amounts could be combined into what Gheziel calls a "global" price for a house, then flats such as hers at the Solar Settlement would be competitive. "Maybe the cost is a very small part of the problem," she reflects. "The rest is political."

Gheziel, who's French and thirty-six, moved to Freiburg from Paris with Neumann, who's German, explicitly to live in Vauban. The couple met while volunteering on a campaign to convince the Parisian city government to construct a green district. In their lobbying, they both brought groups from Paris, including politicians, urban planners, and journalists, to Vauban (among other places) to show them the possibilities. "Eventually we won, but everything got so watered down," Gheziel told me of their work in Paris. From their junkets the couple realized that their politics and daily life would come together most fully in Vauban. "We want to live this way, to show it can be done. To find solutions," she tells me. "We didn't want to always be fighting."

The Solar Settlement is the residential component of a live-work development; the commercial building is called the Sun Ship. The Settlement comprises five rows of attached terraced houses, with fifty units in all. Each has a balcony and a garden and is painted a vivid red, blue, green, or yellow. On the Settlement's eastern side is woodland, and to its west is the Sun Ship, which also has the long, rectangular form common to energy-efficient architecture. The Ship's gray tile and abundant windows present a steely facade softened by brightly colored shutters. Inside are four stories of offices accommodating everything from an alternative-energy company to a bank. On the ground floor is retail space with a café, health-food market, and drugstore. Atop the Sun Ship are nine penthouses and a rooftop garden. No cars are allowed inside the Settlement, with parking spaces on the development's periphery. The only parking on the grounds is for a single vehicle from Vauban's popular car-sharing program.

The Solar Settlement and Sun Ship are the work of another local architect, Rolf Disch, and they were assembled with some of the most cutting-edge materials and designs that push low-energy and *Passivhaus* technologies to the next level. These are "plus-energy" buildings, and as their name suggests, their breakthrough is that they produce more power than they use. After participating in the pivotal nuclear protests in Whyl as a young man, Disch devoted himself to building structures that would require little energy and could generate their own power from renewable sources. Completed in 2006, the Solar Settlement and Sun Ship projects together form Disch's largest development to date.

As with other supergreen buildings, the Solar Settlement and Sun Ship are oriented to the south to maximize sun exposure for passive solar heating through large windows, and electricity generation with photovoltaic panels. The construction materials and methods echo those used in a typical *Passivhaus*: triple-glazed windows, superthick rock-wool insulation, heat-exchanger ventilation systems, and airtight construction. Disch's project also pulls in new technology such as wallboard made with tiny spheres of paraffin wax that are invisible to the eye. The wallboard was developed up the road at the Fraunhofer Institute, which devises energy-saving building materials, high-performance solar panels, off-the-grid power sources, on-the-grid renewable power generation, and even hydrogen technology. On a simmering summer day, wax in the spheres of the institute's wallboard liquefies as it absorbs heat, thereby lowering the temperature of the room; then during the cooler hours of the night the wallboard releases its stored warmth and the wax solidifies again.

In addition to such innovations, what makes the Settlement and Sun Ship different is that the roofs are literally made of photovoltaic panels; their surfaces are a slick of shimmering blue cells encased in transparent sheets of glass. The roofs are pitched to the south so they capture the most light throughout the day. In summer when the sun changes position, the roofs' overhangs shade the south-facing windows, keeping interior spaces cooler.

Disch's development is economically feasible in part thanks to the EEG, or Renewable Energy Sources Act, a nationwide law passed in 2000 that requires power companies to buy—at a premium—renewable energy generated by private owners, such as those at the Settlement. What's more, the utilities are obliged to purchase green power from each producer for twenty years. The EEG, also known as the "feed-in tariff," covers wind, solar, hydropower, biomass, and geothermal (power captured from heat stored in the earth), creating a guaranteed return to householders on their investment. Under the feed-in tariff, utilities must pay more than double the market rate for solar power, or about €.45 per kilowatt-hour. This high price lets solar panel owners recoup their costs faster, leaving them well over a decade of pure profit. Money for the EEG doesn't come from the government or the utility companies, but from an increase in rates for all customers of about €.01 per kilowatt-hour. Everyone who uses electricity contributes to what essentially is a fund that then goes straight into building a renewable energy infrastructure.

At the Solar Settlement, and almost all the other homes I visit in Freiburg that are decked out with photovoltaics, the solar panels exist essentially as generators. Instead of being hooked up to the house's wiring, as has been common practice in the past, the cells are plugged directly into the central grid, the physical network that delivers energy to consumers. (The grid system was created over a century ago and has historically moved energy in one direction—from fossil-fuel-burning centralized power plants owned by utility companies to houses, offices, factories, etc. But any grid-connected building that generates its own supply, say, with solar panels, can send voltage back out to the network for others to use.) The two-way connection provides greater stability for those with solar panels—no need to fret over lack of power on cloudy days—and eliminates the hassle of storing unused energy in clunky batteries installed somewhere in the house. Significantly, this setup also allows solar panel owners to earn back their initial outlay faster than if they used the juice themselves. Largely considered a success, in the five years after the EEG went into effect, the amount of renewable energy fed into Germany's grid more than doubled.

One afternoon I meet Disch at his office in the Sun Ship. It's quiet and most of the lights are off, to conserve energy I guess. We sit at a large table in the sunny conference room. Disch is in his sixties, wears a charcoal herringbone jacket, and has downy gray hair and a bright countenance. I ask the architect how solar can beat out conventional fuels, and he stresses, "The oil companies are the most powerful companies in the world and they're not going to give up easily." To deal with this, Disch believes the role of government is crucial. "Just because of the EEG law Germany became top in wind and solar. The law made many investors react immediately." No technological barriers exist, according to Disch, and no significant economic ones either; he believes that plus-energy buildings can be erected on a wide scale immediately. "The problem is in our heads," he says, index finger to temple.

In addition to practicing architecture, Disch spends a lot of time reaching out to government officials; creating a truly green future demands education about what's possible. In 2008 he launched a campaign he calls "A PlusEnergyHouse for Every Community." Disch initially sent information on energy-efficient architecture to seven thousand mayors throughout Germany. More than two hundred municipalities responded, and as of 2009, one solar-housing development is in the works, with three more in the pipeline. However, Disch explains, government's role must extend well beyond planning decisions. "Only the state can put taxes on the things that are destructive for the environment. With taxation we must bring out the real costs so that the one who creates the pollution pays the damage." He then tells me the economy should serve the greater good of supporting life and well-being for everyone, and not the other way around. "Capital is to be seen as part of society. It doesn't stand for itself."

CHASING THE SUN

Part of what has slowed BedZED in fully achieving its aims is that the proper technology and support services don't yet exist in the UK, as they do in a place such as Freiburg. When BedZED's biomass system went down, adequately skilled repair and maintenance workers were hard to come by. When I was at BedZED, Dunster was also meeting with rep-resentatives from a biomass equipment manufacturer to negotiate the purchase of a new unit. Dunster told me he hopes this one will work, espe-cially because the technology is so expensive. If Dunster and BioRegional had access to the know-how available in Vauban—which uses a larger-scale and higher-tech version of the same type of power plant—BedZED would most likely be tooling along. Why these resources have flourished in Germany and specifically Freiburg is no mystery. The city's dedication to renewable energy and superefficient architecture is the result of signal historical events and the consequent social awareness that fomented polit-ical engagement. This perfect storm continues to be reinforced by events unfolding today.

On January 1, 2009, not long before I arrived in Freiburg, Russian prime minister Vladimir Putin took the drastic measure of turning off the natural gas from Russia to Ukraine, which transships large quanti-ties to Europe. A week later, Russia blocked gas exports to the EU, accus-ing Ukraine of siphoning off the European supply. With no reserves of its own, Germany is among the EU countries that rely heavily on Rus-sia for natural gas. Despite its green credentials, Freiburg only derives 5 percent of its electricity (although far more of its heat) from renewable sources. According to Thomas Dresel of the local Environmental Protec-tion Agency, Freiburg generates fully half of its voltage by burning natural gas imported from Russia via Ukraine. The constant pressure Putin had exerted in the preceding three years—reducing supply in both 2006 and 2008, ostensibly over price disputes with Ukraine—helped animate Ger-many's push for renewables and conservation.

The day I left Freiburg the nearly two-week gas stoppage ended as Rus-sia finally opened the tap. Not long after, Germany, together with Spain, Denmark, and seventy-two other countries, launched a multilateral gov-ernmental body called the International Renewable Energy Agency, or IRENA. (Neither the United States nor the UK joined, but the Obama administration is showing interest.) The body is charged with spurring the growth of renewable energy globally. These events illustrate the ongo-ing dynamic in Germany that keeps the country pursuing green solutions.

Had the forceful protests against nuclear energy in the 1970s and 1980s failed or not taken place, and had Chernobyl not melted down, perhaps Germany would have ignored renewables in favor of uranium as did its neighbor France, which currently gets 80 percent of its electricity from

nuclear. And had large parts of Freiburg not been bombarded and leveled during World War II, perhaps its residents would be less afraid of
future disaster. All of these forces come together against the backdrop of
Germany's political underpinnings of strong social welfare and the regulation of industry. Absent this, perhaps Germany would be faltering on
the environment. I ask Professor Weber at the Fraunhofer Institute (who
worked for years with Obama's energy secretary, Steven Chu) what it will
take for the world's other major economies, especially the United States,
to embrace green architecture powered by renewable energy. "I'm expecting a climate 9/11 event," he says. "Just think about a hurricane that goes
through Manhattan or Houston. This will be what finally convinces people we need renewable energy. I hope not, but, personally, I think this
might be true."

I make two final stops in Vauban before I leave. First, I visit Hedda Jarvis, who moved to the quarter three weeks ago and is living on her own.
I then meet with Jörg Lange, one of the founders of Forum Vauban, the
group that planned and settled the district. From the newcomer and the
veteran I want to find out what the future holds.

The building where Jarvis lives is still under construction. Since her
kitchen has yet to be installed, she's set up a kettle and a hot plate on a
small table to make do. Her three-bedroom apartment is cluttered with
partially unpacked boxes, and ornate antique furniture sits askew around
the living room. A sixty-seven-year-old grandmother, Jarvis has a small
build, fluffy blond hair, and wears reading glasses.

When I ask about her thoughts on renewable energy and ecologically
sound architecture, she, like so many others I've talked to, mentions Whyl.
The protests helped solidify her conviction that nuclear power was a bad
idea, then Chernobyl had a truly profound effect on her. Having recently
moved back from England with her husband and three young children,
Jarvis was horrified at the disaster and its aftermath; she was among those
who searched for uncontaminated food for her family. Chernobyl convinced Jarvis, having already experienced major destruction as a child—
she grew up in post–World War II Freiburg, witnessing firsthand the city
in ruins—to completely reject nuclear energy.

While she considered power from wind and solar a good idea, before
living in Vauban the retired German-language teacher didn't think much
about energy conservation. In her previous house, a spacious single-

family home on the posh Winterer Strasse, the heating bills were exorbitant because the aging structure was so poorly insulated. Not until Jarvis moved to Vauban did she realize she could live comfortably in an energy-efficient home. But, she confides, she decided to rent instead of buy because she was apprehensive about Vauban. That sentiment has quickly changed, however. "I find it great that [Vaubanites] care for alternative energy," she tells me. "I'd love to have been involved in the planning of this building with the *Baugruppe*."

Although the dwellings in Vauban (and BedZED) are recently constructed, new homes make up only a small fraction of the housing stock in most countries. In Germany, 73 percent of existing housing was erected before the first insulation standards were enacted in the late 1970s. In the United States as of 2008, just 5 percent of all homes had been built in the previous four years. The rate of new construction in the UK is similarly low. In other words, the vast majority of homes around today are old and poorly insulated and so hemorrhage heat. While BedZED and Vauban were built largely from scratch, the green breakthroughs they both exploit can be applied to existing structures as well. High-quality insulation methods, heat and electricity from cogeneration power plants, rooftop solar water heaters, photovoltaic panels, green roofs, and catching the sun's rays for indoor heating aren't just for new homes; they're readily adaptable for updating aging structures. Of course, building new or renovating housing costs money. To put Freiburg's green architectural accomplishments in perspective, the town is in the state of Baden-Württemberg, one of the wealthiest regions in one of the world's wealthiest countries. Although the money doesn't flow as freely as some would like, without access to strong financial resources Freiburg may not have achieved its environmental prominence.

Jörg Lange sits across a wood table from me in his office, and as we talk, he keeps fidgeting with a piece of paper. We are in a building called Wohnen und Arbeiten, which translates into Living and Working, and Lange does just that (his flat is on another floor). In the mid-1990s, the Vauban pioneer and some friends assembled a *Baugruppe,* pooled their money, hired the local eco-architect Michael Gies, and built the four-story apartment house. Wohnen und Arbeiten was among the first multifamily *Passivhaus* structures in Germany and was one of the initial new buildings put up in Vauban. Lange is in his midforties, tall with spiky blond hair, and is at once soft-spoken and high-strung. And he is very serious. He's a trained biologist and spends his time researching and experimenting with the latest in resource-frugal building techniques. For Lange, an ecologically sane future isn't just about having the right technology, but rather how those tools are applied.

With Vauban almost fully settled, Lange is nowadays focused on a program called the 2,000-Watt Society, put forward by a group of scientists at the Swiss Federal Institute of Technology. The idea is that each person would consume an equal amount of energy, whether he or she lived in Burkina Faso, Mexico, or England. The Swiss scientists calculated that the planet could support 6 billion–plus inhabitants only if everyone kept his or her consumption level at two thousand watts per day. The two thousand watts are allocated to five hundred for consumption in the home, five hundred for transportation, and the remaining one thousand for everything else (all the energy needed to grow the food we eat, construct the buildings we live and work in, and manufacture and distribute everything we need and use from heavy machinery to cell phones). Current energy-consumption levels in Germany are just over four thousand watts per person each day; in the United States it's almost double that.

Lange participated in the *Baugruppe* that employed Gies to build the Kleehauser, where I'm staying. They planned the structure based on the 2,000-Watt Society model. That means in the Kleehauser each person consumes just five hundred watts of energy a day. I tell Lange I had no idea I was participating in such an experiment. "Then you see that it's not that big of an issue to reduce energy consumption," he says.

Lange could seem like an extremist to some. No doubt when he and his collaborators first started their work in Vauban, he was labeled an idealist, a troublemaker. But now the quarter is the type of place that a retired grandmother such as Hedda Jarvis wants to live. Perhaps if Lange and his community continue to explore and push the boundaries of what constitutes a high standard of living, the 2,000-Watt Society or some iteration of it might take hold. "The government believes they can solve global warming with renewables alone, and this is a grave miscalculation," Lange states. "You also have to cut how much we use." Around the world, many politicians, the conventional-energy sector, and manufacturers of all kinds oppose any major reduction in consumption. If people start using less, then economies based on consumption—such as that of the United States, where buying goods and services comprises 70 percent of all economic activity—will be forced to undergo a colossal transformation. Lange clearly doesn't believe in technological fixes; he says for a solution to be viable it must also address the social forces that keep consumption rates too high. At the root of the projects Lange supports is a sentiment Bill Dunster also expressed, that an ecologically sustainable world requires that no one use more than he or she needs. As Lange explains, "The 2,000-Watt Society says that everyone on the planet deserves an equal amount of power."

PART III

Transportation

CHAPTER FOUR

The Fuel of Forests: Biodiesel

Nestled deep in the tropical rain forest on the island of Borneo, the village of Pareh is a collection of about sixty weathered wooden houses, perched on stilts and enfolded by coconut palms, banana trees, and the dappled green overhang of the towering forest. Pareh's inhabitants belong to the indigenous tribes of Borneo collectively identified as Dayaks. They have lived here for centuries hunting and gathering, as well as cultivating small crops within the forest. Raising rubber trees, pumpkin, cassava, and rice, the Dayaks of Pareh also harvest wood for fuel and lumber, gather native vegetables, and venture into the trees for wild boar and other game.

In 2005, a group of village men went hunting in the ancestral forest several hours from Pareh and stumbled on a clearing in which the trees had recently been cut. That was how they discovered that Perseroan Terbatas Ledo Lestari, or PTLL, a subsidiary of an Indonesian company named Duta Palma Nusantara, was seizing their land. The rain forest on Borneo is among the world's vastest, and the patch around Pareh is big enough for a company such as PTLL to start clear-cutting trees without the villagers finding out for weeks or even months. PTLL's aim was to establish a massive plantation of oil palms, a tree whose oil is rendered and refined into biodiesel. (One of Duta Palma's major customers is Wilmar International Ltd., a Singapore-based firm in which U.S. agribusiness giant Archer Daniels Midland holds a 16 percent stake.)

Over the next two years PTLL destroyed fifteen thousand acres, which the Dayaks of Pareh say amounts to three-quarters of their "customary forest"—land that's vital for their survival and to which they have certain rights under Indonesian law. The plantation also uprooted monkeys and wild boar, which began raiding the community's food supply. Because

PTLL replaced diverse forest with a monocrop, pests invaded Pareh's subsistence gardens. Rice crops failed. With the help of an environmental group called the Indonesian Forum for Environment, known as Walhi, the village leader, Momonus, filed complaints with regional and national officials; at one point the community commandeered one of PTLL's bulldozers (an offense for which Momonus and Jamaluddin, an elder, served jail time). The clearing went on.

Increasingly desperate, in 2007 the people of Pareh offered PTLL a drastic compromise. The villagers would surrender every acre the plantation had illegally seized if the company would agree to take no more land. There was no response. Soon after, a villager obtained a PTLL map showing the company's long-term plan: it aimed to clear-cut fifty thousand acres, more than three times as much land as it had already taken. On the map both Pareh and its sister village Sumunying were gone.

Later that fall, another hunting party was searching for wild game when the men heard the unmistakable whine of chain saws. This time, they didn't write up a complaint—they assembled a posse. More than sixty people from Pareh and Sumunying descended on the site. They found a clear-cutting crew in action, guarded by Indonesian army troops. Based on interviews I conducted and the effects I observed on the ground, such protection—from both the military and police—is commonly a favor granted by venal local and state officials getting bribes or other kickbacks from the plantations. By way of protest, the Dayak villagers seized eleven chain saws. "If we didn't do anything, our land would be gone," a defiant Jamaluddin told me.

In the search for less polluting options for transport fuels, biofuels have been trumpeted as the green solution because, when burned, they release a fraction of the CO_2 petroleum does. Ethanol, an alcohol-based replacement for gasoline and primarily made from crops such as sugarcane and corn, emits 20 percent less carbon dioxide than fossil fuel. Biodiesel, an oil-based substitute for diesel that's refined from the oil of crops including rapeseed, soy, and oil palm trees, releases just a quarter the carbon of its petroleum counterpart. With governments and consumers scrambling for alternatives to fossil fuel, worldwide demand for biofuels has gone through the roof; in Europe, where more than half of all new automobiles and a third of the entire fleet run on diesel, consumption of biodiesel is set to triple by 2010. U.S. subsidies for biofuels, mostly ethanol, will cumulatively top $400 billion between 2006 and 2022, and further cash infusions that go to biofuel producers internationally, especially in developing countries such as Indonesia, come in the form of development money from the World Bank. The upsurge appears set to continue as laws mandating biofuel use exist in the UK, European Union, Brazil, parts of China, and the United States, where President Barack Obama has said he aims to up the mix of biofuels as part of a "national low carbon fuel standard."

But amid the hype, problems have emerged. When production—and the destruction of ecosystems in the developing countries where many biofuel crops are grown—is factored in, some biofuels may actually emit more carbon than petroleum does, the journal *Science* reported in 2008. Indonesia makes room for oil palm plantations by profoundly altering its two main ecosystems—tropical rain forests and peatland forests—the climatic effects of which are devastating. Clear-cutting rain forest most often goes down in two phases: first crews use chain saws and bulldozers to cut, then fire to clear. Leveling the rain forest, as PTLL is doing around Pareh, smashes an important CO_2 repository formed by the native trees; once they're down, they can't sop up any more carbon. Making matters worse, burning the rain forest unleashes the massive CO_2 load the trees absorbed and stored throughout their life spans.

Toppling peatland forests is no less catastrophic. Peatlands are tidal wetlands in which evergreen mangrove trees grow on their gnarled, stilt-like roots. Establishing plantations on peatlands requires ripping out the indigenous trees as well as draining the wet soil, which is composed of decaying vegetation and can reach as far down as twenty feet. Although peatlands cover just 3 percent of the earth's land surface, they store twice as much carbon as all the world's forests combined. Once the trees are gone and the soil loses its moisture, CO_2 and other greenhouse gases that the ecosystem kept locked away are uncontrollably dumped into the atmosphere. Worse still, dried peat is highly combustible, and once it catches, CO_2-spewing flames spread underground where they're virtually impossible to extinguish.

The effect is devastating: the Institute for Food and Development Policy has found that one ton of palm oil can generate thirty-three tons of carbon dioxide emissions—ten times more than petroleum. Despite what oil palm growers assert, the plantations they install can't absorb nearly as much CO_2 as rain forest and peatlands. A happy solution might seem obvious: raise biofuel feedstock in places already converted to cropland. But even if vegetable oils and alcohols (for ethanol) originate on long-established farms in Iowa or the German countryside, biofuels pressure native environments around the globe—including the rain forests of Borneo—because there's only so much land to grow on. When cropland in America and Europe is shifted to raise fuel, new cropland to cultivate food (and yet more fuel) must be established elsewhere. Thanks in large part to oil palm plantations, Indonesia has earned the unsavory distinction of being the world's third-largest emitter of CO_2, trailing only the United States and China.

Regardless, Indonesia, the planet's chief oil palm grower, aims to expand the acreage allocated for plantations from its current 16 million acres to almost 26 million by 2015. If the country's deforestation, which is due largely to oil palm, continues at the present rate, 98 percent of Indonesia's forest—one of the three remaining large rain forests on earth—will be degraded or gone by 2022. Although Indonesia has strict environmental regulations and formally recognizes some land rights of indigenous groups, those laws are only as effective as the local bureaucrats enforcing them. "For the permit certification, a guy just comes to your office and you just pay him off. This is how it works," explains Ong Kee Chau, a former Wilmar International Ltd. executive responsible for most of the company's oil palm plantations and mills on Borneo. For everyone from national politicians to struggling villagers, biofuel represents opportunity. "Oil palm is one of our areas of competitiveness," explains Dr. Herry Purnomo, of the Indonesia-based Center for International Forestry Research. "We can't compete with information technologies, or in auto manufacturing, but we have plantations."

PAREH

The only way to get to Pareh is to travel up the Kumba River, typically in a traditional wood boat fitted with an outboard motor. In May 2008 I make the trip with a researcher from Walhí. We start to Pareh, which is in the northern reaches of the state of West Kalimantan, after a rough seven-hour car ride and just as the sun is setting. The banks are lined with trees and tall grasses, and the sky is filled with corpulent thunderhead clouds; steely gray and electric white, their bulging extremities catch the orange-gold of the dying day. As we glide through the night, a warm rain descends and lightning circuits overhead. Piercing the darkness, the quick flashes illuminate the glistening water, the upcoming bend in the river, and the rain forest that sprawls all around.

When we arrive two hours later, Momonus and his wife, Margareta, receive us in their home. (The people I meet in Pareh all go by single names.) They have no furniture, so we sit in flickering candlelight on the plastic tablecloths that cover the floor. Pages of newspaper are pasted over gaps in the walls, and in one room I read a story about kidnapped girls being used as sex slaves by plantation workers. After a meal of fiddleheads and banana flowers gathered in the forest, rice from the family paddy, and canned sardines, the front room begins to fill with village men. The crowd spills out onto the front porch, and a few women linger in the kitchen doorway. All the men wear freshly washed T-shirts and jeans or khakis and sit cross-legged on the floor. And all the men smoke except Momonus—through the gray haze that now fills the room, I see the red snap and spark of sweet cloves burning amid the tobacco, the typical Indonesian blend. Momonus is thirty-eight, has a tall forehead, a low, solid body, and a thin mustache. He is calm and does not crowd the conversation.

The men tell me that if the government and Duta Palma continue to rebuff them, they will resort to their machetes. Dayaks are notorious for their history of head-hunting in previous centuries, and as recently as 1997. At that time a vicious conflict erupted between Dayaks and a nonnative ethnic group called the Madurese. Lasting several months, the fighting unfolded in the region surrounding Pareh. While both parties engaged in skirmishes, the victims were primarily Madurese. As houses were torched and crops decimated, at least five hundred people were killed—some by beheading—and thousands more displaced including twenty-five thousand Madurese. Although it wasn't that long ago, according to anthropologist Nancy Lee Peluso the Dayaks of today deploy their warrior reputation, ancient and recent, more to inspire fear than carry out the gruesome act of head-hunting.

The community of Pareh is angry and desperate to keep its land as the palm plantation breaks the intricate agroforestry system Dayaks have developed over centuries. In what is generally referred to as swidden agriculture, crops are raised amid the forest trees, using frequent rotation to prevent soil depletion. My guide from Walhi talks about how the media sometimes portray global forest destruction as the result of slash-and-burn farming by indigenous and peasant peoples. However, maintenance of the health of the forest has always been incumbent on groups such as Dayaks if they are to survive. Large-scale deforestation and fires did not arrive in West Kalimantan, my guide tells me, until the big timber and plantation concerns did. As we talk with villagers in Pareh and elsewhere, I realize there is no word for clear-cutting in the native tongue of Dayaks, in Madurese, or even Bahasa Indonesia, the official language of the country. As the meeting in Momonus's house winds down, Julian, a young father of two, asks if anyone has been to the boundary between the forest and PTLL's plantation. Another young man says that he was recently there and didn't see any logging.

The next morning, I go with Momonus, Julian, and two other villagers to see the deforested area. On motorbikes, we navigate the ribbon of slick mud that passes for a road. After two perilous hours, we reach the land PTLL has grabbed.

The contrast between past and future is extreme. The ancestral forest has an understory of ferns and flowers; monkeys swing from the branches of wild mango, teak, and ironwood trees, and soaring above it all is a majestic canopy of dipterocarps. One of the rain forest's iconic treasures, dipterocarps bloom irregularly, perhaps once every four years, but miraculously do so in unison, their vivid red flowers erupting over hundreds of millions of acres.

Across the road is a moonscape. Charred skeletons of trees lie prone as far as the eye can see. Torn and beaten up, the landscape is being transformed into blank cropland; on the horizon is a thin seam of emerald green—the encroaching column of palms. Duta Palma has also planted seedlings in a narrow band along the border of the community's land, like a message written in green: this forest belongs to the palm.

The midday sun stings a million sharp pricks on the skin, so we decide to move. Back on the bikes, we head to the area denuded last fall. Tucked into the forest, it's not visible from the road, and not that big. But, as Momonus tells me, these things start small. Thick logs are scattered about, motionless branches, mud. We spot the military guard post set up to protect the loggers. There are no soldiers and the deforestation seems to have stopped, at least for now.

Farther along we find a camp. A blue tarp is pitched over a platform covered with bedding and folded clothes. Momonus lifts the lid on a pot of freshly cooked rice; it's still warm. Dishes and a toothbrush sit on the edge of a nearby stream. "They're hiding from us," Julian says. "They heard our motorcycles and ran into the trees." Momonus takes a stub of wood from the cooking fire and writes on the platform in thick black letters, *Stop destroying the ancestral forest!!!*

We hit the road again. After a few miles, our bikes abruptly halt—several recently downed trees are blocking the way. Almost instantly a young man appears carrying a bright orange chain saw. He sets it down and pulls the starter, but the engine won't turn over. He says nothing and doesn't look at us, but keeps pulling the cord. The drone of chain saws reverberates from just within the forest, as three more workers emerge from the trees. These men are not from here—unlike the people from Pareh, they have tattered clothes, black teeth, and a remoteness fixed in their eyes. Momonus calmly exchanges words with one of them and heads into the forest to see what's going on. When he returns ten minutes later, his eyes shine with rage. Then another man, better dressed than the laborers, comes barreling toward us on a white motorcycle. He, too, looks furious. Momonus orders us on the bikes, and we speed away. When we finally stop, Momonus reminds me where I've seen the man before. He was the villager at the meeting last night who said the clearing had stopped. He is Momonus's brother-in-law.

I have just witnessed the palm companies' modus operandi in miniature. Operatives will proposition community members to assemble a logging crew in return for a sum that is insignificant to the company but a fortune to a villager. Some people will say no—Julian refused $6,000. But the company will keep trying until someone says yes, and someone almost always does. Buying people off helps the plantations expand into the forests, but, even more important, it sows betrayal and division that undermine the communities' opposition to clear-cutting.

A few days after I leave Pareh, I get a text message from Momonus saying a group of villagers went back to the clearing and confiscated twenty chain saws.

MUARA ILAI

Of course, not every community rejects plantations outright. In 2000, an oil palm company struck a deal with the residents of Muara Ilai. This Dayak community is buried in the equatorial rain forest about ten hours by river and road south of Pareh, also in the state of West Kalimantan. Muara Ilai is made up of a string of what are referred to as subvillages, collectively inhabited by four hundred families. For villagers here, like the people of Pareh, the forest is absolutely vital to their cultural identity and daily survival. The people of Muara Ilai struck an agreement with an oil palm plantation common in Indonesia, known as a plasma scheme. The details can vary, but generally fall along the same lines. Individual families consent to surrender a set amount of acreage to the estate in exchange for a smaller plot planted with oil palm for them to farm. Establishing a palm grove is well beyond the means of forest denizens because it requires expensive seeds, fertilizers, pesticides, and, since the trees can take anywhere from four to eight years to yield fruit, plenty of time to recover costs. The community of Muara Ilai embraced the opportunity to break into the lucrative palm business, seeing it as their chance at a better life.

One of the leaders of Muara Ilai, whom I will refer to as Asmoro, recalls that when the plantation firm first arrived, it made great promises to improve their livelihoods and invest in public infrastructure. But after planting just 15 percent of its acreage, Asmoro explains, the company collapsed from mismanagement and the project stalled. In the ensuing six or so years, smallholders such as Asmoro and his brother-in-law Norman Wicaksono, as I'll call him, watched other oil palm plantations in neighboring communities unceremoniously abandon their lofty pledges and raze the forests their fellow Dayaks relied on. Residents of Muara Ilai thought they'd dodged a bullet until, in 2007, another firm bought out the original concession and proceeded with the plantation.

Aiming to develop twice as much land, the new owner, Perseroan Terbatas Borneo Ketapang Permai (PTBKP), was far more ambitious than its predecessor. The revised project would be twice the size, with the area designated for oil palm crops fully engulfing three hamlets and shearing the forest right up to the front doors of thirteen other villages, including Muara Ilai. Not only did PTBKP come in with a more aggressive plan, the company claimed that villagers couldn't back out of participating in a plasma scheme. Asmoro explains that PTBKP is now strong-arming his community to accept a deal that requires each villager to turn over twenty acres instead of the thirteen they'd previously consented to, and that reduces by over half the oil palm acreage the farmers would receive in exchange.

The community opposes the offer, and in January of 2008, 250 people from Muara Ilai went to the PTBKP office demanding their land back. They were met by police, who threatened to throw the group's leaders in jail unless they dispersed. A month later, PTBKP changed its approach. The company summoned the heads of four villages, including Asmoro, for a meeting in Pontianak, the capital of West Kalimantan. PTBKP paid for their transportation, put them up in one of the swankiest hotels in town, and gave a PowerPoint presentation promising the standard package: development, higher incomes, schools, hospitals, and well-maintained roads. "It looks good, but we know it's not," Asmoro remembers thinking. At the end of the meeting, one by one, each of the village leaders unequivocally rejected the offer.

Thanks to the stark imbalance of power that marks the establishment of oil palm estates, any social and ecological protections that exist are most often trashed. In addition to forbidding the use of fire to clear trees, Indonesia's rather strict environmental laws require palm oil companies seeking to establish estates to secure a series of permits. Plantation firms are required to conduct extensive environmental impact assessments, including finding sites where the ecological effects will be marginal, and seeking input from local inhabitants. Only after state officials approve these reports can an oil grower secure permits from the national departments of Forestry and Plantations. Somewhat surprisingly, though, the Forestry and Plantations divisions must then send their opinions back to the rural government for final approval from the much lower-ranking district head, or *bupati*.

Since the collapse of the Suharto dictatorship in 1998, the national government has implemented a program to rapidly devolve power to the provincial and district levels. The idea behind this massive restructuring is to undo the centralization now commonly seen as having enabled Suharto's lock on power. By distributing decision-making to the regional and local levels, the reasoning goes, there will be greater accountability, thus protecting ecosystem health and social rights. Instead, much of what seems to be happening in West Kalimantan is interagency rivalries and the creation of fiefdoms by previously powerless officials. Local governments now typically side with plantation firms when land disputes erupt, looking the other way or even dispatching the military and police to suppress protests.

The head of the provincial Environmental Impact Monitoring Board, Tri Budiarto, believes this situation can change, even though he is witness to countless instances of blatant disregard for the law. "No one can force communities to give up their land," he tells me when we meet. "The people have to know they are as strong as the company, that they are equal, so they can make decisions together on how to use the land." Even from the most optimistic angle, achieving this is a Sisyphean task.

Indonesia's infrastructure for exploitation runs deep, beginning in earnest over four centuries ago under Holland's Dutch East India Company. Operating with the blessings of the central government of Holland, the conglomeration of trading firms used terror and brute force against Indonesia's inhabitants to maintain control over the lucrative spice trade. In the 1800s the Dutch colonial government declared all unclaimed land and forest its domain and forced local peoples to labor in state plantations. Dutch control continued through the 1940s.

After just two decades of independence, the military dictator Suharto seized power in the mid-1960s and embarked on a bloody communist purge, in which half a million people are believed to have been killed. Simultaneously, Suharto opened the country to Western companies, welcoming among others the American mining giant Freeport-McMoRan Copper & Gold, Inc. In short order, the Arizona-based multinational, one of the world's chief gold producers, commenced operations on the pristine island of West Papua (formerly known as Irian Jaya). In 2005, Freeport was found to be making direct payments for protection of the mine and the company's interests to local police and military, which are known to have committed serious human rights violations. Freeport's carved-up corner of Papua is now home to the planet's largest gold mine, where twenty thousand laborers toil. The current devastation of Borneo's rain forests for oil palm plantations is just the latest chapter in a long history of violent repression to ease the looting of Indonesia's rich natural resources.

Since Asmoro and his fellow leaders' rejection of PTBKP's offer, life has got complicated for the people of Muara Ilai. A few days after he returned from Pontianak, Asmoro says he was approached by two men at the village café. "They said it directly to my face—they said they wanted to kill me," he recounts. "They had clubs and almost swung at me."

Sitting across the conference table from me in the Serikat Petani Kelapa Sawit (Oil Palm Smallholders Association), or SPKS, office, Asmoro's eyes are bloodshot, his dark, wavy locks are turning gray, and he constantly has a cigarette stuck between his thick fingers. He takes out his cell phone and reads off the date, the names of the men who threatened him, and all the people who witnessed the event that afternoon at the café. His cell phone is where he keeps track of the harassment. He pulls up the details of another incident, this time at the hands of military troops who called him a pro- vocateur and threatened to arrest him. The *bupati* and PTBKP posted the army near Muara Ilai to protect the plantation. Due to this harassment the community complained, which Asmoro and Wicaksono tell me forced the army's withdrawal. However, Asmoro says, police were immediately dispatched to take over.

Pressures weigh on other members of the community as well. Wicak- sono takes a folded envelope out of his pants pocket. Inside is a letter from the police calling him to appear in court. He's being charged with steal- ing palm oil seeds from what is now the PTBKP estate. Asmoro has been summoned to testify as a witness against Wicaksono. The men tell me that at least fourteen people they know have recently either been charged with crimes or called to appear as witnesses against each other. Wicak- sono explains that the intimidation he's experiencing began in April just weeks after his wife and two of her friends erected fences around the land they had agreed to give to the first plantation company. Straightaway, the husbands of these women became targets of police harassment. Accord- ing to Wicaksono, a week ago, an officer and thirty workers from PTBKP came to his land and took down the fence. His wife and her friends were there but could do nothing to stop the men.

I ask about the charges against him. Wicaksono seems stunned as he speaks. PTBKP alleges that he stole oil palm fruit—which contain the valuable seeds—seven years ago from one of the small parcels the for- mer owner had planted. Wicaksono now grows oil palm on some of his land and explains that he got his seeds from fruit that had fallen on the ground. He tells me he took only what would have gone to waste. The let- ter from the police says, in addition to stealing, Wicaksono is accused of "disrupting the business of the plantation." He is supposed to appear in court tomorrow morning.

Despite numerous requests from residents of Muara Ilai, the men in the SPKS office tell me, PTBKP has never produced a legitimate permit for the plantation to begin operations. "The companies are not allowed to start clearing until they have the legal letters from the Forestry and Plan- tations departments," explains Cion Aleksander, a small oil palm farmer and founder of SPKS. "But usually the companies start clearing before they get the permits and just use a letter from the *bupati,* but it's not legally valid." This may mean the plantation company has been asked for bribes and kickbacks in exchange, Aleksander says. I ask Asmoro if he's scared and he says no. "The question now is whether the community can stand up to the police. Right now the chances are fifty-fifty."

MEGA TIMUR

Is conflict really the only option left for forest people? To answer this question, I visit an older oil palm plantation, Perseroan Terbatas Bumi Pratama Khatulistiwa (PTBPK). PTBPK—not to be confused with PTBKP in Muara Ilai—is owned by Wilmar International Ltd., the ADM-affiliated company that buys oil from Duta Palma. The PTBPK estate is located in the coastal district of Pontianak, near the village of Mega Timur. This terrain used to be peatland forest, an ecosystem covered with evergreen trees and shrubs rooted in swampy earth comprised of centuries' worth of decomposing plant matter. To establish its PTBPK plantation, in 1996 Wilmar began razing the native groves and dug deep canals to drain the soil. Now the land is a uniform grid of oil palms. According to Greenpeace, the destruction and degradation of peatlands in Indonesia alone releases 4 percent of the world's total greenhouse gas emissions.

Unlike the Dayaks I met in Pareh, the peasants of Mega Timur embraced the plantation and accepted its transformation of the peat forest as a step in the development they believed would benefit everyone. Mega Timur is a village made up of smaller subvillages that dot the banks of the Malaya River. Most of the peasant farmers who live here are among the Madurese ethnic group, who came to Borneo as part of the country's decades-old transmigration program, which relocates the destitute from overcrowded islands such as Java and Madura. The government issues each family a modest parcel on which to farm and build a house.

Strung along roads, most of these dwellings are small, beat-up shacks that seem abandoned, but they're not. A wood house with crooked window frames, no glass, no shutters, offers the faintly visible profile of a woman inside. From behind a door hanging off its hinges a child emerges carrying a kite. A faded one-room hut is hooked up to a massive satellite dish. In the ten or so acres surrounding their homes, these smallholders cultivate crops to sell such as black pepper, pineapple, rubber, and aloe vera (the plant is referred to as crocodile teeth by locals). After having settled and worked their land for a generation, the peasants of Mega Timur could survive, but oil palms seemed to offer a better future. That's why, like the Dayaks of Muara Ilai, these smallholders welcomed the new plantation with its plasma scheme. They were also enticed by the prospect of jobs at Wilmar's estate and other benefits the company pledged, including schools, mosques, and roads. But today's reality diverges rather sharply from the promises made more than a dozen years ago.

On a May afternoon I visit Mega Timur with Amiriyanto, a young leader in the community who brings me to the village. If the weather is good, Mega Timur is less than an hour's drive from Pontianak; if a deluge hits, the journey can take much longer. On our way the steamy sky dumps rain, but it recedes quickly, and before long we arrive at the house of a peasant named Nazit.

About a dozen family members and neighbors, who are either smallholders in PTBPK's plasma scheme or workers at the plantation, assemble on the front porch to talk. They all flick off their plastic flip-flops into a pile at the bottom of the front steps and take seats on the smooth wood deck. Most of the men don't speak Bahasa Indonesia, only their native Madurese, and they don't read. Nazit is a plasma farmer, having given up much of his land to the company over a decade ago. Nazit doesn't know his age because he has no birth certificate. His body is slight and weathered, his hair has gone white; he supposes he's fifty-five or sixty, but looks much older. He wears a woven plaid sarong around his waist and a clean white T-shirt with a silkscreen of two politicians who lost in the most recent provincial elections.

Not everyone participates in the plasma scheme, however, especially those who had no land to give. Instead, like Rahmat, one of Nazit's sons, who is in his midthirties, they get jobs at PTBPK. Rahmat tells me that even though he's grateful to have work, the conditions are tough. Many of his coworkers agree, so two months ago, a group of PTBPK laborers staged a protest to demand higher wages. Gathered outside the main plantation office, the workers chanted and yelled to their bosses. No one from the company ever came out to speak to them. In the twelve months preceding the laborers' action the price of crude palm oil had almost doubled. Three days after the protest sixty of the demonstrators were summarily fired. Among them was Marnaki, a man in his late thirties who worked at the plantation for four years. Sitting on Nazit's porch, Marnaki explains that he wasn't told why he was fired, nor were any of the others. "I've been traumatized by oil palm!" he says with a weary chuckle.

As the late afternoon drags the heat lethargically into night, a prayer call rings out and a few of the men excuse themselves before heading to the village mosque. Nazit invites us inside. His house has no running water or toilet and his living room is furnished solely with a table upon which sits a television. The house, however, does have electricity. Through a doorway at the far end of the front room I can see into the kitchen, which is clearly the domain of the women. One in a *jilbob*—a head scarf—is seated with a baby on her lap, speaking to another woman who is standing; their voices are inaudible from where I am. Their forms are bathed in pale fluorescent light and framed by the kitchen doorway, through which I see the flicker of children chasing each other back and forth behind them.

Nazit recently passed along his five-acre plasma plot (the size everyone was allotted by PTBPK) to his youngest son, Jhari. The father's plan was to then get a job as a fieldworker at PTBPK. But when he went to the plantation to ask for work, he was refused; Nazit thinks it's because he's too old. Now he must rely on his sons for help.

Jhari is twenty-three, lean and bright eyed. His short hair is wet from his having just bathed in the river after a day working his palm grove. The most important aspect of this labor is picking the fruit: dark red berries the size of dates that grow clustered on spiky pods a little larger than a football. Inside the fruit's flesh is a seed that contains the valuable oil; these palms are among the most efficient oil crops, with higher yields per acre than any other oilseed crop including rapeseed, sunflower, and olive. Jhari and the other men tell me that although their families gave PTBPK acreage near their houses, the company took that land for itself and gave the peasants parcels on the outer reaches of the estate, which spans thousands of acres. It now takes Jhari an hour to walk to his plot. And since most plasma farmers are too poor to pay for adequate field help and hauling, they're unable to maximize their earning potential. Jhari explains that what he earns from his harvests isn't enough to support his family, including his wife and child. "I want Wilmar to give our family's land back," he tells me.

Only over time have the smallholders of Mega Timur come to realize they are bound to PTBPK in ways they couldn't have anticipated. When families received their parcel sown with palm, they were also issued debt. Despite having received free land from the peasant farmers, the plantation charged them for the initial oil palm planting—paid for with loans arranged by Wilmar and third-party banks. The smallholders now find themselves locked into an arrangement that somewhat resembles sharecropping: The peasants are obliged to sell their harvest to the company at a set price, regardless of the market rate. The Wilmar plantation siphons off half the money as payments on the planting loans; it also deducts fees for roads and drainage systems, fertilizer and pesticides, harvest collection, security and administrative charges, and a deposit into a mandatory savings account. After almost a decade of working with the company, none of the smallholders I talk to know how much they've earned, how much they've saved, or what portion of their loans they've paid.

The people of Mega Timur do know, however, that they must endure the environmental effects of the oil palm estate. According to Wilmar, at PTBPK they spend 65 percent of maintenance costs on petrochemical fertilizers. In addition, to keep bugs, rodents, and weeds away, the plantation uses heavy doses of insecticides and herbicides. These hazardous effluents drain into the Malaya River, along which most of the community's houses sit. The river here, as is common on Borneo, provides water for bathing and washing (although it is not a source for food and most people catch rainwater for drinking). Since Wilmar's plantation was established, the community has noted a marked increase in skin rashes and cases of diarrhea. The fertilizer that leaches from the plantation also encourages growth of river grasses that form damlike blockages. The sitting water creates breeding grounds for mosquitoes, increasing risk of malaria, and can easily force the Malaya to breach its banks.

In fact, floods and droughts, once rare, have become a standard feature of life for the peasants of Mega Timur. Wilmar's clearing and draining of the peat forest has undermined the land's ability to absorb rainwater or to retain moisture past the wet season. Now the dry months are tough on crops and not all survive. And while PTBPK's land is engineered to channel floodwaters away within three days, Mega Timur's is not. The year 2007 alone brought four major floods. During one that lasted two full weeks, not only were daily lives thrown into disarray and family farms destroyed, but also the community had difficulty evacuating and lacked access to basic necessities such as food and clean water.

This, then, is the rain forest dwellers' unenviable choice—they can enter into a life of indentured servitude to a multinational corporation, or they can continue to fight oil palm until the plantations swallow their homes. In the West the choices appear less menacing: regular gasoline, or a bio-fuel blend at the pump.

SURREAL SUSTAINABILITY

Responding to outcry from activists over palm oil's dire effects on rain forests and their communities, the industry's major plantation owners, processors, traders, and commercial consumers joined an initiative of the World Wildlife Fund to create a voluntary international oversight body. The Roundtable on Sustainable Palm Oil, or RSPO, was formally established in 2004 and counts among its members Wilmar, Duta Palma, Archer Daniels Midland, and Cargill, the latter being another biofuel player and owner of oil palm plantations on Borneo. While palm oil is rapidly seizing market share in the biofuels sector, it is most commonly milled into edible oil. Those bottles that line the grocery aisle labeled as vegetable oil are often straight palm oil. The substance is widely used in a plethora of processed foods, with huge producers such as Unilever, Nestlé, and Cadbury Schweppes among the biggest consumers of palm oil. These firms also played key roles in establishing the RSPO and continue to support it.

The organization tasks itself with delineating high-minded standards, embodied in its "Principles and Criteria for Sustainable Palm Oil Production." The RSPO also aspires to facilitate the implementation of "best practices" by its members, in part through its own verification system. In unadulterated corporate-social-responsibility-speak, the RSPO website states its aim is to "promote the growth and use of sustainable palm oil through co-operation within the supply chain and open dialogue with its stakeholders."

However, the group's "Principles and Criteria" might come as a surprise to someone who has visited areas affected by oil palm plantations on Borneo. For example, Criterion 7.5 states, "No new plantings are established on local peoples' land without their free, prior and informed consent, dealt with through a documented system that enables indigenous peoples, local communities and other stakeholders to express their views through their own representative institutions." Other criteria pledge to leave primary forest intact, compensate local people for land they relin-quish, and not discriminate against plantation workers based on union membership or age. When I asked about the situation in Pareh and the conditions in Mega Timur, the RSPO's representative replied, "The RSPO is a voluntary organization and can only do so much."

Several Indonesian nongovernmental and community-based organi-zations have ventured into the gulf between assertion and reality to try to contain the destruction. In the summer of 2007 two activist organi-zations, Lembaga Gemawan and KONTAK Rakyat Borneo, along with Milieudefensie (an environmental group based in the Netherlands), released a report titled *Policy, practice, pride and prejudice,* a study of three other Wilmar plantations on Borneo, in the West Kalimantan dis-trict of Sambas. The document details illegal acts at the estates, which include logging protected areas, using fire to clear trees, draining and burning peatlands, coercive and forced displacement of indigenous peo-ple and small farmers, and inadequate or nonexistent permits. These activities violate Wilmar's own social-responsibility policies, as well as the standards of the RSPO and the International Finance Corporation (IFC), a World Bank agency that has provided Wilmar tens of millions of dollars to expand its business. Due to its support of oil palm businesses, the IFC is also a member of the RSPO. After considerable pressure from Indonesian activists, both the RSPO and the IFC, through its Compliance Advisor/Ombudsman (CAO) office, launched separate audits of Wilmar. Because of the scrutiny, Wilmar temporarily halted expansion of its oil palm cropland during the time I was on Borneo. When I visited one of the company's newly established estates in the district of Landak, I inter-viewed a low-level manager who illuminated what Wilmar's definition of halting expansion is. He explained that because of the controversy they had to put down their chain saws for now, but "we've just stopped tem-porarily." He was confident the work would resume, so kept the planta-tion's crews busy surveying the more than thirty-five thousand acres to be razed and tending the oil palm saplings that will be planted.

At the end of 2008 the RSPO completed its probe and gave Wilmar the all clear to continue expanding its cropland throughout West Kaliman-tan. Six months on, however, the IFC's CAO issued its findings, which were damning: "For more than twenty years IFC had information at its disposal on significant governance as well as environmental and social risks inherent in the Indonesian oil palm sector" but took no action to address these matters. To speed dispersal of moneys to Wilmar, the World Bank's finance branch dismissed warnings from its environmental staff and disregarded its own procedures for allocating funds. The IFC deliberately misrepresented Wilmar as a "low risk" investment to avoid obligatory accounting for social and environmental costs. Further, the body failed to ensure that Wilmar was in compliance with Indonesian law. Consequently, the CAO concluded, human and ecosystem health were sacrificed while "deal making prevailed."

Lely Khairnur, executive director of Lembaga Gemawan, tells me that to promote justice and accountability, nongovernmental organizations such as hers are not just leaning on the RSPO and the World Bank's IFC in the case against Wilmar. They're employing a range of tactics that include direct action, organizing, educating forest dwellers about their rights, and positioning candidates for local office. "This is a long process," Khairnur tells me. "It's not just about five demonstrations or a series of public hearings. . . . We are not fighting against one company, we are fighting a system."

Of course, the system reaches not only into the world's most powerful corporations, but also its highest political offices. The Obama administration proudly supports what are called next-generation biofuels, as do mainstream environmental groups, including the Sierra Club. The concept behind second-generation biofuels is to use nonfood inputs such as algae, crop wastes, or cultivated plants, including perennial grasses that require no tilling (which releases CO_2) and help prevent soil erosion. These potential future blends are viewed as an improvement on first-generation crop-based ethanol and biodiesel, which have inflicted so much damage. However, such fuels do not yet exist. According to Obama's own energy secretary, Steven Chu, next-generation biofuels are at least five years away. As some may recall, this is what we were told five years ago.

Meantime, Lisa Jackson, head of the EPA, recently stated that the administration would continue to support, through mandates and subsidies, crop-based eco-fuels, which she says are "a bridge to the next generation of biofuels." The promise of second-generation biofuels is helping to keep us hooked on the crop-based variety, whether this is the intention or not. Most gas sold in the United States today must have a blend that uses 10 percent ethanol, an amount that's set to increase under current policy. In 2009, the U.S. government also committed support to automakers in expanding production of so-called flex-fuel vehicles, which can run on gasoline blended with as much as 85 percent ethanol, or E85. So we'll keep pumping the disastrous first-generation stuff into our tanks for years to come. As was true of the IFC in its business with Wilmar, even though most Western leaders are aware of the staggering toll crop-based fuels impose on people and the planet, deal making indeed prevails.

Before leaving Indonesia I visit the Center for International Forestry Research, a serene, wooded compound where more than one hundred top scientists are working out ways to protect the world's forests and their peoples. Researcher Dr. Herry Purnomo is helping shape a United Nations–sponsored initiative to pay developing countries to leave their trees standing. Known as Reducing Emissions from Deforestation and Degradation, or REDD, the program, Purnomo explains, is projected to cost about $12 billion annually worldwide—not bad considering that the U.S. government has spent over $126 billion on post-Katrina reconstruction. But, as of my meeting with Purnomo, international agencies and Western governments had promised only $1 billion so far—"nowhere near what there needs to be," Purnomo says with frustration.

However, even if the money for REDD comes through, the program has serious problems. It doesn't account for the rights of indigenous peoples nor does it explicitly include them in decision-making. What's more, REDD relies on the UN's definition of forests, which treats monoculture plantations as equivalent to biodiverse native ecosystems. That means the displacement and clear-cutting for oil palm in Indonesia would be declared ecologically sustainable. The people in places such as the rain forests of West Kalimantan are up against formidable forces, which include not only the world's most powerful corporations and their friends at the World Bank, but also bureaucrats who might appear to be helping.

While I was in Pareh, some village men asked if I wanted to see the eleven chain saws they'd seized the previous fall. They led me to a hiding place and took out the orange-handled saws one by one, carefully placing them in a straight line on the ground. A few minutes later they meticulously arranged them in a circle. I could tell how proud they were: the chain saws were trophies of their bravery. I also realized that despite all they'd been through, the villagers continued to regard the saws as bargaining chips, a monumental misperception of the size and scope of their opponent.

CHAPTER FIVE

Green Machines:
Ecological Automobiles

Almost no one expected it, but when Toyota introduced the hybrid gas-electric Prius, first in Japan in 1997, then three years later in overseas markets including the United States and Western Europe, sales almost immediately outstripped supply. The concept was captivating: use less fuel but still go wherever you want. The Prius automatically switches between its gasoline-run internal combustion engine and its electric motor, fed by on-board batteries. At slower speeds the car rolls strictly on voltage, while the internal combustion engine kicks in at higher speeds. Cleverly, energy given off during braking that would normally be lost is captured to recharge the battery while driving. Those who wanted a Prius of their own had to join waiting lists and take whatever color was available; that first year in the United States thirty-seven thousand people signed up but only twelve thousand got one. Despite the car's drawbacks—it cost about $3,000 more than an equivalent nonhybrid model, and the initial Prius was jerky and slow to accelerate—eco-conscious shoppers, including such celebrities as Leonardo DiCaprio and Cameron Diaz, now had a car they could feel good about driving.

The Prius represents an important shift toward greener automobiles. By coupling the two propulsion systems—an internal combustion engine with an electric motor—hybrid technology creates an opening to begin shifting away from greenhouse-gas-spewing vehicles. Hybrids also remedy the most vexing problem that plagues fully electric cars, their limited range. A typical all-electric vehicle may only go twenty, thirty, or forty miles before its batteries die, and standard recharging takes hours, not minutes. The hybrid concept rather brilliantly overcomes this limit by giving the batteries a backup, allowing the driver to cruise on electric as far as possible, with the gasoline-powered engine taking it from there. Although the Prius doesn't get drivers off fossil fuels, in upping efficiency and conferring upon its owners a badge of ecological responsibility, the car taps into a pool of consumers the big U.S. auto firms had for so long insisted didn't exist.

In 2004, when Toyota's second-generation Prius debuted, sales in the United States exceeded fifty thousand and within a year nearly doubled again, accounting for almost 60 percent of the global Prius market. According to the Environmental Protection Agency's tests, the 2008 model had a combined average fuel economy of 46 mpg, beating most other American sedans, in some cases by double digits. In the spring of that year, with record oil prices nearing $150 per barrel (driving people away from buying gas-hungry SUVs), and before the global economic recession peaked (driving people away from buying much of anything at all), Toyota boasted cumulative worldwide Prius sales of more than 1 million, helping the firm build its green credentials and nudge past General Motors as the planet's top automaker.

Up until 2007, Ford, Chrysler, and GM had yet to seriously commit to energy-conserving power trains, even though the firms cultivated appearances to the contrary. By then they'd all started producing "flexfuels," vehicles that can burn either straight diesel or gasoline, or a mixture of fossil fuels and veggie-based biofuels. And both Ford and GM had introduced gas-electric hybrids into their fleets. But the big Detroit firms did not apply hybrid and flex-fuel systems to turn out more efficient and better-designed cars to compete with the Prius. Instead the top U.S. auto companies chose to achieve fewer gains, installing the technology in their ever-more-enormous, ever-more-polluting passenger trucks and SUVs, such as the GMC Yukon hybrid, which gets a maximum of 22 mpg. As late as 2004 GM's vice chairman of global product development—a job that involves creating greener rides—Bob Lutz, wrote off hybrids as "an interesting curiosity."

The largest auto firms have a solid reputation for fighting changes that might erode profit margins even when a revamp would be beneficial for people and the planet. Carmakers' belligerent resistance to adding safety features and lowering emissions illustrates the point. Seat belts, headrests, steel reinforcements, and air bags were all fought by the auto industry because adding these features increased costs. The auto firms—including such eco-minded outfits as Toyota—unfailingly marshal their cadres of lawyers and lobbyists to beat back tougher emissions rules. For more years than some care to remember, established U.S. environmental organizations including the Sierra Club and the Natural Resources Defense Council as well as newer pro-EV groups such as the California Cars Initiative and Plug In America, have been targeting politicians and the biggest vehicle makers with campaigns and lobbying for factory production of cleaner cars. Only after SUV and pickup truck sales tanked, first due to unrelenting oil price hikes and then a broken economy, among other reasons, did GM finally cotton on to the gravity of the situation. In a frantic effort to hedge its product-line bets and promote itself as green, at the 2007 North American International Auto Show held annually in Detroit, then chairman Rick Wagoner unveiled a concept car that GM declared would be the next-generation eco-ride: a plug-in gas-electric hybrid called the Volt.

GM subsequently announced details including that the Chevy four-seat sedan would get the equivalent of over 200 mpg in the city and would sell for $40,000. While it was on the upper end of midpriced cars, middle-class families could still afford a Volt, and GM initially pledged they could be behind the wheel by 2010. Research, design, and manufacturing schedules for a new standard internal combustion vehicle are typically five to six years, start to finish. GM sped up the more complex production of the Volt in an effort to update its behind-the-times image and earn some street cred among the ecologically inclined. Wagoner's introduction of the Volt and the subsequent and sustained flurry of PR and news coverage helped trigger a wave of announcements for juiced-up hybrids from at least eight other rivals, including Toyota.

Similar to regular hybrids, plug-ins have both an electric motor and an internal combustion engine, but with key differences. Plug-ins are known as extended-range hybrids; a higher quantity and quality of batteries can propel these cars farther solely on electric current. Only after the batteries grow depleted does a scaled-down internal combustion engine fire up, but not to run the car as in a standard hybrid. Instead the engine acts as a generator to keep the battery going strong. With a fully charged battery, GM says the Volt will go forty miles before any gas is needed. Another major difference between the two hybrids is that once the cells in the more advanced version are empty, the vehicle must be plugged into an outlet— hybrids such as the Prius are never plugged in—and recharging takes considerable time, eight hours for the Volt. Relying less on petroleum, plug-ins might achieve higher efficiencies than today's standard hybrids, yet these vehicles open up new questions about running cars on coal, the number one contributor to global warming.

So why the delay in mass-producing ecologically responsible vehicles? Ask the average person why Americans don't have more green modes of transport—from superefficient cars to reliable mass transit—and most often they'll proffer two theories. First, the automotive establishment is in bed with Big Oil, so they want us to keep swigging down petrol. Within auto industry and environmental lobbyist circles the notion that carmakers are colluding with oil companies is laughable even though drivers pumping thousands of dollars of gas into their tanks every year might consider the idea a real possibility. The second common explanation is that Detroit suppresses electrics and other alternative technologies to stifle any threat to its market dominance. Although it may sound absurd that the Detroit Three snatch up and bury greener technologies, such speculation is not so wild, considering that U.S. companies sell superhigh-mpg vehicles abroad. Unquestionably, the auto establishment and the oil sector share priorities, but finding the minutes from the backroom meetings is difficult. Nonetheless, it's true that the leading auto firms have either underutilized or outright neglected game-changing technologies for decades even though these solutions exist.

If you ask the major U.S. automakers why we still have so many gas-greedy rides, they'll also offer two explanations: consumers haven't been willing to pay for higher fuel economy, and greener technologies haven't been ready for the big time. During the climatically crucial years of the 1990s up through 2008, the Detroit Three justified continuing to push hulks by citing their own—proprietary—market research. Their data consistently affirmed that consumers wanted SUVs and pickups. In other words, Americans just preferred gas-guzzlers.

It's true that most American drivers haven't ponied up for more efficient cars, while they have thrown around thousands of extra dollars per vehicle for more space, power, and luxury—all of which destroy fuel economy. Until recent years, SUVs and light trucks accounted for half of new car sales in the United States. But why haven't drivers wanted to burn less gas? People in other countries consume a fraction of the fuel Americans do, buying subcompacts with manual gearshifts that take a few more seconds to hit sixty miles per hour. There's nothing inherent to human nature about wanting a vehicle that can seat ten, tow a boat, and haul home six months' worth of paper towels, juice boxes, and hot dogs from Sam's Club. It's a practice we've learned, in no small part from the automakers themselves, who are among the top advertising spenders in the United States. Perhaps the American penchant for hogging gas is also the product of what automakers want. Since each SUV offers thousands of dollars more in profits than a lightweight subcompact, which typically brings in just a few hundred dollars in profits, the auto majors have had a strong incentive to avoid greener cars.

Much of the information the public gets in the media about the viability of today's eco-technology is a faithful detailing of cool-as-hell breakthroughs, and what lies on the horizon. A steady stream of news and magazine stories tell us about scientists and engineers who are working around the clock on such projects as concocting the right chemistry for a battery pack that's durable, doesn't weigh too much, holds a strong charge, and isn't too expensive. This narrative reinforces the assumption that vehicles remain dirty because the technology we really need remains just beyond our grasp.

Meanwhile, however, the very American firms that insist they need more time to get high-mpg cars on U.S. roads already sell them—profitably—in Europe, Asia, and Latin America. The overseas operations of Ford and GM make small, well-engineered internal combustion cars, some of which get over 80 mpg. Further, even though the auto majors have yet to release superefficient plug-in hybrids, full electrics, and hydrogen-fueled vehicles, these rides are already tooling along U.S. highways—homemade conversions or the products of upstart luxury carmakers. All of this makes apparent that mass-producing greenmobiles isn't so pie-in-the-sky.

In the winter of 2008 I go to Detroit, epicenter of the world's largest auto market from the industry's earliest days until 2009, when China overtook the United States. My aim is to learn more about why Americans have had so few alternatives to polluting. When I'm in Detroit, the transfer of power from the pollution-abetting Bush administration to the more eco-oriented presidency of Barack Obama hasn't yet happened. With the change in the White House green vehicles look increasingly accessible. Straight out of the gate, Obama pushed the auto industry in a more ecologically prudent direction—although not far enough for many. The new president issued a nonbinding target calling for 1 million plug-in hybrids on the road by 2015. His stimulus package, the 2009 American Recovery and Reinvestment Plan, expanded tax credits for plug-in hybrid purchasers (a much smaller scale program was initiated under Bush) to encourage more drivers to make the switch. And within a few months of taking office, Obama raised fuel efficiency standards for cars and trucks, requiring each auto firm to have a fleetwide average of 35.5 mpg by 2016. Soon both the press and carmakers began talking about fuel efficiency as a positive selling point. In this context, pressure for ecologically sane transportation continues to mount amid louder calls for energy independence and ever more terrifying scientific reports on the effects of global warming. As of 2010 business and government leaders who want to maintain their position have to cultivate what might be called environmental capital because if they're seen as unresponsive to ecological crises such as global warming, they risk losing public support.

Sooner or later, the world's top carmakers will release plug-ins for the masses, whether or not a postbankruptcy GM gets the Volt into full production. But a fundamental question remains: are the obstacles we face technological or do they reflect the underlying economic pressures and incentives that led automakers, and therefore the rest of us, to become addicted to gasoline and diesel in the first place? While encouragement to make and buy plug-in technology may be an important step, it doesn't mean automakers will necessarily begin prioritizing environmental wellbeing. Capitalism's market imperatives, which have remained mindbogglingly unchallenged in the pall of economic collapse, dictate that profitability comes first. The trajectory of the auto industry delineates what happens when the bottom line trumps all else—the social good, including environmental health, invariably takes the hit.

The current moment is a turning point; in the coming years fuel-saving cars will be more widely available. But it will take time for automakers and suppliers to ramp up manufacturing enough to get out the quantity of cleaner vehicles needed to meaningfully cut greenhouse gas emissions. Consider the Prius. Despite its rock-star status Toyota keeps annual production volumes of the Prius relatively low, only recently boosting output to several hundred thousand units globally. To put this in perspective, worldwide auto production has ranged between just under 40 million to almost 55 million units per year over the last decade. Accounting for commercial vehicles, total annual production jumped to 70.5 million in 2008. As of 2007, more than 800 million cars and trucks were rumbling along the planet's roads, a number that's expected to breach 1 billion by 2020.

Because the preponderance of existing autos run on fossil fuels, as will be true with most vehicles built in the coming decades, achieving environmentally sustainable passenger vehicle transportation is a long way off. But it doesn't have to be. Given the tremendous technological resources available, why aren't more eco-cars already on the road, and what happened to mass transit?

DEARBORN

The Ford Motor Company's Rouge Factory, located on the periphery of Detroit in the town of Dearborn, was once a fetid cauldron of industrialized mass production but is now held up as a shining example of ecologically responsible manufacturing. In the early 2000s the forward-looking Bill Ford Jr., great-grandson of Henry, brought in the high-profile eco-architect William McDonough to redesign parts of the factory. The idea was to usher the company into the environmental age and help disperse perceptions of the auto industry as toxic and an agent of global warming. Unveiled in 2004, McDonough's improvements are considered by many as an important incursion into the notoriously polluting realm of automaking. Building vehicles represents the largest manufacturing sector not only in the United States, but arguably the world.

The Rouge facility has a glitzy tourist center with an observation tower that looks down onto one particular factory building. The structure's flat, rectangular roof stretches over ten acres and is covered with snow, beneath which, my group's tour guide assures us, is a carpet of dense sedum, a succulent ground cover. She explains the "living roof" absorbs and cleanses rainwater, preventing it from unnecessarily flowing to the wastewater treatment plant. The rooftop garden also helps regulate the building's temperature, retaining warmth in the colder months and coolness in the heat of summer. Studding the factory's roof are raised skylights that allow sun to beam down onto the assembly line inside.

Our guide directs my group's attention out another window to a set of solar panels. She explains that the small array sends a modest supply of energy to the factory and says the company hopes to expand its solar capacity in the future. Planted on a strip of grass alongside the tourist center are three stiff rows of bare crab-apple trees. Come spring, our guide announces, the trees' fruit will supply food to migratory birds. The final feature of our visual eco-tour is the parking lot just beyond the trees. Composed of a newfangled porous material, the lot's surface channels runoff into a reconstructed wetland system where plants filter the water, some of which is then recirculated on-site.

As part of the tour, visitors are invited into the sedum-covered factory to view the assembly line in action. Once inside, I stop at the washroom. There I find a sign affixed to the wall that explains the water in the toilet is cloudy because it comes from the parking-lot-to-wetland system. This demonstration neatly concretizes the ecological technologies and processes my group just spent half an hour hearing about. Meanwhile, on the other side of the door, hundreds of workers are busy fitting radios, dashboards, power-steering units, air-conditioning parts, and rows of seats into F-150 trucks, a longtime Ford bestseller. The F-150 is one of the least fuel-efficient automobiles on the road.

On a glaring, bitingly cold afternoon I visit Ford's offices, also in Dearborn, a few miles from the Rouge plant. The modernist office block is now dated, its foyer quiet, only the voices of security guards echoing off the polished marble floor. The lobby is cluttered with parked cars, models from the company's previous century of production. While I'm waiting for my escort to the office of John Viera, Ford's director of sustainable business strategies, I check out the iconic Model T. Having first emerged from the Ford Piquette Avenue Plant in Detroit in 1908, this quintessential horseless carriage is now a relic, but it offers a compelling contrast to today's auto culture. The Model T has shiny black paint—the only color offered—two bulbous headlamps, and a simple mechanical setup: a steering wheel, gearshift, and brakes, and a hand-crank starter. No frills are inside the buggy either: a windshield, but no side windows, and narrow bench seats in the front and back. Referring to the Model T, a Ford advertisement from the 1920s reads, "[The company] wants every owner of one of these cars to run it as long as possible at a minimum of expense." Ford built the Model T to get 26 mpg.

A few feet away sits the latest Ford F-150 pickup truck. The hulk has a glistening red paint job; the power windows are rolled down to reveal overstuffed leather seats and a dashboard bulging with a range of gadgets for climate control, navigation, and entertainment. The average mpg for a 2008 Ford F-150 four-wheel drive, like this one, is just under fifteen.

In addition to being famous for its passenger trucks, Ford is also known for sport utility vehicles, or SUVs, a type of full-size ride that caught on big in the early 1990s with such models as the Ford Explorer. Surviving a gory string of rollovers that led to hundreds of crashes and dozens of deaths—caused by poorly made Firestone tires but arguably worsened by the Explorer's top-heavy vehicle design, which was more prone to flipping over—the SUV emerged a winner. Amid the decade's dot-com bubble, SUVs became a must-have status symbol for yuppies, outdoorsmen, and suburban soccer moms alike.

For Detroit's big automakers, the SUV offered an enticing opportunity for profitability. The automakers could build SUVs on existing truck chassis using existing assembly lines, which would dramatically contain production costs. And by constructing SUVs on truck frames the vehicles could be categorized as "light trucks" under the government's fuel efficiency regulatory system. That meant SUVs would be exempt from stricter fuel economy standards applied to cars, thereby lowering engineering and manufacturing costs further still. Compared to the margins on small cars, which typically loiter in the hundreds-of-dollars range and can even fall into the red, each SUV could (and does) fetch $5,000 or more in pure profit.

Another reason Detroit's firms fell in love with the SUV (and the pickup truck) was a result of U.S. restrictions on imported light trucks resulting from an obscure trade dispute involving—of all things—frozen chicken. To protect its poultry farmers struggling to compete with low-cost American imports, in the early 1960s the newly created European Economic Community (then just six countries in Western Europe) imposed a steep tariff on frozen chickens. The United States retaliated by slapping duties—which, because of existing rules, applied to all international trading partners—on a handful of products including light trucks. At a staggering 25 percent, the tax effectively eliminated foreign competition. The only way outsiders could get around the tariff was to manufacture SUVs and pickups on U.S. soil, a dauntingly expensive undertaking that wouldn't happen for another quarter century. In the meantime, American automakers had free rein in a market segment their foreign rivals couldn't afford to access. On the consumption side, SUVs qualify for a U.S. federal tax deduction if they are used as work vehicles for at least 50 percent of the time, and if they weigh over six thousand pounds. SUVs that fall into that weight category include the Cadillac Escalade, Dodge Durango, and Lincoln Navigator. Under the code the full price of an SUV can be recouped within five years, with a write-off of at least $25,000 in the first year. This not only encouraged more people to buy SUVs, it also gave manufacturers incentive to build flabbier models that emitted higher levels of greenhouse gases.

John Viera's secretary takes me from the lobby to his office, which is at the end of a long, soundless corridor. On the way we pass one vacant office after another, a symptom of the company's fantastic financial losses.

Viera is young with short, dark hair, and a crisp button-down shirt, and has squeezed me in before he catches a flight for a meeting with other auto company sustainability executives. I am a little surprised when he says the most important ecologically responsible innovations Ford is currently working on are improved internal combustion engines. I was expecting something a little more politically correct. Viera enthusiastically launches into a rap about the company's EcoBoost program, which entails creating greater fuel efficiency by downsizing engines to remove weight, then adding "turbocharging," which gives the smaller engines more gusto. This is important because Americans, he tells me, are used to oomph when they're at the wheel, unlike European drivers, who are accustomed to less powerful machines. Ford has only deployed its EcoBoost technology in a few models so far, however. The main holdup is cost; if consumers choose a more efficient V-6 over a V-8, but still want the power of the latter, they must pay to add EcoBoost. Since the green tech costs more than a standard V-8, not everyone is willing to take the plunge, Viera says. As for the company's other green offerings, Ford is also dabbling in plug-in gas-electric hybrids, but Viera offers no details and speculates these won't be ready for a few more years. Likewise, he reports, the company's efforts in hydrogen-fuel-cell technology won't bear fruit for decades.

The eco-machines Ford has on the road in large numbers are its flex-fuels. Viera estimates that in 2008 the company will sell almost 3 million vehicles in the United States, and 15 to 20 percent of those can run on either ethanol or biodiesel. Ford and the other Detroit majors began manufacturing flex-fuel vehicles, according to their PR, because it was the environmentally responsible thing to do. But flex-fuels also allowed the firms to more easily meet the fleetwide gas mileage standard set by the federal government under the corporate average fuel economy (CAFE) rules. Automakers could earn credits from flex-fuels to make up for the petrol-sucking pickups and SUVs they were selling so many of. "Without the credits, Ford and GM wouldn't have met mileage goals for light trucks in 2003, 2004 and 2005 and would have owed fines," explains an article in the *Wall Street Journal*. A cut-rate way to meet mileage requirements, flex technology entails a relatively simple computerized device that detects ethanol in the fuel tank and tells the engine to operate accordingly. Not until gasoline prices jolted upward and the Toyota Prius proved people cared about cleaner cars did Ford (and GM) begin slick eco-marketing campaigns for their ethanol-capable trucks and SUVs. Before that, many owners had no idea they could fill their tanks with corn—the primary feedstock for ethanol in the United States—and many still do not. Crucially, car companies receive CAFE credits regardless of whether flex-vehicle drivers roll on ethanol.

As for ecological sustainability, biofuels have been widely discredited. The energy efficiency achieved with ethanol is dubious and a source of much debate. While some researchers say more energy goes into making ethanol than the alt-fuel can supply, others estimate a positive energy balance. A commonly cited figure is that for every gallon of fossil fuel used in production, only 1.3 gallons of corn-based ethanol can be refined. Either way, by now it's apparent that biofuels pressure both ecosystems and the access to food. Cultivation methods for ethanol feedstock such as corn entail industrial farming using monocultures, petrochemical fertilizers and pesticides, and massive amounts of irrigation. Further, the practice triggers demand for more cropland, which is then carved out from native ecosystems, and it forces people to compete with machines for food. Nevertheless, companies such as Ford and GM continue pursuing flex-fuels while powerful governments in both advanced and emerging economies move forward with subsidies and mandated consumption targets for biofuels.

I ask Viera about Ford's hybrid offerings. As part of his green awakening, in 2005 Bill Ford, the company's then CEO, pledged the firm would have 250,000 hybrids on the road by 2010. The goal was quietly dropped in 2006 less than a year later. As of 2008, when we meet, Viera tells me Ford currently offers just one model, a gas-electric SUV called the Escape, which gets about 33 mpg. As far as profitability, Viera says, "Hybrids don't make any money; depending on the vehicle, you actually lose money." Ford's gas-electric Escape goes for between $19,000 and $27,000, which is $3,000–$4,000 more than the equivalent nonhybrid model. This premium covers only half the additional costs the company incurs to make each hybrid. Ford can't ask the full $6,000–$8,000 extra, Viera says, because no one would buy it.

REN CEN

The hub of downtown Detroit is the Renaissance Center, a shimmering five-tower high-rise complex built in the 1970s in an effort by local officials and auto magnates to recover from the city's brutal riots of 1967. As its name suggests, the idea behind the Renaissance Center was to revitalize downtown to help prevent social instability from sparking again. In 1996, General Motors relocated here from its previous headquarters, which were just up the street from its biggest local factory, the Pole Town Plant. The Ren Cen, as locals call it, is a sleek, modernist city within a city that contains corporate offices, a shopping mall, health club, several restaurants, and a Marriott hotel. Everything can be accessed via an indoor, multistory network of retro-futuristic glass and cast-concrete walkways, which, around lunchtime, teem with women speed-walking in their office attire and chunky sneakers.

After clearing security, I step into an external glass elevator that shoots up over the Detroit River. Ice floats in silvery sheets along the water toward Lake Erie. It's been an unforgiving winter; so far the area has received more than double its normal snowfall.

I'm here to meet Terry Cullum, GM's director of corporate responsibility and environment and energy. He advises the firm on its social and ecological policies and helps with political lobbying. A lifer with the company, Cullum has a small build, thinning hair, wears a tailored blue suit, and is a year away from retiring. I ask what GM is doing to address the environmental crisis, and he explains the company's capabilities are limited. GM focuses mostly on the near term, Cullum says, meaning what's being manufactured now and in the next three to five years. "The long term, twenty years out, we just can't think about that. That's not how our industry works."

As at Ford, Cullum first stresses the importance of GM's improvements to the tried-and-true internal combustion engine. Then he wants to talk about hybrids. The firm has eight gas-electric hybrid models currently in showrooms, with a "major rollout" coming soon. But, like Ford, GM has installed hybrid technology mostly in its fuel-bingeing SUVs such as the mammoth Chevy Tahoe and Cadillac Escalade. On the subject of gas-electrics, I expect Cullum to talk about the Chevy Volt. Oddly, he doesn't mention it. Instead, the energy and policy guy grabs GM's upcoming annual report and flips to a double-page spread about the firm's hydrogen-fuel-cell trial called Project Driveway. Cullum is effusive about the program's potential to deliver a carbon-free future.

Although hydrogen is extolled by many as the best means for energy salvation, it's no magic bullet. Hydrogen is one of the most abundant substances on earth, so, unlike oil, there's plenty to go around. Most significant, hydrogen contains no carbon, so emits no CO_2. However, H (its symbol) doesn't exist alone. To be made into an energy carrier, hydrogen must be released from its bonds in other substances, such as water or natural gas. Once refined hydrogen can be used to power an internal combustion engine or a fuel-cell motor (essentially an electric motor) with no greenhouse gases coming out the tailpipe, only clean water. Rendering hydrogen for fuel, though, requires substantial energy, most of which comes from highly polluting coal. Compounding that, more than half of today's hydrogen fuel supply is derived not from water, but from natural gas—the main by-product being CO_2.

A few weeks after Cullum and I talk, a *Wall Street Journal* report from the Geneva Auto Show says both GM and Toyota are "doubtful on [hydrogen] fuel cells' mass use." GM's Bob Lutz tells reporters these vehicles remain far too expensive to introduce on a large scale: "We are nowhere [near] where we need to be on the costs curve." Toyota president Katsuaki Watanabe agrees: "It will be difficult to see the spread of fuel cells in ten years' time." Project Driveway may well be a genuine effort, but it also serves as a distraction—a no-strings-attached gesture that, whether GM makes low-impact cars or not, proclaims the automaker's fealty to an environmentally healthy tomorrow.

Peeking from under the papers pinned to the wall above Cullum's desk is a photo of the concept Volt. The slick image looks like an ad for a Batman movie and is part of GM's full-on campaign to promote the car. I point to the picture and ask about the plug-in electric's progress. When Cullum answers, he de-emphasizes the Volt, explaining that it's part of the firm's larger "E-flex" program that isn't about just one car. A few days later I come across a front-page story in the *Detroit Free Press* profiling the Volt and its product-line executive, a German engineer named Frank Weber. In terms of technology, the article is singularly focused on the Volt, and it reads like ad copy. I find it hard to reconcile Cullum's lack of enthusiasm with GM's lavish PR for the Volt and the constant flow of flattering coverage it receives in the press. Maybe Cullum's tired of talking, or maybe he's hedging because he's doubtful. Perhaps it's safe to crow about hydrogen vehicles because they're nowhere near being production-ready. But talking up the Volt is riskier because it's more real. Once the car hits the road in 2010 and more widely in 2011, its lofty technological promise may well go unfulfilled.

I call Miguel Chavarria, a veteran worker at GM with thirty-one years on the shop floor. I want to find out more about how the automaker is gearing up to manufacture the Volt in 2010, the production date initially announced. Chavarria and I meet at the grimy Anchor Bar in downtown Detroit, not far from the Renaissance Center. It's early evening on a weekday, and he's just got off his shift at GM's Pole Town Plant, which is where the Volt is scheduled to be assembled. Chavarria is in his fifties, has a stocky build, thick black hair, and a ready smile. We sit at a table in a cramped wooden booth next to the bar's makeshift kitchen; the crackling sound of the deep fryer overpowers the jukebox from time to time.

He's stressed-out and tells me that just last month half of the workers at Pole Town were laid off. Those remaining have been offered early retirement and buyout packages. He's weighing his options and confesses the buyout is tempting, even though he'd like to keep his job. It's a gamble: if he stops working, he won't have as much money in the bank, but if he stays on the job, he might get laid off with little or no severance. Amid such financial distress, the prospect of GM's launching a new vehicle seems like a godsend.

I ask Chavarria what he thinks about the Volt, and he says that although he questions the veracity of global warming, he hopes GM gets the car into production at Pole Town. "Right now I don't see any investment being made. Usually when a new model comes, we have a team already being assembled, a launch team." But that's not happening with the Volt. According to Chavarria, it can take up to a year and a half to get the assembly line ready to build a new model, and that's using the same car frame and a standard internal combustion engine. But the Volt will require a totally different platform, necessitating new heavy machinery such as dies. There's also the equipment they'll need for mounting the banks of lithium-ion batteries. Regardless of whether the Volt gets built on time at Pole

Town or elsewhere, serious questions persist about the plug-in's environmental prowess and economic viability. Despite an increase in ecologically sensitive government policy and a marked consumer shift to cleaner cars, between 2008 (when I am in Detroit) and 2010, when the first few hundred handmade Volts go on sale, the future of the plug-in remains uncertain.

For one, the car's efficiency isn't such a straightforward matter. According to GM, the plug-in has the potential to reach the equivalent of 230 mpg. But to hit that number, a Volt driver will have to follow a somewhat inflexible regime. The battery must be fully recharged daily, and the driver can't venture farther than forty miles on most days. Using this formula, a Volt owner can roll gas-free much of the time. Citing Bureau of Transportation figures that report nearly eight in ten Americans drive fewer than forty miles per day, GM says relying on the battery alone will be a cinch for Americans. But what GM doesn't clarify is that this number reflects strictly the miles racked up commuting from home to work. Running a few errands and picking up the kids can put a driver over forty miles in no time. What's more, the Internet auto magazine Edmunds.com calculated that if you go for a 230-mile spin on a single afternoon, the fuel economy of the Volt plunges to 38.3 mpg equivalent. At this point, nobody really knows what mpg the Volt will get because GM hasn't issued enough information and the EPA has yet to test the vehicle. The Edmunds.com finding also raises questions about how standards for setting mpg equivalents on plug-ins will be determined and by whom.

Having eco-cars such as plug-in hybrids on the road can cut greenhouse gases when they're driven less rather than more. So far, however, consumers who buy greener hybrids tend to spend greater time behind the wheel than those with conventional vehicles—about 25 percent more, according to a 2009 study. The reasons why aren't clear based on the report's findings. I can propose one possible explanation offered by a Prius driver I interviewed. She said that because the fuel-efficient car made her feel that she was polluting less, she indulged in more trips.

No matter how the fuel-efficiency math works out, the underlying economics of the industry remain unchanged. The same core sticking points that existed before the Democratic electoral sweep of 2008 and the auto sector meltdown the following year weigh on the future of the Volt and other green vehicles like it: What if only a few people buy the Volt—will GM continue offering it in coming years? And if the plug-in hybrid sells well, will the recently bankrupt GM be able to carry the losses that will accrue until production can achieve sufficient volumes to bring down costs? In other words, can a major automaker stay competitive while losing money on a product that's more than twice the price of a standard model? And most important, if plug-ins succeed, will automakers truly use them as a bridge to ever-greater fuel efficiency that no longer relies on fossil fuels, including coal-fired power? Or once the technology reaches a politically acceptable mpg, will automakers plow future efficiency gains into more-profitable luxury features yet again?

As our meeting ends, I ask Chavarria why firms such as GM haven't worked harder to turn out ecologically responsible automobiles. "They're not going to make a car more efficient if it costs them more. If they could sell the same thing year after year without making any changes, they would." Although it's typically consumers who are charged with stubbornly clinging to gas-guzzlers, Chavarria thinks that something embedded in the culture of the auto industry leadership yearns for stasis. "Right now people in power who want to make the money, if they made such a big change [to green transportation], they wouldn't be able to control their destinies."

A few weeks before I talk to Chavarria, GM's Lutz, whose job closely involves the Volt, slips up in front of the press. He tells reporters in a closed-door session that global warming is a "total crock of shit." Although clearly off-message, a taunt such as this from Lutz isn't so surprising. After all, the former marine was party to the early development of the breakthrough SUV, the Explorer, in the mid-1980s when he worked for Ford. Having also occupied executive posts at Chrysler and BMW, GM's "car czar," as he's often referred to, has played no small part in keeping the auto industry on its highly polluting course. On the personal side, Lutz is famous for his machismo, arriving to work in his private helicopter, and flying around in his own fighter jet—brand name Alpha.

To better understand the position we're in today—hooked on greenhouse-gas-belching internal combustion rides made by extremely powerful companies with global-warming deniers at the helm—it's important to consider why most Americans don't have other choices. Most obviously, what about mass transit and greener cars? Highly functional tramway lines, most powered by electricity, once circuited cities and towns across the United States. But the network was bought up and systematically dismantled by the most influential auto interests globally, led by GM. The car business saw it could thrive by turning all those riders into drivers. The industry's band of good old boys was not only capable of junking mass transit, throughout the twentieth century they also kept their own experiments with alternative technologies—gas-electric hybrids and full electrics among them—off the streets.

In the early 1920s, General Motors realized that its main competitors weren't just Ford and other automakers but the myriad public transit lines that connected people with home and work. At that time, a mere 10 percent of Americans owned cars, while public transport systems abounded, offering frequent service throughout neighborhoods and into downtown areas. To create more of a market for itself, GM forged a clandestine joint venture with Standard Oil of California, Firestone Tires, and other auto industry players to procure local transit firms and replace streetcars with buses, which would then yield the road to cars. In the late 1930s, these coconspirators created a company called National City Lines, or NCL, to serve as a front for their activities.

NCL presented itself as a mass-transportation firm, and it grew by acquiring local routes everywhere from Cedar Rapids, Iowa, and El Paso, Texas, to Los Angeles and Baltimore. Although it's little known today, these towns and scores of others once had comprehensive, efficient public transit systems. After NCL bought up the lines, the firm would systematically cut service while keeping fares steady or raising them, effectively making public transit more of a hassle than a help. Running existing networks into the ground made it easier for NCL to claim rail transit schemes weren't viable. That justified making the switch to buses—manufactured by none other than GM—which NCL assured could offer superior service. This in turn facilitated paving over trolley tracks and tearing down overhead electrical cables, making the transition to individual autos all the easier.

An internal memo, written to the head office not long after NCL acquired the public system in Tampa, Florida, outlines the firm's standard practice: "In the event we maintain a 5 cent fare in Tampa without transfer privileges, my thought was to terminate all routes downtown. In other words, eliminate all crosstown [sic] through service."

In the midst of its dirty work, NCL, GM, Standard Oil, and Firestone were indicted on federal antitrust charges in a case that went all the way to the U.S. Supreme Court. In the 1949 ruling, which stood, the companies were found guilty of conspiring to monopolize the transit business.

However, the Court fined each firm a paltry $5,000, and the colluding executives were each ordered to pay exactly $1 as a penalty for their transgressions. Facing such leniency, the auto interests continued unencumbered in their deconstruction of America's public transit networks.

Over the ensuing three decades, NCL, along with two other front companies, Pacific City Lines and American City Lines, bought up public transportation routes in more than eighty U.S. towns, affecting millions of people. Regardless of public opinion, which showed clear support for the expansion of mass transit—as in post–World War II Los Angeles, where polls revealed 88 percent of those surveyed wanted more, not fewer rail lines—the automakers' plans went forward apace. Ultimately, NCL's efforts were successful. Replacing the mass-transit networks that NCL wiped out has proven politically and financially impossible, leaving the vast majority of Americans with no choice but automobiles.

As automakers carried out their conquest of transportation systems, they didn't solely pursue gas-guzzlers. Well-known companies also experimented with and, in some cases, manufactured alternative vehicles. In the United States however, the Detroit Three refused to put greener cars into full production.

A hundred years ago Dr. Ferdinand Porsche, the German car builder, constructed his first roadster, which was an electric vehicle, or EV. His second was a gas-electric hybrid with an internal combustion engine that spun a generator to power electric motors in the wheel hubs. Running strictly on its battery pack, the Porsche hybrid had a range of thirty-eight miles, much farther than today's commercial gas-electrics. Several other small companies, such as Detroit Electric and Woods Dual Power, turned out EVs and hybrids over the ensuing decades. Henry Ford and Thomas Edison both drove Detroit Electrics.

Well before the oil shortages of the 1970s, hundreds of thousands of Americans were buying gas-saving compact Volkswagen Beetles, and the BMW Isetta, which got 50 mpg. In 1969 GM made a hybrid prototype called the 512. It could also go fifty miles on a gallon of gas and featured a futuristic body that flipped open instead of using doors. Like current hybrids, GM's engine ran on electric in low gear and switched to the internal combustion engine at higher speeds. The fastest it could go, however, was a meager forty miles per hour, which eliminated the possibility of its entering the mass market.

After flopping with the gasless Electrovette in the 1980s, GM embarked on its most well-known foray into emissions-free cars, the EV1 and its successor, the EV2. Through its Saturn division, the firm leased a thousand of these full electrics to drivers in California in the 1990s. As depicted in the 2006 documentary film *Who Killed the Electric Car?* the company controversially did away with the project in the early 2000s, ending leases regardless of whether consumers wanted to keep their wheels or not. When devotees and a Saturn manager in charge of the program, Chelsea Sexton, claimed GM failed to adequately market the car, the company rebutted that drivers just weren't interested. Once all the EVs were collected, amid protests from pro-electric groups, GM sent the cars to be crushed for scrap.

A simultaneous venture into alt-tech was the Supercar. In 1993, Vice President Al Gore and his boss, Bill Clinton, joined forces with the CEOs of the Big Three to form the Partnership for a New Generation of Vehicles, or PNGV. The program was a collaboration between the federal government and industry to fund and facilitate research for a Supercar: a four-door family sedan that would get a remarkable 80 mpg, wouldn't ask consumers to sacrifice comfort, performance, or styling, and would be in showrooms by 2003. The public-private partnership that would bring this about entailed $1.5 billion in government money, plus resources from a wealth of federal research labs and government agencies. In exchange for the automakers' participation in the nonbinding goals of the PNGV, the Clinton administration backed away from increasing CAFE standards.

The companies unveiled their prototypes in 1999, and according to a story in the *Chicago Tribune,* each car came close to the project's goals: Ford's and Chrysler's greenmobiles both got 72 mpg while GM's hit the 80 mpg target. All of them were sedans built with superlight materials and powered by diesel-electric hybrid drivetrains. But after all the newspaper and television stories ran, the automakers didn't gear up their assembly lines because, they said, cost posed an insurmountable obstacle.

While the other two kept quiet on specifics, Chrysler claimed its Supercar ran $7,500 above what it could realistically charge customers. As GM's EV program and the Supercar reveal, the auto firms know how to make highly efficient vehicles, but they don't dedicate their assembly lines to eco-cars because the financial risk is too great, at least in the short and medium term.

Say Chrysler put its Supercar on offer and it was a washout. The company would have sunk a fortune not only into R&D but also factory retooling and building up whole new parts supply chains, all for naught. Alternately, if the Supercar was a sensation, then the automaker would lose thousands of dollars on each sale. The more units people bought the more losses the company would rack up. Only over time—as supply chains for the exotic new parts were established and production was ramped up and perfected to achieve economies of scale—would profits begin to materialize. Getting to that point would be slow and financially painful. Giving new and costly technologies the time and nurturing needed for them to take root would also require a board of directors willing to buck the short-term concerns of shareholders. Going for long-range outcomes and "intangibles" such as ecological well-being are moves that usually get board members kicked out in short order. Following the rules of business, it was economically responsible for the Detroit Three to forgo ultraefficient vehicles and stick with what they knew was profitable—trucks and SUVs.

What's more, with a presidential election in 2000, the major auto firms likely held out for a sympathetic Republican administration. And George W. Bush obliged. The new president promptly named as his chief of staff Andrew Card, who was then serving as GM's top lobbyist in D.C. Prior to that, Card spent five years as president of the American Automobile Manufacturers Association. One year after Bush entered the White House, his energy secretary, former Republican senator from Michigan Spencer Abraham, appeared at the 2002 Detroit auto show to present the spoils. He announced that the PNGV was over. Supercars never went into production.

AUBURN HILLS

Chrysler headquarters is about thirty miles north of Detroit, not far from the posh suburbs of Bloomfield Village and Birmingham in a place called Auburn Hills. The firm used to have its offices and a key factory in Highland Park, a small incorporated town in the center of Detroit. In the 1980s, as the Motor City slipped further into poverty and social disarray, Chrysler retreated to its current, more exclusive location. Snow is still falling from the previous night's storm, and in contrast to the city, out here the blanket of white is unspoiled. Chrysler's campus sits within the gentle slope of a hill; a metal fence traces the perimeter and surveillance cameras are everywhere.

Inside the place is bustling. The interior resembles a multilevel subur-ban shopping mall, with an open central corridor crisscrossed with stairs and escalators, and offices with plate-glass windows facing outward, like shops. Max Gates from the communications department, who's serving as my chaperone, tells me the building's architect normally designs com-mercial retail space. "If things don't work out, the idea was that it could always be used as a shopping mall," he says with a chuckle. As the compa-ny's prospects stand today, that might just happen.

Gates takes me to the office of Reginald Modlin, Chrysler's director of environment and energy. Modlin dresses in old-school preppy: kha-kis, jacket, oxford shirt. After earning a degree in aeronautical engineer-ing, he started at the firm and has been here his entire thirty-five-year career. Among his duties at Chrysler are making frequent trips to Wash-ington, D.C., like GM's Cullum, to serve as a resource for auto industry lobbyists.

When Modlin starts on the subject of green vehicles, like his counter-parts at Ford and GM he explains that Chrysler is primarily focused on improved gasoline engines and diesels. He admits that Chrysler has yet to produce any eco-vehicles, but it plans to get out its first two hybrids—both large SUVs—by 2009. (However, as soon as the automaker debuted its Dodge Durango and Chrysler Aspen gas-electrics in fall 2008, it announced the scrapping of its entire hybrid program due to the com-pany's unraveling economic security.) Modlin touches on hydrogen and flex-fuels, neither of which the company produces. Most of what Chrysler still sells is internal combustion SUVs, pickups, and minivans, which, as of 2007, comprised about three-quarters of its sales.

The company is moving so slowly on clean vehicles Modlin proffers because it's not up to the Chryslers of the world to forge greenhouse-gas-busting breakthroughs. "That's for the entrepreneurs to do," he says. "And when they've got something really good, we'll come in and either buy that product from them or buy their company." I ask if large corporations such as Chrysler are risk-averse and therefore unwilling to deploy greener tech-nologies. "We don't know which technology will take off, so we have to be careful about what we invest in," he responds. "There's a lot at stake, and we don't want to be left with all our eggs in the wrong basket." Sitting on Modlin's desk is a framed illustration. The image is of two construction workers atop cranes, each building two halves of a rainbow that will meet in the middle. The section of rainbow on the left has its colors stacked one way, the right half has the same colors, but inverted. The speech bubble above one of the workers says, "Aw shit!"

During our conversation, Modlin mentions that significant efficiencies have been achieved in internal combustion engines over the last thirty years. These, he says, could have been applied to improving gas mileage, but instead they've gone into making cars bigger and more luxurious. Gates—who has worked as a journalist and lobbyist in the auto sector for decades—interjects that had these gains been applied directly to engine functions, they would have created an annual 1–1.5 percent increase in fuel economy. So cars that now clock 27.5 mpg, the CAFE standard, could be getting 35–39 mpg. Larger vehicles such as SUVs that are supposed to meet the CAFE required 22.5 mpg would see a boost of 6–10 mpg. Not only does this explain why some of the first automobiles such as the Model T got superior mileage to many of today's vehicles, it also highlights that we don't need to wait for some elusive engineering feat to drive less polluting cars. For every increase of five miles per gallon, 20 percent of a vehicle's annual CO_2 emissions are eliminated. Instead, total U.S. carbon dioxide releases have surged by 17 percent between 1990 and 2007.

When I'm in Detroit, I talk about this with John German, manager of environmental and energy analysis at Honda, a company known for its fuel-frugal cars. He says consumers haven't been willing to put their money on higher mpg because they don't believe they'll get it. The fuel economy listed on a car's sticker, since the inception of such estimates, has notoriously overstated how many miles a vehicle will go on a gallon of gas. Consequently, the information is often doubted. Fuel economy can only be determined once the gas tank has been filled a few times, but by then the driver has already bought the vehicle, which can't be returned even if the mpg is lower than the sticker stated.

"Performance is much easier to quantify," German offers. "You have one test-drive and you have a pretty good idea of what the performance is, so there's a lot less uncertainty. Luxury, you go down there, you can see the leather, you can see the accessories, these are things that are all very, very certain." For many people a new car is the most expensive purchase they'll ever make, and, understandably, buyers want to be sure they'll get what they paid for. "And so I think that is why the industry's been widely criticized for using this technology to improve performance and all these other features instead of fuel economy," German says. "But this is why we do it."

ANN ARBOR

The U.S. Environmental Protection Agency's National Vehicle and Fuel Emissions Laboratory is on the fringes of Ann Arbor, a straight forty-mile shot on I-94 from downtown Detroit. The EPA opened this facility in 1971 to monitor pollution levels of auto emissions, including CO_2; after the first oil shock of 1973 the lab also began checking fuel economy. It remains the only U.S. government facility to perform these jobs. The sticker on all new passenger vehicles including cars, light trucks, SUVs, and minivans bears the numbers the lab's tests produce—the city average, the highway average, and the combined average fuel economy, which tells consumers what mileage a new car will get. I've come here to talk to Jeff Alson, senior policy adviser for transportation and climate. I want to know why the lab's fuel-economy estimates have been so unreliable, leaving consumers doubtful they'll get what they pay for.

Alson shows me where the tests are conducted—in small rooms called cells. We go inside one and find a vehicle in a bay with its rear wheels resting on a giant silver dynamometer, a high-tech treadmill that allows a car to run in place at top speeds by absorbing the force of propulsion. Hanging from the ceiling on a thick metal arm is a computer monitor that charts out a travel path, which is readable from the driver's side window. The computer program offers two options: city, which is full of stops and starts that translate into a jagged line; or highway, the uncluttered curve of acceleration and cruising.

Throughout the 1970s the agency designed and established the standards for fuel economy testing in the United States and, in its first decades, conducted all its own trials. But due to budget cuts that grew steeper under the Bush administration, the EPA lab is now unable to keep its cells fully operational. Alson explains that this facility currently tests emissions and fuel economy on just 10–20 percent of American consumer vehicles; the remainder is now conducted by the carmakers themselves. (He assures me they adhere to strict EPA specifications.) It's a Friday afternoon, which perhaps accounts for it, but as we walk around, I see only a handful of people working, and most cells sit in darkness.

Tall, fair-haired, and lean, Alson started working here three decades ago, and says he knows fuel-economy estimates have been inaccurate for years. He explains that the agency's tests have failed to account for a range of driving styles, and variations in weather conditions. For instance, a driver who "jackrabbits"—steps hard on the gas during acceleration—might use 5 or 6 percent more fuel than someone with a lighter foot. Weather such as strong winds and searing heat can also push mileage downward.

When we were in the cell, visible on the monitor perched at the driver's side window was the most recent test, which had been performed on the highway graph. On the screen were two lines, the test route in red and the technician's path in white. The white line sat almost directly on top of the red. These trials have no unexpected lane changes or sudden braking, no tailgaters or dangerous drivers forcing a speedup to get out of the way, no storms or air conditioners on full blast. What's more, the technicians who carry out the tests are real pros—some have been at the job for over twenty years—and they can navigate the routes blindfolded. "If you tried to drive that, you'd be all over the graph," Alson tells me. "But these guys, they really know what they're doing, they stay right on target." This uniformity was intended to create a level playing field for all cars. While it may sound good in theory, in practice it has meant the lab registers the highest possible gas mileage, something no real-world driver could achieve. The discrepancy created by a higher number listed on the sticker but lower realized mpg is part of what has fostered consumer doubt of fuel-economy statements. It has also facilitated the automakers in getting away with engines that used more fuel and spewed more greenhouse gases than they claimed.

In 2008 the EPA at last adjusted its testing methods in an attempt to more accurately capture what on-the-road petrol consumption might be. I ask Alson what took so long. "At one-dollar-a-gallon gasoline we didn't think anybody cared," he says. "From 1986 until 1999 nobody cared. We didn't care, the auto industry didn't care, politicians didn't care. We were all fat and happy. And"—implausibly—"no one knew enough to care about global warming." Alson assures me that future CAFE estimates listed on a new car's sticker will be more reliable, producing fuel-economy numbers about 10 percent lower than the old methods. "At least we're doing better with stickers," he says. "Now people can start trusting us more."

Far from disregarding fuel economy, people have expressed a potent desire for more efficient vehicles. In 2007 the Pew Campaign for Fuel Efficiency conducted a survey of voters from both parties in swing states and found a "broad consensus for mandatory auto fuel efficiency increases." Eighty-eight percent of Ohio respondents wanted the standards upped, as did 90 percent of those asked in Kentucky, and 89 percent in Florida. "Support for increased fuel efficiency standards . . . is overwhelming and unwavering," said Mark Mellman, president and CEO of the Mellman Group, which was among the companies conducting the poll. "Americans are clear: they want standards that are higher, come into force sooner, and are not capped."

THE FUTURE IS NOW

A 1932 mural of the Ford River Rouge plant by the famous Mexican painter Diego Rivera is housed in an atrium at the Detroit Institute of the Arts. Originally commissioned to paint two murals, Rivera ended up spending almost a year in Detroit and covering all four of the room's walls, floor to ceiling. He was deeply moved by the industrial project of mass assembly-line production, seeing in it a larger social purpose. The muralist and his wife, the painter Frida Kahlo, spent weeks in the Rouge factory, observing the workers, watching the machines. He made drawings and took photographs. Ultimately, Rivera painted a multiracial labor force, weaving in spirituality, the earth's elements, the potential of medicine, the miracle of life, and the hazards of war. But most of all Rivera painted the wonder of technology, the possibilities it held for delivering the whole of society from inequality and suffering to abundance: a transformation of the fire of greed and the burden of deprivation by the rhythm of shared labor and efficient production, remaking the world with forward movement leveraged through inspired innovation.

This belief in technology seems to motivate Stanford R. Ovshinsky. Since he and his late wife, Iris, established Energy Conversion Devices in 1959, this self-taught scientist has spent much of his career perfecting energy generation and storage. In a profile, the *Economist* magazine referred to Ovshinsky as a latter-day Thomas Edison. He is the inventor of the nickel-metal hydride battery (NiMH), which made the Toyota Prius and other hybrids possible and is still used in the most current gas-electrics. Ovshinsky also built the batteries for GM's EV1 and EV2 and continues, at the age of eighty-four, to forge ahead with alternative-energy technologies aimed at addressing environmental ills while allowing people to continue tooling around in their own vehicles.

His latest innovation is a hydrogen car. Instead of building one from the ground up, Ovshinsky adapted his Prius by replacing the gas tank with a thick-walled storage canister. His hybrid still employs an NiMH battery to power the electric motor, but rather than gasoline, its engine runs on hydrogen fuel. While most hydrogen fuel is refined from natural gas using nonrenewable energy, Ovshinsky employs a cleaner recipe. He makes hydrogen from water through electrolysis, whereby electric current is used to break apart the H_2O. Since he uses only solar power—generated with photovoltaic sheeting that he also invented—Ovshinsky's hydrogen is virtually carbon-free. "It's bigger than what Toyota and the Big Three say, we absolutely need new technology," he tells me. "If we don't advance society with new technology, then we erode society—there's a terrible crisis that brews."

Although Detroit's Big Three have led the way in failing to turn out cleaner cars and continue—even in the Obama era—to defend their right *not* to make them, the technologies are already here and in production.

Despite all its bluster over the Volt, GM missed the chance to introduce the world's first production plug-in gas-electric hybrid. That distinction goes to the F3DM, as it's called, which was released in December 2008 in China. Manufactured by BYD, that country's leading cell-phone-battery producer, the four-door sedan seats five and has a top speed of ninety-three miles per hour. The F3DM can go sixty miles on its batteries alone, then another three hundred miles with the help of its internal combustion engine; its batteries take seven hours to recharge. While BYD plans to offer the vehicle in U.S. and European markets in 2011, currently the company only sells the F3DM in China, for about $22,000. Although that price might sound cheap compared to the Volt, in China it's a lot of dough. BYD's own highly skilled engineers would have to spend about three years' wages to buy one.

A class of mini two-, three-, and four-seater full electrics barely larger than golf carts are gaining increasing popularity in Europe, although as yet none are for sale in the United States. (Several automakers have EVs in the works, including Nissan with its Leaf, a five-seater full electric set to hit the streets in Japan, the United States, and Europe in late 2010.) Among the current producers are the Indian carmaker REVA with its G-Wiz, the Norwegian firm Th!nk with its City, and Mitsubishi's i MiEV. Most models are curved and podlike, resembling a cartoon rendering of a car. Looking at the different offerings on the web—where the G-Wiz is exclusively sold—I half expect to see two large white eyes with solid-black pupils appear in the windshields. These vehicles can hit between fifty and ninety miles an hour, with a range of between seventy-five and one hundred miles, and can take anywhere from six to fourteen hours to recharge. The G-Wiz starts at just under £16,000, or about US$25,000, and Mitsubishi's i MiEV costs almost US$45,000. The Th!nk City goes for about €25,000 or just over US$35,000, but is projected to cost around US$20,000 when it debuts in the United States. That price does not include the battery pack, however. Th!nk requires its drivers to pay a monthly battery rental fee of about €65, or US$90. Clearly these rides are not for everyone.

Taking EVs up a step, the automaker Tesla began selling the Roadster, its luxury all-electric sports car, in 2008. Able to roar along at 125 miles per hour, the Roadster has a range of 220 miles, and according to the company, the two-seater's batteries can be recharged in just three and a half hours. However, the sleek electric sports car is only for those with deep pockets, ringing in at $109,000. Having ramped up production, in 2012 Tesla will roll out the Model S, which the firm projects will sell for a much lower $50,000.

Key to a shift in transportation technology is a support infrastructure including refueling, servicing, and parts. Two nascent refueling options attracting attention today are both for electric vehicles: recharge spots and battery-swap shops. High-voltage power points installed on public streets, as well as in office and shopping-mall parking lots, will allow EV and plug-in hybrid drivers to quickly rejuice their packs and get back on the road. Battery-changing stations allow drivers to pull in and have their depleted cells switched for full ones in minutes. Better Place, a northern California start-up—part of the Silicon Valley green-tech movement—is planning a global rollout of both types of facilities, which can be powered by solar. In 2009 Better Place opened its first switching post in Yokohama, Japan.

The main obstacle to greener automotive technology isn't that it's new and unproven. Hybrid and full electric systems have been around for over a century. Even EV refueling stations are not a novel idea: in the early 1910s Thomas Edison envisioned public charging points along trolley lines. Current vehicles such as the Tesla and G-Wiz demonstrate that alternative drivetrains work. The primary holdup is that internal combustion engines have been so much more profitable. The market hasn't brought us eco-cars; it's brought us SUVs. Consequently, we're waiting not so much for great technological breakthroughs as for the major auto firms to figure out how best to profit from them.

By way of contrast, where sizable fuel levies (a form of carbon tax) are in place, auto firms produce and consumers buy the world's most efficient cars. In Europe, petrol taxes are about 60 percent of the total retail price, while in the United States drivers pay a mere 13 percent in federal and state tariffs for transportation fuel. Europeans doling out more than double what Americans pay at the pump creates an incentive to consume less through greater efficiencies. One way to do that is to use diesel, which burns 30 percent cleaner than gasoline (over 50 percent of all new vehicles in Europe are diesels). Another way is through avoiding fuel-hungry cars. Consequently, industry standards on the Continent as well as in the UK call for smaller, lighter vehicles that use a fraction of the fuel burned in American cars.

As many efficiency-seeking Americans thwarted by the big U.S. firms already know, companies such as Ford and GM supply a robust market for petrol-thrifty models overseas. Consider the latest Ford Fiesta ECOnetic. The 2009 model gets a staggering 88 mpg on the freeway and 61 in the city. While it's a subcompact, the car can seat five, and starts at about $17,500, far cheaper than a hybrid or full electric. With much fanfare, Ford has announced that a modified Fiesta is slated for the United States in 2010. However, it will have a disappointing fuel economy in the low 30s. This number fails to exceed legally mandated U.S. CAFE standards, which could mean that if more ecologically beneficial regulations were put in place, U.S. drivers might just gain access to the cleaner rides we can't get today.

On the larger question of plug-ins' and full electrics' real environmental impacts, the jury is still out. According to a recent study by the Natural Resources Defense Council, and the Electric Power Research Institute, a utility trade group, juicing up a plug-in electric with coal-fired energy can produce more CO_2 than comes out the tailpipe of a standard hybrid that runs on fossil fuel. Carbon dioxide levels drop when voltage comes from alternate sources such as natural gas, hydropower, and nuclear—although these are less frequently used than coal (and present their own problems). Today China derives three-quarters of its electricity from coal, while the United States gets more than half its voltage from the black stuff, a potent source of carbon dioxide and other hazardous emissions, including mercury, a known neurotoxin. Overall, more than 40 percent of the world's electricity and almost a quarter of the energy used in industry comes from coal. These numbers are poised for a steep rise in the coming years. Electric vehicles can help cut greenhouse gas emissions only if they are part of a larger transition to renewably generated power.

Many people think the shell-shocked, toxic city of Detroit represents a past—the riots, the racism, the corruption—that has never been overcome. But perhaps Detroit is instead an indication of what lies ahead. Maybe the Motor City reveals what a highly polluting society can create for future generations.

Grand is a wide boulevard that forms a U-shaped outline of the central city of Detroit, connecting the west side to the east side, and linking GM's former headquarters to its Pole Town Plant. As I drive the path, I see blocks of obsolete factories, five stories tall. These buildings were deserted en masse after World War II when carmakers, seeking to intensify production, adopted more automated manufacturing methods that required single-story, sprawling assembly lines such as Pole Town. I come to a bridge. Rain has begun to dissolve the snow that accumulated last night. The road is wet, and the windshield wipers are barely keeping the water from blurring my view. The defrost is on but the windows are fogged up anyway. Suddenly the wheels start banging, sinking deep into potholes, hitting the bridge's metal support structure that used to be covered with cement. I slow to a creep. The surface of the road is cratered. Below the bridge are more brick shells of old factories, brittle, broken things. I stop the car and look back, convinced I accidentally drove onto a bridge that has been condemned. It seems as if at the top there will be nothing, the bridge will simply drop off, it will not deliver me to the other side. But when I glance back, I see no bright orange signs, no flashing lights. Instead I catch the glint of another car coming up behind me. I push the gas pedal.

Eventually my drive takes me to Highland Park. Cruising down Woodward, Highland Park's main artery, I find the factory the Ford Motor Company used before relocating to Dearborn. The abandoned building is easy to miss, blending in with the surrounding decay. Up and down Woodward sit check-cashing places, shuttered gas stations, used-car lots, defunct discount shops, strip clubs, and liquor stores with flashing signs advertising lotto tickets for sale. More buildings are empty than occupied. I pull off the main road to follow the haunted residential streets. Some dwellings are merely blank with absence. Others are bludgeoned, hollowed out, roofs missing, bits of sky visible through crumbling walls. Clothes, night-stands, and couches are in piles on curbsides, slowly disintegrating in the winter snow and rain. Many corners lack street signs, so I just roll through and try to guess where I am. At a single intersection on Woodward sits a large, windowless public school, a power plant with a FOR LEASE sign, and a public library wrought in the carved stone of neoclassical architecture with a plywood sheet erasing its doorway.

Ford's Highland Park factory is where the company, in the early 1910s, invented the moving assembly line, a key innovation that transformed industrial capitalism. Frederick Taylor, the famous rationalizer of the labor process, spent time in the plant with Henry Ford and his workers study-ing their systems. The established method of building a car had been for a small crew to put together a single vehicle from start to finish. Radically reconfiguring the process, Taylor broke the assembly into discrete tasks so that each laborer performed a pared-down job repeatedly throughout the shift. Taylor also introduced a giant conveyor belt so that workers would stand in place as the vehicles under construction rolled past, creating greater efficiencies and giving management direct control over the speed of production. In addition to forging new heights of worker alienation, the moving assembly line dramatically upped productivity, decreased manu-facturing costs, and marked the ascendance of mass consumption.

In more recent decades, the auto majors have typically justified their avoidance and undermining of greener technologies by claiming that increased costs would do the industry in. And they're right; such sweep-ing changes may well decimate corporate balance sheets and autowork-ers' livelihoods, crippling the overall economy. But, as we saw in 2009, other forces can drag the industry down as well. Even though the U.S. government handed out billions of dollars to Chrysler and is now the largest shareholder in GM, no automaker is obligated to get radically cleaner cars into full production. Nor is the U.S. government repurpos-ing shuttered auto plants to manufacture equipment such as windmills needed for a green-energy transformation. Mass production like that achieved at Ford's Highland Park plant was supposed to deliver a high standard of living, creating greater equality and less hardship as Diego Rivera imagined. For decades it did, but at what we now know has been a staggering cost, both social and environmental. The onslaught of global warming, the trashing of towns such as Highland Park and Detroit, as well as the auto industry's unwillingness—indeed incapacity—to mass-produce highly efficient cars aren't disparate phenomena. On the contrary, they're deeply interconnected—all results of a system ultimately unable to factor the larger well-being of the environment and human health into its accounts.

Like its surroundings, Ford's obsolete factory is now derelict. There is no observation tower as at the Rouge plant, no tourist center. Instead, the windows that are not boarded up are smashed. The rooms inside are weathered and torn. You'd never know how historically significant the place was if it weren't for a small bronze marker planted in a patch of grass near the building's former entrance. It tells a brief but familiar narrative, which reads, "Here at his Highland Park Plant, Henry Ford in 1913 began the mass production of automobiles on a moving assembly line. By 1915 Ford built a million Model T's. In 1925 over 9,000 were assembled in a single day. Mass production soon moved from here to all phases of American industry and set the pattern of abundance for 20th Century living."

CHAPTER SIX

The Price of Air: Carbon Offsets

G udibanda is a string of dusty villages about sixty kilometers north of Bangalore in the southern state of Karnataka, India. The landscape is rocky and dry, its windswept hills are solid granite, which can rise slowly or jut dramatically into the sky. Men wearing traditional lungis squat on the faces of these massive rocks, tapping chisels along fractures to set loose slabs they can sell to earn a living. People with land grow peanuts, and during the wetter parts of the year, just after the monsoons, rice. Some also raise mango trees and dairy cows. Across fields, herds of goat and sheep amble to and fro and come in like waves at the end of the day following the whistles and shouts of their minders.

Gudibanda would seem an unlikely place for the top British rock band Coldplay. But in 2002, when the group took the ecologically vanguardist step of "neutralizing" the carbon dioxide emissions generated from its second album, *A Rush of Blood to the Head,* the network of Indian villages that comprise Gudibanda figured prominently. At the time, awareness of, and guilt about, the devastating effects of global warming were beginning to seep into the daily lives of Western consumers. Since CO_2 is the biggest contributor to global warming, Coldplay's actions seemed like a no-brainer. As detailed in a 2006 story by Amrit Dhillon and Toby Harnden that ran in the *Sunday Telegraph* (London), the band paid a British offset firm called Future Forests, since renamed The CarbonNeutral Company (TCNC), £33,000, just under US$50,000, to plant ten thousand mango trees in fields around Gudibanda. The move was met with a flood of publicity that helped glamorize the act of shrinking one's carbon footprint. So enthusiastic was Coldplay that they began encouraging their fans to buy trees, too. "You can dedicate more saplings in Coldplay's forest, a specially-selected section in Karnataka, India," its website read at the time. For £17.50, about US$25, eager fans could buy a piece of the offset action; in return they received a certificate conferring their participation in establishing "The Coldplay Forest."

The rock band was ahead of the pack and has since been joined by increasing numbers of fellow musicians, including the Rolling Stones, the Dave Matthews Band, and KT Tunstall. To answer the call, more companies began forming in the United Kingdom, Europe, Canada, and the United States to sell the notional product of carbon offsets. It was becoming easier not just for celebrities but also regular consumers and businesses to pay a little extra to chip in for tree-planting endeavors or renewable energy projects to try to counteract the damage from hopping a plane or hitting the highway.

Broadly speaking, there are two types of offsets. The kind Coldplay purchased is referred to as "voluntary" and is sold by independent firms to organizations, businesses, and individuals who want to reduce the effects of their carbon output. The second type are mandatory offsets, generated as part of the Kyoto Protocol. Under this system, if a company exceeds its emissions cap it must either buy additional CO_2 credits from another firm that didn't use its full allocation or it can invest in creating new credits—offsets—via what is known as the Clean Development Mechanism (CDM). CDM and voluntary offset projects are essentially the same in their implementation, the primary difference being that the former are overseen by a UN body. This chapter focuses primarily on voluntary offset projects because currently they are the only option for Americans seeking to settle their carbon debt. Since carbon offsetting will doubtless be a key facet of any cap-and-trade legislation U.S. lawmakers eventually pass, scrutinizing the impacts of current voluntary efforts is crucial. (Also, many voluntary projects are now seeking and winning official CDM status.)

As it typically goes down, an outfit such as TCNC sells its voluntary offsets in the West, then collaborates with an entity, often a nongovernmental organization, in the place where the project will be implemented, often in a developing country. Some portion of the money consumers pay is channeled to the NGO, which then forges local contacts in areas where, say, a mango plantation would be welcome. Such an endeavor can also involve regional elected officials, village leaders, local community self-help groups, and individuals who decide or are chosen to participate. On their websites, most offset firms boast the win-win benefit of attaining lower CO_2 levels while boosting livelihoods for impoverished local residents.

For the Coldplay grove, TCNC partnered with Women for Sustainable Development (WSD), a Bangalore-based NGO that recruited a slew of peasant farmers to receive and care for saplings. As opposed to non-fruit-bearing varieties, mango trees made sense because they could provide income for years to come. This created a built-in incentive to tend them well and protect them from becoming firewood or construction material. WSD distributed the saplings, promising the farmers a small sum from the offset money, fertilizer, and supplementary water in case of shortages. The project sounded great; however, things didn't quite work out.

As exposed in the widely publicized *Telegraph* story, the project was poorly executed and fell dramatically short of its clean-air promises. Only eight thousand trees were ever distributed, and of those many didn't survive. By the time planting got under way, Gudibanda was in the throes of a severe multiyear drought that showed no signs of letting up. Since 1995 the monsoon rains hadn't adequately filled the arid region's reservoirs, which it relies on to feed its crops during the parched months. Nevertheless, WSD stuck with the plan. In one village WSD gave saplings to just a single family out of the 130 that lived there. "No one else got any trees. Some of us were offered saplings, but we don't have any water," a farmer's wife explained to the *Telegraph*.

When WSD pulled a no-show with its water truck and other supports, parts of the Coldplay Forest withered and died. One farmer, Jayamma, told the *Telegraph* she was given 150 trees by WSD, out of which just a third survived and only because she had a well on her land. "I was promised two thousand rupees"—about US$40—"every year to take care of the plants and a bag of fertilizer. But I got only the saplings." According to the report, Anandi Sharan, head of WSD, said her organization was unable to fulfill its responsibilities due to inadequate funding from TCNC. The offset firm said WSD dropped the ball. Of the trees that actually made it into the ground, it's impossible to know how many are still standing.

Critics in the UK latched onto the ill-fated mango plantation as emblematic of the inability of CO_2 offsets to cool a warming planet. The story also tapped into a growing international grassroots opposition to selling greenhouse gas credits instead of limiting emissions outright. A few years prior, in 2004, the "Durban Declaration on Carbon Trading" was drafted in South Africa and signed by almost three hundred environmental groups, people's movements, academics, and others. The document says the signatories "reject the claim that carbon trading will halt the climate crisis" and calls offsetting a "false solution." It goes on, "We denounce the further delays in ending fossil fuel extraction that are being caused by corporate, government and United Nations' attempts to construct a 'carbon market.'" The mango debacle created an opening for dissenting voices such as this to be heard. After all the bad press, TCNC said it took the mango tree project off its carbon ledger and made up for the loss elsewhere. But the impact reached beyond just one project, as people in places such as Europe and South Africa continued questioning whether the abstract process of carbon offsetting could really work.

The website is the primary tool for carbon-offset firms. Here they promote themselves and sell their wares; they have no storefronts, their projects are often in remote locations, their customers never bump into each other at the cash register. The sites telegraph responsibility and simplicity, the antithesis of consumption. The aesthetic is usually spare, lots of white space and green lettering, with photos of towering windmills and resplendent banks of solar panels. The electronic pages are accented with what most people imagine when they think of nature: radiant flowers, waves crashing ashore, thickets of trees. "Ever wished you could do something about global warming?" asks a leading U.S. carbon-offset company, TerraPass, on its online shop. "The first step you can take to fight global warming is to reduce your carbon footprint through conservation. Drive less. Turn down the thermostat. . . . Then use TerraPass to balance the emissions you can't reduce." Carbonfund.org has a similar message: "Reduce what you can. Offset what you can't." Another entity, the Swiss-based Myclimate, reassuringly tenders "climate protection" against dangerous greenhouse gas emissions. And TCNC says on its website that settling one's carbon debt by procuring greenhouse-gas-neutralizing credits makes sense "because it should be easier and more enjoyable to be 'greener,' shouldn't it?"

Filling the chasm forged by the guilt and concern of the world's most wasteful consumers, the voluntary CO_2 offset industry is thriving. Not only does Al Gore pay to counteract his heat-trapping gases, so too does Hillary Clinton, Arnold Schwarzenegger, David Cameron (head of the UK Tory Party), and a host of other influential leaders and celebrities. TCNC has serviced the likes of Brad Pitt and the Rolling Stones while its current customers include Coldplay, Jake Gyllenhaal, and Sky, the UK-based television and communications firm. Myclimate counts Coca-Cola, Ben & Jerry's, Virgin Atlantic, and Unilever among its clients. Gatherings including the 2006 G8 summit and the 2008 Democratic National Convention as well as high-profile annual events such as the Oscars also procure voluntary offsets. Joining along are surging numbers of everyday fliers and drivers headed to business meetings and vacations. Growth in voluntary offsets has spiked in recent years, and the market is expected to be worth $4 billion by 2010.

But as the industry matures and expands, some crucial aspects of retail offsets marketed to the public remain obscure. Differing from credits generated via cap-and-trade policies mandated under the Kyoto framework—issued primarily to large companies, not individuals, and monitored by a United Nations agency—retail offsets are entirely voluntary. They're also entirely unregulated. Offset brokers are not compelled to meet any standards, have no required inspections, project approvals, or reviews, and no obligatory follow-up assessments to ensure the efficacy of the carbon remediation. Although organizations exist that offer certification for projects that meet a set of guidelines, such as the Gold Standard, these efforts are in no way mandatory. And, as I found out, the certifiers don't always maintain the highest standards themselves.

Even the more visible aspects of offsetting such as pricing are dubious. In this market the product for sale is the "credit," which is equal to a ton of CO_2. Emissions caused by activities that require burning fossil fuels, such as running errands in the car or taking a flight to visit family, can be measured, but these metrics vary widely. Each offset firm comes up with its own formula to calibrate its website's "carbon calculator." The calculator prompts the conscientious eco-shopper to confess the miles he or she plans to travel, and whether it's air or road; those seeking full absolution will also find inputs for daily energy use. After entering the information, out comes a pollution quotient and a correlating dollar amount. In part because the market is still new, no standard prices exist so the numbers are all over the map. Consider the varying fees to neutralize the CO_2 emissions from a round-trip New York City–Mumbai flight. The CarbonNeutral Company offers three options that range in price between $36 and $87. To do the same job, Myclimate charges considerably more: for their credits a consumer would pay $250 to contribute to an offset project in a developing country such as India, or $760 toward a project in Switzerland. Beyond cost, there's no official industry registry so it's impossible to know how many credits exist for any given project, and how many have been sold and to whom. Consequently, it's impossible to know if companies are vending the same credits multiple times. The industry is riddled with inconsistencies and an overall lack of transparency, leaving tremendous room for fraud that cheats consumers and the atmosphere.

Further, to get the job done, greenhouse gas neutralization doesn't happen immediately but only over the life of the project. That means trees planted to sop up carbon from today's long-haul flight or cross-country tour will only absorb the CO_2 over the life of the tree, which could be one hundred years or more, depending on the species. Since CO_2 absorption is lower in saplings than in mature specimens, it takes time for a newly planted tree to reach meaningful sequestration levels. The remedy might seem obvious: plant trees with shorter life spans that reach maturity sooner. However, these trees also die sooner, and upon expiring—as is true with all trees—begin releasing the entire carbon load they've soaked up. In other words, even when trees have full, healthy lives (unlike Coldplay's mango forest), they invariably dump the CO_2 they've absorbed right back into the atmosphere. Trees with shorter life spans of, say, thirty years as is the case with willows, or fifty years, as with birch (TCNC uses both varieties in reforestation projects), if planted today will begin releasing their stored CO_2 between the years of 2040 and 2060. At that time, it's likely the world will still be struggling to bring down carbon levels; how will we handle those deferred emissions then? Alternately, when trees take in CO_2 over a much longer time, say a century, greenhouse gas levels continue to rise in the immediate future, precisely when they need to come down.

Sadly, marketing the prospect of neutralizing a consumer's greenhouse gases conveys to people that their contribution to global warming can successfully, and quickly, be annulled. Statements of relief about this from the British pop musician KT Tunstall indicate how misleading this system can be. To cleanse the greenhouse gases from her release *Eye to the Telescope,* the musician paid TCNC to plant fifteen hundred trees in Scotland. "I can now say that producing this album hasn't harmed the environment at all," Tunstall told a reporter in 2005. "It's going to be carbon neutral for me from herein. Each time I use the tour bus, each time I play a gig, more trees will be planted." The musician explained how shocked she was when TCNC told her she emitted almost seventy times more carbon than the average Brit. "I said immediately whatever proportion of my earnings it takes to put back into the environment what I've taken out, that's fine. I just wanted to put back in what I've taken out."

Stuffing the global-warming genie back into the bottle is the tough task offset companies promise to fulfill. But what's actually going down in the places where these guilt- and carbon-scrubbing projects materialize? In addition to tree planting, offset money also funds renewable energy projects such as wind, solar, and biomass meant to provide power that would otherwise come from fossil fuels. India is host to more than a quarter of carbon-offset ventures globally, in part because it costs considerably less to build these projects in developing countries. In the fall of 2008, I visit the southern state of Karnataka, which has its fair share of CO_2 neutralization projects; here some light might be shed on what transpires after a consumer sitting at his or her computer in New York City or London clicks the OFFSET MY CARBON NOW button and pays up with the credit card.

GUDIBANDA AND BANGALORE

It's nighttime and I'm at a cooperative dairy in a remote village that's part of Gudibanda. I'm here to find out what happens to the vestiges of a failed offset project, in this case the Coldplay mango forest. In the room with me are about nine men; most of them are standing because there are only a few chairs. I am sitting, and they are all staring at me. The room is dank and the air musky with the smell of milk just out of the body of a cow. The green paint on the concrete walls is faded and chipped and, in some places, splattered with mud. The president of the dairy has positioned himself behind a beat-up metal desk. His hair is coiffed and oiled, and he wears slacks and shined shoes. It's the uniform of a man on the take; he clearly doesn't earn his living as a farmer. All the other men do, and they're scruffy, their lungis are soiled and they have cheap plastic sandals on their feet. Resting on the desk, the president's fists are studded with a dazzle of gold rings.

More men gather in front of the building outside the room's only window, which has bars over it. The drone of the cooling vats where farmers deposit their day's milk muffles any sound from outside and, I realize, any sound that might come from this room. "I don't know what you're talking about," the dairy president says to me, smiling through his combed mustache. His expression comes across as menacing, and as I ask more questions, the tension mounts. Back in 2002 the dairy president was a member of the local governing body known as the panchayat. I am told by current panchayat members that he would at least have heard of the mango project. In a specious manner, the president tells me of some development projects that have come along in the last few years, but he can't remember the names of the NGOs involved. He consults with the farmers; everyone says he knows nothing about the Coldplay mango forest.

Most of the farmers here raise livestock or grow peanuts, millet, or lentils; others have mango plantations. One mango farmer sits down next to my translator and confesses that he remembers the project. The president interrupts, blustering that the man doesn't know what he's talking about, then stares him down. The terse, nonverbal exchange is over within seconds. The farmer doesn't say another word. Some of the nut growers have brought handfuls of dried peanut plants into the room and set them on the desk. The president sifts through the leaves for the shells, cracks them open, and eats the nuts raw. They are shriveled like raisins. The men talk about the ongoing drought and how this year's harvest is stunted. As he eats, the president lets the shells fall across the desk and onto the floor. Someone else will clean them up.

A couple of farmers offer to roast some nuts. A few minutes later, in the dirt patch in front of the dairy, they use matches to light the bundles on fire. The flames are short and fast, streaks in the darkness. One of the men stands over the burning, staring as if in a trance. Soon he lifts his leg and stamps the fire out. The scorched peanuts taste like soot and smoke and make me nauseous. When my translator and I get up to leave, the president asks us to stay a little longer. My translator suggests we don't. The group of men escorts us to our car.

As we drive away, our headlights shoot their beams on darkened houses made of granite. In this part of Karnataka the rock is more abundant than wood, so peasants drag thick slabs from the hillsides back to the village to build their shacks. The village is quiet and no one is around. I spot a tiny shop; from inside, the green-white glow of a fluorescent tube washes onto the dirt road. We pull over to talk to the couple crammed behind the counter. I buy some fried lentil biscuits, and as I'm paying, my translator asks if they know anything about the mango forest. The woman keeps her mouth shut as the man steps forward. He begins to answer, but then his eyes wander. I turn around and the man with the rings is behind me. The shopkeeper immediately tells him we were asking about the mango trees. "You believe *me,*" the president of the dairy commands in a low voice. The farmer who told us he knew of the project is also here and invites me to come with them; he wants to show me his farm. It's pitch-black outside, I say no. The man with the rings insists. My translator and I jump into our car and get the hell out of there.

Anandi Sharan's name is listed on the website of a renewable energy company called Decentralized Energy Systems India Private Limited, or DESI. The firm is based in Bangalore and is chaired by Anandi's father, Dr. K. S. Sharan. The green-energy outfit is focused on a project to bring renewable biomass electricity to one hundred villages and is currently receiving money from Myclimate, a trusted Swiss voluntary offsetter. DESI purchases biomass gasifier generators for its project from a company called NetPro, which it shares an office with and which is owned by Dr. Sharan's brother. And rather astoundingly, the certifier of the hundred-village venture is Anandi Sharan herself. After the mango tree fiasco, she didn't back away from offsets but has instead expanded her reach. Her company is called CER India Private Ltd.; among its services are verification of the feasibility and efficacy of both voluntary and UN-regulated CDM projects. Apparently, the Sharans offer one-stop CO_2 offset shopping.

Every time I call to make an appointment to interview someone at DESI's Bangalore office, the woman on the other end of the line tells me no one's there and to try again in a few days. Finally, one afternoon I just show up. The office seems deserted; the lights are off and only a few people quietly mill about. The company's development engineer, Kaveri Uthaiah, agrees to an interview. She is tall and thin, only a few years out of college, and has a bad cold. Having graduated with a degree in environmental science, Uthaiah now works on DESI's hundred-village project, being carried out far from here in the northeastern state of Bihar. It is India's poorest, least developed, and most lawless region. In the last two years, DESI has installed four NetPro biogas electricity-generation units in three adjacent villages in Bihar.

Uthaiah explains that her job is to oversee the women's self-help groups DESI initiated to encourage business activity in the villages with the aim of strengthening demand for electricity. ("If we didn't, we wouldn't be able to generate the power and offset the carbon," she tells me.) Stemming from this work, dozens of businesses have been established, she proudly states, which means the project serves both the environmental and social good. When I ask for some examples, Uthaiah stammers, then says she knows of a rice mill and a workshop. What kind of workshop? "I'll have to get back to you with that information."

What Uthaiah does have is a video about NetPro's biogas technology. She hits PLAY on a laptop and a bold classical score, clearly influenced by *Star Wars,* issues forth from the tinny speakers. As the video rolls, it becomes clear that its aim is to obscure rather than illuminate. The movie doesn't show any images of real equipment, but instead begrudgingly leads the eye through a 3-D animated version of a biogas power plant. All of the equipment is rendered only as a series of cylinders, boxes, and rectangles, with no views of what would be happening inside the machine, no explanation of what the fuel source is, and not a word about how much energy can be produced. What I'm watching more closely resembles an experimental art film than an industrial video.

I ask if I can see pictures of the power plants and the new businesses in Bihar. Uthaiah says she doesn't have any. "They're all on Dr. Sharan's laptop, which he has with him"—and he's not here. Anandi Sharan's cousin Aklavya, who's an engineer at NetPro, comes into the room and says he has photos in his office. I wonder why DESI works in the remote and dangerous region of Bihar. Aklavya tells me Bihar is where the Sharan family comes from. "Our grandfather was a lawyer and earned the people's respect, so everyone will do what we say now," he states. Aklavya also boasts, as did Uthaiah, that in 2006 DESI won a $200,000 award from the World Bank for its initial work in Bihar.

At his computer Aklavya clicks through a PowerPoint presentation, scrolling to a photograph of a real biogas power generator. "This is what it looks like," he says. "But this isn't a machine that's in Bihar, this one is in Tamil Nadu," a state in the country's far south. I press for something that depicts the work they're doing in Bihar. He offers two other pictures. In the first a row of five or six women dressed in brightly colored saris pose for the camera with the countryside in the background. The other shows about twenty women seated in a room for what looks like a meeting; evidently this is one of the women's self-help groups. Aklavya says he has no other photos.

I ask Uthaiah and Aklavya—representatives of this award-winning renewable energy company that's helping lift the most vulnerable out of poverty—for a brochure detailing its activities, but DESI has no such literature. Before I leave, Uthaiah says that in the coming year DESI will expand its hundred-village project to twenty more locations—an ambitious plan from a company that has just five employees. I subsequently find a news article in which Dr. Sharan says this expansion will be accomplished in eighteen months. The article also says that, according to Dr. Sharan, DESI gets 50 percent of its investments from selling carbon credits, so the faster it gets projects on the books, the fuller its pockets will be.

The Sharans make the biogas units, they get the carbon offset money and run the social programs, they do their own offset verification, and they are politically influential in the region where the projects are implemented, which is a dangerous place for outsiders to visit uninvited. It's a self-contained system, one that's effectively closed to people such as me who might check on the validity of their offset enterprise.

Perhaps the project in Bihar is happening; perhaps micro-entrepreneurs are getting green power and gaining opportunities they wouldn't otherwise have. Maybe the biogas plants work and truly are renewable, maybe they are keeping CO_2 from spilling into the sky. Ultimately it's impossible to know what's really going on with voluntary offset ventures. Official CDM projects require more documentation, audits, and verifications, yet even this information is limited in its ability to truly capture what's happening in situ. For any given CO_2 offset endeavor, the official "project development documents," letters from host countries, and stakeholder comments offer convincing assurances that this endeavor will eliminate carbon dioxide and most certainly improve the livelihoods of the rural poor. But that isn't always the case.

MALAVALLI

The power is out again in the hamlet of Heggur, in Karnataka State. Manini, as I will call her, moves from her kitchen into the small brick-and-mud dwelling's only other room and flicks the switch once to make sure. No current. The mother of two teenage children feels with her hands for the kerosene lamp that's fashioned from a used glass flask and a short line of twine. It's stored on the room's only shelf, near the narrow wood bench that also serves as the family's bed. The match pops when it lights and gulps brighter when it touches the fuel-soaked wick. Her brother, who

has been talking with some friends after a day laboring in the fields—
it's sugarcane-harvesting season and they have work for the time being—
reaches for a second lamp in the dim glow. Manini resumes her work in
the kitchen; the small ceramic stove that rises about two feet off the floor
radiates heat, but not much light. She knows where everything is, though;
she feels for the silver water jug and pours the liquid into the pot that's
heating on the stove as a faint trail of smoke begins filling the enclosed
room.

The electricity comes back on in about half an hour. In this impoverished rural farming region of Karnataka, blackouts are normal and it can
take six, seven, or more hours before voltage again courses through the
village lines. Most power from the central grid is absorbed by the teeming
city of Bangalore, home to almost 6 million. According to the people I talk
to in the village of Heggur, the Indian government first installed transmission cables through this part of Karnataka in the 1970s, but the supply has
always been unpredictable. With the rise of India as a global economic
force, and Bangalore as the Asian hub of the information technology sector, millions of new city dwellers and power-intensive businesses now
draw on a supply that cannot keep pace.

A new kind of energy company, Malavalli Power Plant Private Ltd., or
MPPL, walked into this situation in 2001. The company had a unique plan
for Heggur and its neighboring villages in an area called Malavalli, from
which the firm derived its name. MPPL would build a forty-five-hundred-
kilowatt biomass power plant, which could burn organic residues such as
sugarcane leaves and rice straw left in fields after harvest, mill wastes, including sawdust, dead palm fronds, and branches trimmed from trees felled for
paper pulp or construction. Unlike coal, oil, and natural gas, which release
concentrations of carbon stored up over millennia, when organic matter is
burned, it emits no more CO_2 than the plant took in while it was alive. The
facility would channel its renewable electricity to the surrounding energy-
deficient villages and provide work and training that would promote higher
living standards, upward mobility, and stable incomes.

Government bodies such as Karnataka Renewable Energy Development Ltd. liked the plan for its environmental pathbreaking; according to
MPPL, no such project had been developed anywhere in the country. The
only problem was that MPPL needed more than just government support
such as tax breaks and subsidies to cover the high cost of biomass inciner-
ation technology. But MPPL knew they could turn to another source: the

emerging retail carbon-offset sector. So when the alt-energy company was approached by Myclimate, they took the deal.

"We are planning on building two more in Karnataka, and over fifty small-scale plants in Punjab," P. Sekhar, the director of MPPL, tells me as we talk in the company's bustling office in Bangalore. "Malavalli is an experimental plant. That's where we worked out the system: establishing the fuel-supply-chain model, processing the fuel, and how to design and build the equipment to adequately take and use this fuel." In addition to Myclimate, MPPL has received money for its Malavalli plant from several other offset entities based in the United States, Canada, and France, including Sustainable Travel International, PURE, and Climat Mundi. Companies like these typically contribute to several projects; the amount paid by a consumer is pooled with everyone else's money, then distributed to the various projects. Myclimate invests both in Switzerland and internationally in endeavors aimed mostly at fostering renewable energy. With a translator I make the 120-kilometer journey from Bangalore to Malavalli to find out more.

Tiny villages and shantytowns dot the lush farmland that surrenders to the swell of granite hills in the water-rich district of Mandya, where Malavalli and MPPL are located. Rutted, narrow roads cut through a patchwork of small plots chockablock with sugarcane, rice, millet, peanuts, and coconut palms. The villages are typically situated up winding dirt paths nestled within the fields. This part of the district also has many shantytowns where the landless live clustered along the main road and near the canals that run throughout the area. Their makeshift shelters are fashioned from dead palm fronds, blue tarps, and sheets of black plastic. Children play between the tentlike structures as women tend smoldering outdoor cooking fires and wash clothes in the narrow canals that run with muddy irrigation water.

Those who live in the villages are decidedly less destitute, having inherited houses and land from their families, who've been here for generations. But times are hard for some who, to give their offspring a place to farm, have divided their parcels so much that little is left for anyone to earn a living from. "It used to be much easier here, it was inexpensive to live and plenty of space," explains the wizened matriarch of a family in another village in Malavalli called Chikke Gowda Halli. "When we were raising our children, we had no worries about how we would survive." Her large family is now struggling, most of them having sold off their land to raise money with the hopes of finding work in one of the rice- or sawmills, or possibly the biomass plant.

One of the matriarch's sons tried to secure a job at MPPL for his own grown son. "But the people there had a lot of favoritism and asked me for a bribe," he recalls, still angry. "They only hired people they knew or people who paid them off." He claims the going price at the time was thirty thousand rupees, US$620, a sum he could not raise. Although the weather-beaten, middle-aged man hoped to see his son with a white-collar job, they both must now search for temporary labor in other farmers' fields, where they can expect to earn about US$1.50 per day.

Back in nearby Heggur, I find some men who are among those fortunate enough to have got jobs at the MPPL biomass station. A man I will refer to as Sakash says he started working there just under a year ago, while a fellow villager I'll call Amalendu got his job a few months after that (neither were asked to pay bribes; in fact the subject never comes up in our conversations). They both work among the hundred or so men who pull the leaves, branches, and husks from the outdoor storage yard into the building to feed the furnaces.

In his thirties, Sakash is lean and has a thick mustache. He wears clean shorts with a collared shirt accented with a terry-cloth towel thrown over his right shoulder and around his neck, a standard local look. When he started at MPPL, Sakash didn't realize the plant had worker safety issues. Neither did Amalendu, who's also in his thirties and sports a mustache and towel. The men say they are given no protective gear at the plant, and that the company has failed to install safety devices on its fuel-processing equipment. When I inquire MPPL tells me the facility provides hard hats and goggles, which are required for workers in the boiler-feeding area. However, the photos of the facility posted on Myclimate's website, which the offsetter and MPPL perhaps haven't reviewed, show men working in the boiler room, and none of them wear hats or eye shields.

Amalendu works the night shift hauling sugarcane leaves, palm fronds, and other fuel from the yard outside the power station into the boiler room. He explains that the leaves and branches stored outside form nests for the many snakes common in the region, which include cobras. The workers use their hands to load and move the material, but are given no gloves, and the facility doesn't adequately light the yard for the night-shift workers to help them avoid snakes. Consequently, workers must endure frequent poisonous bites. Amalendu was recently struck in the forearm; after a week's recuperation—without pay—he was back to good health. But that's not always the case. Sakash confirms that the workers are in constant fear of snakebites and tells me of a coworker who died from a bite he got on the job.

The equipment the plant uses also presents hazards. Before wood goes into the fire it must be sent through a shredder. The mouth of the machine is so large, Sakash tells me, "an entire human body could fit through it." But, he says, it has no safety guards, a charge neither MPPL nor Myclimate disputes in our communications. Sakash speaks of another laborer who lost his hand when he reached in to clear a jammed piece of wood. When I ask Amalendu about precautionary measures at the plant, he tells me there basically are none. "What goes on in the factory is a hush-hush thing," he says. "When Westerners come, you don't let them into the factory." Indeed MPPL denied my request to see the power station.

The MPPL website, like Myclimate's, paints a very different picture of its biomass project from what I found. MPPL's take highlights the benefits that are accruing to villagers such as those in Heggur with a flow-chart tracing the social and environmental good works of distributing its carbon neutral power locally and creating jobs.

According to MPPL's website, the green energy leaves its facility, enters a "switch yard," and flows out for "rural electricity distribution." Since the peasants and laborers in the surrounding area lack an adequate supply, increased access to electricity would undoubtedly improve quality of life. A case study currently available from one of MPPL's certifiers, the Gold Standard, states that the facility "provides reliable energy for 18 hours per day, and with improved voltage." However, that's not an accurate depiction of what daily life in Malavalli entails. The energy produced at the biomass plant isn't sent by special lines to the nearby villages, but instead goes into the central grid. Everyone I ask in several of the surrounding villages says they get a maximum of twelve hours of power, six in the morning and six in the evening, riddled with unpredictable blackouts.

In terms of jobs, MPPL says the biomass facility's presence has created more than 400 jobs in the community. Myclimate says the project generates $1 million annually for local farmers who sell their crop wastes and that it has led to 650 new jobs. According to MPPL those include positions for metering and issuing bills, as well as bill collection and "complaints recording," the latter two performed by women's self-help groups, as the company's website states. Yet there are no metering, billing, or customer service jobs. Household power bills are ascertained, issued by, and paid directly to the state government, the same system that was in place before MPPL's power plant arrived. In mid-2009, when I ask about the discrepancy between what I found and what MPPL claims, the company says the jobs were part of a pilot project that was active from June 2004 until April 2005. MPPL's chairman, K. Krishan, tells me the firm has been "remiss" in keeping its website current on this point.

The flowchart on MPPL's website also illustrates that the company is composting its only by-product, ash, into a usable "organic fertilizer," which creates more jobs. MPPL's Krishan says the company employs twenty workers to process waste ash with cane trash and cow dung into fertilizer. In addition, the company's website states, outside jobs are generated because women's self-help groups sell the compost to area farmers. In mid-2009 MPPL sends me photos it says were recently taken at the composting operation, and maps of where the facility is located. It's in the village of Heggur. Everyone I talked to over the two days I'd spent in Heggur—a tiny village—including farmers and MPPL workers, however, said no compost facility exists (not to mention any fertilizer-selling women's self-help groups, which, in our exchange, Krishan admits were also part of the long-defunct pilot project). Further, when I was in Heggur, no ash-processing operation was visible in the countryside around the village. Perhaps MPPL is composting, but I saw no trace of it.

As for the jobs that have materialized, I meet no one in the villages around MPPL who has been given a chance to work in the power plant's offices, where fifty people are employed. Everyone I talk to says these better-paid positions are reserved for outsiders who've already earned higher degrees. The only direct jobs the villagers seem to have access to is loading the fuel into the boiler, which number about one hundred. Other new jobs that have come about are with hauling contractors who collect crop wastes to deliver to the plant. According to MPPL these jobs total almost four hundred, which, based on interviews I did with two contractors, seems slightly high but nevertheless realistic.

Environmentally, the one undisputable success of the project is that it generates energy without burning fossil fuels. This has created a booming local market for combustibles, however. Consequently, people such as Manini, who earns $1 a day when she can find work, must often buy wood whereas before she could gather crop wastes and dead branches as needed. The effects on the poorest are substantial because they make fires multiple times a day for cooking and to heat water for washing. And with more people buying firewood, vendors are felling increasing numbers of trees to meet demand. What's more, Sakash tells me he cuts trees on his land to sell directly to the power station to earn extra money. He knows others who do the same. While MPPL's chairman says the company does "not at all contribute to residents cutting down trees," Amalendu as well as Manini's brothers say they've seen an uptick in tree clearing since MPPL opened.

Sakash assures me that he plants saplings to replace whatever he's cut down, and perhaps the others do, too. But either way, what's happening inevitably puts pressure on the land, and on water systems, which suffer when trees are felled. When organic materials are used for fuel, they will compete for soil with either food crops or natural ecosystems. Using what are truly wastes to generate electricity is a viable solution, but it has limits that are easily disregarded.

MPPL's biomass plant carries a seal of approval from the Gold Standard, the most highly respected third-party certifier in the over-the-counter offset market. The Gold Standard is a nonprofit entity started in 2003 by a small group of nongovernmental organizations, including the World Wildlife Fund, or WWF. According to WWF's website the Gold Standard (GS) was formed to "ensure top quality projects." To do so GS dispatches inspectors to verify a project's social and environmental claims. When I contacted GS, the representative said what I had found at MPPL was "alarming" and that "this project in particular has been subject to extensive reviews, research, and monitoring both by the carbon community and independent groups." (She also tells me that GS has yet to issue its license to MPPL from 2008, even though both Myclimate and MPPL continue to use the GS logo.) That professionally trained inspectors miss what an outsider could learn in days begs the question of whether it's realistic to think any certification body can and will keep up with what's actually going on. Maybe some inspectors are lazy, or on the take, but what seems most likely is that such a job—of making sure carbon is reduced while the surrounding ecosystem is protected and social well-being is improved—simply can't be done.

NAGARLE

Harish Hande doesn't like carbon offsets. "It's a load of rubbish," he tells me when we meet at the Bangalore headquarters of his firm, Solar Electric Light Company, or SELCO. "Windmill companies, carbon offset verification companies, they're all pitching projects as investments to make the most money in the quickest period of time. It's not about renewable energy, it's about making money, that's it, that's all." He's pissed off. "Good things could be happening with this money, it's not that I'm opposed to companies paying to help subsidize renewable energy, it's just that it's not being used that way. It's criminal."

Despite his scathing criticism, Hande accepts money from The CarbonNeutral Company. He uses the funds to help propel SELCO, a for-profit maker of solar panels and lighting systems for "underserved households," mostly the rural poor. Hande sees himself not so much as an environmentalist as a social entrepreneur. While SELCO is primarily a manufacturer of micro-solar systems, its business model includes assisting many of its customers in securing loans from rural banks to purchase the firm's products. By doing so, SELCO hopes to take away a barrier that keeps those with few resources from tapping into off-grid energy: the initial outlay for the hardware. A typical SELCO package includes a twenty-watt panel hooked up to two light fixtures, and a battery that stores enough power for three to four hours of juice. It costs about $260. Although the price is high for someone who earns $2 or less a day, in the world of photovoltaic technology, that sum is low. SELCO is able to get the cost down by pruning the system so that it provides light but not much more. "We work with people to figure out what they need. Not what they *want*, but what they actually *need*," Hande explains. In other words, if they're willing to scale back, even the world's poorest can have renewable green power.

To see the offset-subsidized micro-solar systems in action, I go with my translator to the village of Nagarle, an hour's drive from SELCO's branch office in the city of Mysore. The company has assigned a young man named Sukumar K., the branch's executive of customer support, to act as my guide. He's a little shy, has a pockmarked face and bright eyes, and tells me that he does sales, installation, and maintenance across the region. The journey to Nagarle takes us along bony, rotten roads, dodging herds of sheep and perilously overstuffed buses whimsically decorated with tassels and flowers.

The large village of Nagarle is lively at midday. The sun is bright and high in the sky. Our first stop is a shop owned by a man named Maranayaka. The closet-size store is made of scraps of wood and bamboo with a roof of dried palm fronds. He sells eggs, rice, sweets, toothbrushes, cigarettes, alcohol, soap, SIM cards, and bright plastic, single-serving packets of cooking oil, pigment, and instant coffee. The stand is located on the main road, which is unpaved and shaded every so often by wide bodhi trees. Inside there's barely room for Maranayaka's aging body, let alone customers, so they must point to what they want from the other side of the narrow, well-worn wooden counter. He sees us coming—Sukumar brings visitors here with some regularity—and to demonstrate his sun-powered lights, he flicks on the two fluorescent bulbs that hang from the ceiling amid the shiny plastic packets.

Before getting his photovoltaic panel, the shopkeeper didn't have electricity, so after nightfall he was reliant on kerosene, which emits greenhouse gases when it's burned. The emissions that are saved when SELCO customers such as Maranayaka use solar instead of kerosene generate the credits that TCNC procures from SELCO. In turn, SELCO uses that offset revenue to subsidize 3 percent of the interest on loans people in nonelectrified areas take out to buy its solar kits. For Maranayaka it's meant he didn't need a chunk of money to buy the system outright and could instead pay it off in installments over three years. Sukumar from SELCO says the shopkeeper's two-light, single-panel unit is cost competitive with kerosene when the payments are spread out over time. Once the solar setup is paid off, the energy will be virtually free for the remainder of the unit's life, which is about twenty years. Maranayaka brags to me that he's got only six months of payments left, then he'll have seventeen years of energy free and clear.

I walk around back to find the photovoltaic cell. The sleek rectangle sits incongruously atop Maranayaka's ramshackle hut; it is a collision of eras. (The previous day, my translator had said that India exists in many centuries at once.) Wires run from the twenty-watt photovoltaic panel down through one of the gaps in the back wall to what looks like a car battery sitting behind the counter at Maranayaka's feet. Each day the battery soaks up enough juice to brighten his lights for the three or so hours he's open after dark.

SELCO installs between ten and eleven thousand solar lighting units each year in remote villages as well as in more accessible spots, some of which are wired to central power lines. But the company sells CO_2 credits to TCNC only from systems bought by people who don't already have grid power. SELCO offers up credits generated by just two thousand of the sets it sells annually. TCNC tells me that SELCO reserves an additional thousand units on top of that to buffer against overcounting of carbon credits that might happen when systems fall out of use, say, if power lines are brought in. Compared to other CO_2 ventures, SELCO doesn't appear to be inflating its offset credits or leveraging them to pump up profits. As Harish Hande told me in our interview, "We use the CO_2 money to get projects off the ground, then we move on and put the money into a new project. We don't just keep collecting on the same project—I'm not using CO_2 offsets to boost my bottom line." He also voiced concern over offset money as a stable means of shifting to renewable energy. "I'm worried that once this [CO_2 offset] bubble bursts the money will dry up. . . . Then you'll have all these solar systems and wind farms that will be abandoned."

According to SELCO, half of its installations are in places hooked up to the grid; the other half are in places with no access. Nagarle is a mix of the two. Although SELCO and TCNC don't appear to be selling CO_2 credits from systems in homes already wired, the stories in Nagarle offer important insights into emerging clean-energy systems in one of the world's fastest-growing economies. The situation raises two crucial questions: What comes of photovoltaics when electricity generated at coal-fired plants shows up? Conversely, is people's use of grid power lessened when photovoltaics become available?

A group of men and children has gathered in front of the shop, but Maranayaka doesn't like people hanging around so he shoos them away. A man who is sitting in a lawn chair tilts back on its plastic legs and announces in English that he can stay because he's rich. The man is tossing peanuts carelessly into his mouth. He has silver hair and wears gold jewelry. When he speaks, bits of half-chewed peanuts fly from his lips and he doesn't care. He announces that he has a SELCO system at his house—

a more expensive two-panel, four-bulb unit—and blurts out that the lights aren't bright enough so he doesn't use them regularly, only when the electricity is out. It's then that I realize the village is wired; it's just the shacks like this shop that have squatted along the roadside and a smattering of houses that lack electricity. I find out that Maranayaka uses grid power at home, no solar. The shopkeeper next door also has a panel for his business but not for his house.

The rich man sends us to his house to see the SELCO system. Mahadevi, his wife, answers the front door in a flowing blue sari. She leads us through the cool, plaster, two-story dwelling to the garden and points to the two panels that adorn the roof. The photovoltaics are hooked up to four interior lights, each mounted in a different room: an office, a bedroom, the foyer, and the kitchen. Lightbulbs glow throughout the house, a ceiling fan whirs in the sitting room, and appliances, including a television and a refrigerator, hum in the kitchen. But none of it is powered by solar even though there's barely a cloud in the sky. On our way out, Mahadevi hits the switch in the foyer to show us that the solar light works, then she turns it off.

I ask Sukumar from SELCO if most people use their systems merely as a reserve for when the grid seizes up. He says people here do use solar over grid power and takes me to the house of another family to prove his point. We knock, and a quiet man in his early twenties named Suresh invites us in. In sharp contrast to Mahadevi's home, this dwelling has only one room and a nook for the kitchen. The cramped space is shared by four adults: Suresh, his older brother, and their parents. The brick-and-mud house is windowless but has two small rectangles cut into its roof that beam sunlight down onto where we sit.

As we settle in, Sukumar boasts that this is the first installation SELCO did in Nagarle and demonstrates the two-bulb, single-panel unit. The solar light flickers on, dim and metallic. To Sukumar's chagrin, Suresh echoes Mahadevi: his family only uses solar power when the grid falters. Because blackouts (or "load shedding" as it's often called) occur daily—typically during peak times, for a few hours in the morning and a few in the evening—the home solar systems in Nagarle are regularly used. But it seems that once the power comes back on, the sun-run lights are flipped off. The people I talk to in Nagarle say they don't rely more on emissions-free electricity because the voltage from the systems they can afford is too weak. At full capacity, the standard solar unit simply doesn't produce enough juice to power the basics such as a radio and hot plate while also keeping the lights on.

Nagarle presents a telling picture of what small-scale green energy systems are up against. When such projects are installed in villages with few prospects of connecting to the grid, they offer the biggest benefit. But when the units are installed in areas such as Nagarle where electricity is accessible, their efficacy drops precipitously. Maranayaka and his neighboring shopkeeper don't have solar at home because power from the grid is so cheap, domestic prices being heavily subsidized by the government. As a result, there's no economic reason for them to switch. The low-watt solar systems for their shops will pay off in savings on kerosene. But the cost difference between the outlay on the more extensive gear they'd need to generate equivalent solar power to what they get from the central lines just doesn't add up.

Another crucial issue these projects raise is who should pay for renewable energy hardware—rural people in developing countries, most of whom are impoverished, or governments that instead currently fund major expansions in coal-fired power plants? Suresh tells me that his family got the solar unit four years ago because his brother, Kumar, thought it was a good idea. Kumar convinced them to work with SELCO to secure a loan with a nearby bank so they could make the purchase. However, since then the family's finances have soured. After Kumar took a steady job—of all things—installing transmission lines that bring voltage from central power plants to the area's villages, the younger sibling followed him into the vocation. But a year and a half ago Suresh fell from a pole and sustained major injuries, including breaking most of the ribs on his left side. He spent three weeks in the hospital and another three months in bed and was on a steady diet of painkillers. His family is still struggling to pay down the resulting medical bills. Due to the effects of his injuries Suresh can't go back to his old job, so now he works with his parents at their restaurant in a shack a few doors down from Maranayaka's shop. The twelve to fourteen hours they put in shopping, cooking, and cleaning every day only reap a total of two hundred to three hundred rupees, or about US$2 each. Suresh tells me it's hard to get out from under all the debt. "We want to pay this [the medical bill] off before we pay for the solar system—I just told the bank we can't pay it now," he says with irritation. "The solar panel is my brother's problem."

The financial aspect of SELCO's project is complex. Sometimes the financing arrangement works, as with Maranayaka, but when it doesn't, this renewable green energy can become a burden. Suresh tells me that if they didn't have all the debt—another loan for his sister's wedding was only recently paid off—his family would have bought some land to build a house with more space. Not only does their current dwelling offer no privacy, but it also has no toilet or indoor running water.

Consumers in the West clicking onto TCNC's website might come across a description of SELCO's work and think that by chipping in they would be contributing to building a renewable energy infrastructure in India. And they can believe that carbon offset money plays a key role in getting these efforts off the ground, working around a stubborn lack of government support. But if green energy (CO_2 offset funded or not) is primarily tapped when more polluting systems go down, or is abandoned when conventional power plants go up, and if the financing of such systems is from unstable or inconsistent sources that aren't part of a long-term policy, then these endeavors won't be a bridge to cleaner energy. Many villages in India don't have access to electricity and won't for years to come; providing light to study and work by in such places is laudable and deeply humane. But we often assume the environmental benefits are just as abundant, which can be far from the truth because these clean-energy systems are designed to replace candles and kerosene lamps, not coal-fired power plants.

The reach of low-power energy such as SELCO's systems in Nagarle is inherently limited, V. Santhakumar, author of an analysis of electricity deregulation in India and an assistant professor at the Center for Development Studies, an economics graduate school in the southern state of Kerala, tells me. "It is not a very socially efficient solution because it doesn't meet their needs," he explains when we speak. The type of solar unit most rural dwellers can afford is one that, like SELCO's, produces a weak current compared to grid power. The professor says that's precisely why these micro off-the-grid options aren't remaking how energy is generated in India. Absent more comprehensive, integrated renewable energy infrastructure programs, when people such as those in Nagarle gain access to central lines, they'll most likely abandon their lower-quality, higher-cost micropower systems. "If I'm putting it bluntly, these types of projects lack the ability to shift people from fossil-fuel energy to renewable energy,"

Santhakumar tells me. Micro-solar and similar low-power systems can fill a need when no electricity is available. But as soon as Suresh's brother and his coworkers roll in with the power lines, the twenty-watt photovoltaics will most likely lose out to fossil fuels. As for people who already access the grid, installing solar photovoltaics to generate electricity is a discretionary cost many won't take on.

Building renewable energy systems needed to "leapfrog" dirty energy is a much larger and politically complex undertaking that requires community members, local leaders, and the Indian government getting on board and forging a far-reaching, well-funded program (subsidized by the world's most developed countries). A serious transformation would come from installing enough renewable energy capacity to eliminate the need to run grid power to these villages at all. Instead, bureaucrats, elected officials, and influential energy companies plow ahead with fossil fuels; India's Electricity Act of 2003 pledges to plug in the entire country by 2010. Although this goal won't be achieved on time, the tight schedule means the plan implicitly relies on fossil fuels, not renewables. A week after I go to Nagarle, the state of Karnataka announces the approval of two new six-hundred-megawatt power stations that will run on coal.

POLLUTER PAYS

So many endeavors coming up short begs the question, is it possible to do a carbon-offset project right? Perhaps, but some serious obstacles have to be overcome. The offset mechanism rests on two rather wobbly legs, "baseline" and "additionality." Without these it is impossible to quantify any benefits delivered by offsetting—necessary to sell the credits—however, it's impossible to firmly establish either.

Baseline is a predicted measurement of emissions that would be released if development continued under a "business as usual" scenario. Both voluntary and official Kyoto projects need to establish a baseline to measure how many credits will be generated by the project, and hence how many can be sold. Involving a huge amount of guesswork, baseline is supposed to pinpoint something quite convoluted: what would have happened if something else didn't happen, and what might that have led to?

It's murky business indeed, and a perfect breeding ground for venality. In Bangalore I hear stories of NGOs that offer generous baseline interpretations that serve to inflate the amount of CO_2 a project might realistically offset, therefore augmenting revenues. If an offset venture claims to be clearing more greenhouse gases than it can, it's obviously bilking consumers, but it's also failing to rein in carbon. (Similarly, and infamously, under the official Emissions Trading Scheme established by Kyoto, baselines were so grossly overestimated that within its first year of implementation, 2006, the bottom dropped out of the carbon market, while emissions continued to escalate.) On top of all this, it is impossible to track the accuracy of carbon credits assigned to the projects I saw because there are no requirements to keep such records.

As for additionality, it easily slips into equally confusing and counterproductive terrain. Additionality tries to establish whether a project would have happened without offset money. If, say, a biomass plant had already secured its funding through investors, then sought offset money, the project would be deemed illegitimate because its costs were already covered. It's only acceptable to ask for carbon funding before a venture is fully financed, the idea being to support endeavors that wouldn't otherwise have been realized. (This is why companies such as DESI get their offset funds *before* they build their projects.) But because additionality is so tricky to nail down, renewable energy companies and other projects that get voluntary, as well as official CDM, money are now factoring the pollution payment into the business plan from the start. In 2005, James Cameron, a London-based carbon trader with Climate Change Capital and a lawyer involved in Kyoto negotiations, said, "You are forcing investors in these projects to lie . . . they have to tell their financial backers that the projects are going to make lots of money, but you have to tell the [UN] that they wouldn't be financially viable" without the subsidies.

Another glitch is that an offset firm cannot know its efforts are truly additional. This is what happened in Guguletu, a decrepit apartheid-era township twenty kilometers outside Cape Town, South Africa. According to an article by Trusha Reddy in the *New Internationalist,* in 2005 the UK-based offset company Climate Care partnered with a local energy consultancy to hand out power-saving compact fluorescent lightbulbs to households in Guguletu. It seemed additional because most residents wouldn't have been able to afford a CFL bulb, which costs about five times more than a standard incandescent. Plus at the time no stores in the area sold them. However, not long after the CO_2 offset–funded bulbs were distributed, due to extensive blackouts the township's energy supplier,

Eskom, adopted an efficiency program that included distributing 5 million CFLs to low-income households. Eskom gave lightbulbs to eighty-six thousand homes in Guguletu, covering the same turf as Climate Care. The complexity and indirectness of the system hobbles its ability to effectively address global warming; since Eskom's initiative reduced the same CO_2 as Climate Care's, the emissions offsets that the company sold were not in fact offset.

Another aspect of additionality is that it can slow the growth of sensible options to fossil-fuel-generated electricity. In reading Malavalli's most recent verification form I come across a line confirming the project's additionality: "It can also be concluded that there are no new policies or regulations, which would mandate the implementation of the project activity." In other words, no laws have been enacted since the last verification that would require this type of renewable energy generation. If national or state laws establish such rules to help build an alternative low-carbon energy supply, then the CO_2 offset industry would suffer. The Indian government, through its Ministry of Environment and Forests, has set up a CDM Authority to streamline approval of projects and facilitate their implementation, with the aim of attracting foreign investors. The authority has already approved more than twelve hundred offset ventures, only four hundred of which have received full accreditation by the UN. India's CDM Authority states on its website that if the UN approves the remainder and the resulting credits are sold at the "conservative" price of $10 each, India will see "an overall inflow of approximately US$5.73 billion in the country by the year 2012." By keeping its energy system dirty, India promotes the value of its carbon market. If the government mandates green energy, on the other hand, fewer projects will be deemed additional, and the country will lose profitable offset projects to competing countries such as China.

According to the logic of the offset trade, both voluntary and mandated, the market creates incentives that will drive the discovery of the most cost-effective ways to cut greenhouse gas emissions. This is seen as more efficient than imposing regulations on sectors such as manufacturing and power generation, which many claim would cripple the economy. A look at official CDM offsets is revealing about what the emissions market can deliver.

Consider trifluoromethane, or HFC-23, which is a virulent greenhouse gas that also depletes ozone. It's related to the banned chemical chloro-fluorocarbon (CFC) and is similarly used to make refrigerants for appliances such as air conditioners. Eliminating the use of HFC-23s creates tradable emissions reductions under Kyoto's CDM. But rather than fix the problem, this seems to be helping support a dirty industry. According to Michael Wara, a carbon-trading lawyer interviewed in a 2006 *New York Times* article, the offset money chemical companies receive is helping finance the expansion of existing factories and build new ones that make HFC-23s. These factories aim to increase production of the chemical to lure even more offset money to boost the bottom line.

EcoSecurities, among the world's largest carbon-offset project implementation firms, which does most of its work in India, says that 80 percent of its endeavors are HFC-23 eradication projects. "There are imperfections" in the offset system, explains Bruce Usher, EcoSecurities CEO, when I hear him speak at a conference in the summer of 2008. He says that the CDM and offsets in general were promoted to help build a renewable energy network in developing countries, but that hasn't happened. Because the offset system encourages finding the cheapest solution, "everyone removed HFCs." As of 2006 two-thirds of all CDM projects were HFC-23 reduction ventures, which pulled in $3 billion in investments that year alone. There's no way to know how many current projects are treating HFC-23 from factories built with the very offset money meant to eradicate the chemical.

Even if carbon offsetting won't thrash the economy (which remains to be seen), it doesn't seem particularly helpful to the environment. The various projects I visited might contribute to the low-carbon energy infrastructure of tomorrow if they were being done well and as part of a larger, coordinated program. There are ecologically beneficial, or potentially beneficial, aspects to all of the projects I saw. Yet the drawbacks are many and don't seem to be flaws with just these few projects, but rather with the process itself.

The renewable energy venture in those one hundred villages in Bihar could hook people up to a truly green and reliable system. It could bring economic activity and from that better access to education, health care, and more comfortable living conditions. Regardless, what DESI is up to is obscure, whether by accident or design. The workings of the offset mechanism don't seem to facilitate transparency.

Micro-solar is useful for delivering voltage to remote villages with no access to the power grid, and for offsetting CO_2 emissions from items such as kerosene lamps. Small-scale solar also has the potential to cultivate a familiarity with and acceptance of renewable energy as part of daily life. Projects such as the one in Nagarle deliver electricity, but inadequate quantities of it even once people have reduced their consumption. The renewable energy hardware required to supplant fossil fuels is simply beyond the reach of the world's poorest who buy the products of a company like SELCO. And why should the rural poor—not the planet's wealthiest countries and companies—pay for the construction of a green energy network?

Burning plant matter to generate power is carbon neutral, so MPPL's Malavalli station could be ecologically sound. To do that it would need to incinerate only material that was truly waste. If this power station were part of a hybrid system that integrated other types of renewable energy such as solar, then there would likely be less pressure on the ecosystem. A biomass plant such as MPPL's also has the potential to provide quality jobs and real social engagement. But the game is such that doing those things costs more, impeding expansion to the next offset project and the next.

While I'm in Bangalore, I meet a man who owns a small solar-panel company. He tells me that Bangalore has the highest concentration of the devices in India. Amid its birth as a tech haven over the last decade and a half, Bangalore's population has mushroomed, stretching its power supply beyond the limit. In response, the city began encouraging residents to install solar water heaters. Almost everyone I meet in Bangalore now has one; washing with water warmed by the sun has become a mundane part of life. All of these people have shifted to solar but they didn't do so for carbon credits nor with an eye on potential offset money. They've embraced heating their water with solar rays instead of fossil fuels because it works, both at delivering heat to the faucet and reducing power consumption. This initiative doesn't require wading into the morass of calculating baseline or establishing additionality, no certification agent must be brought in, no abstract swapping of pollution for credits. The carbon credit system—a series of convoluted financial instruments that serve Wall Street and the City by allowing them to use the earth's atmosphere as a casino—is poised for mass adoption worldwide with the successor agreement to the Kyoto Protocol. But what if sunny towns in Western countries went ahead, as Bangalore did, with the truly voluntary installation of solar water heaters? Greenhouse gases would fall and jobs would be created for manufacturing, installing, and maintaining the equipment. Internationally, what if the West authentically supported developing countries in creating viable, sustainable, and integrated renewable energy networks today? This is the type of direct change that carbon offsetting can easily distract us from.

Assessment

When I set out on this journey, I'd never been to most of the places I visited. The rain forest was an abstraction, as was organic farming in the global south. Countless times I'd noticed various countries' names on the oval label stuck to the organic apples I would buy at the supermarket. Because of the dearth of reporting on how these growers operated, I could only wonder what such farms might be like. I'd seen dramatic pictures of clear-cut tropical rain forests in magazines such as *National Geographic,* but never thought I'd witness this firsthand. Carbon-offset projects were obscure as well. They seemed ethereal and convoluted, yet possibly leading to climate-protective progress on the ground. Eventually, I found that imagining these places and events wasn't enough. The blind spots in the stories we've been telling ourselves about how we're saving the planet were too big. I made this journey in an attempt to witness and better understand the concrete ways we're addressing today's grave ecological turmoil.

Everywhere I traveled I saw that the social and environmental are intimately linked. Talking about the damaging effects of monocropping in Paraguay is impossible without also discussing the economic prospects of the campesino farmers. On Borneo, ecological upheaval is inseparable from the division and betrayal within indigenous communities. Likewise, the decline of the island's rain forests and wetlands is intertwined with the opportunism and corruption of many government officials, plantation firms, and multinational corporations. From these remote locations all the way to the Hudson Valley of New York State, the interconnectedness of humans and the environment was inescapable. The way the New York small farmers tend their land and animals is about how humans connect to cultivation. And the eco-villages in Freiburg wouldn't successfully have been conceived, built, and maintained without social movements and community engagement.

When some people think about nature, they imagine a sandy beach with crystal clear water or perhaps a mountain peak surrounded by pristine forest. Typically these scenes include no humans. But people have always coexisted with nature, each influencing the other. Protecting the environment isn't about ending this connection, but instead apprehending it more fully as an interaction. The point is not to leave nature untouched; removing people from forests or any other ecosystem is not a real solution. A different approach could be to work with nature in an authentic way so that we can take what we need to live without trashing the place.

Keeping our attention trained on what we purchase can make a difference, to be sure. I shop my conscience when I can afford it, and I believe that doing so can have a positive impact. But these consumer-based actions lack the ability to reach the goals we're aiming for. Convincing ourselves that we're solving our environmental problems when we aren't is a catastrophic game of denial; the problems run deep and so must the solutions.

The new green economy operates on a lot of assumptions and misperceptions, often emanating from advertisements, corporate boardrooms, and politicians' offices. Consumers might trust that any food labeled organic is good for the earth, and that crop-based fuels are ecologically smart. People may believe they can erase their CO_2 emissions with the click of a mouse. Just as many might accept that green transport, eco-architecture, and renewable energy aren't available to the masses because the technology is flawed or still prohibitively expensive. The public is encouraged to believe that some solutions are successful when they can't possibly be, and that other clearly feasible options are unattainable. In researching this book I found solutions that work and saw that we know how to implement them—truly organic farming, green architecture, and energy-efficient transportation. But instead, political and corporate leaders, and some in the environmental establishment, are putting aside what works in exchange for what poses the least challenge to established power structures.

Large-scale organic exemplifies this dynamic. Although Azucarera Paraguaya's mammoth sugar plantation doesn't spray its organic acreage with chemicals, it does monocrop, uses chicken manure from factory poultry farms as fertilizer, and is benefiting from the felling of trees to expand its organic cropland. The small farmers who supply the company also seem to be cutting down diverse native forest and replacing it with fields of cane. Further, being registered Fair Trade offers no guarantee that the campesinos will earn more—or any—money from their crops. Even though its representative in Paraguay knows what's happening, Imperial Sugar's Wholesome Sweeteners continues buying AZPA's product. Yes, the events in Paraguay could be anomalous, but they're probably not. Because AZPA is one of the biggest suppliers of organic sugar globally and is certified by Quality Assurance International, among the largest validation firms in the world, what happens in the sugar maker's fields reflects at least some of what goes down in the organic trade more broadly. As organic goes mainstream, its methods increasingly resemble the environmentally disastrous commercial practices it was meant to challenge. This is the result of choices organic farmers and processors must take based on economic sense, which apparently limits how green they can be.

Among the most disastrous solutions out there, crop-based biofuels come at a dear ecological and social price. On Indonesian Borneo I met Dayak communities that were being driven from their ancestral lands by agribusiness firms growing oil palm used for making biodiesel. I witnessed a plantation company clear-cutting a community's forest. I met small farmers who were working under what amounts to a sharecropper system, obliged to sell their fruit strictly to a single processor—a major multinational corporation partly owned by Archer Daniels Midland. I talked to men and women being threatened and harassed by the police and military for opposing plantations in their forests. What I saw dispelled thoughts I had that maybe the deforestation was for crops not intended for biofuels, or maybe the forest destruction was an exaggeration. The ecological and social toll exacted by this "green" fuel is extreme. Precisely when we need forests to stay intact and perform the vital function of absorbing and storing CO_2, they're being ripped away in the name of stopping global warming.

With carbon offsetting I found blatant failures, and some projects that showed degrees of success. The biomass power station in Malavalli, MPPL, which bears the coveted Gold Standard assuring integrity and is supported with funds from the offset firm Myclimate, looks promising on paper. However, the energy plant doesn't live up to its online profile. Even though the company wasn't directly delivering electricity to the surrounding villages, it continued for years to say it did on its website. And although both MPPL and Myclimate dispute these claims, from what I saw and was told, the biomass plant has questionable working conditions and has created an incentive for people to cut healthy trees to sell either to the station as fuel or to villagers as firewood. The micro-solar project that receives funds from The CarbonNeutral Company brings much-needed light to villages with limited or no access to electricity. As such, the project is effective at replacing CO_2-generating kerosene lamps. But because this type of effort cannot compete in terms of price and performance with energy from coal-fired power plants, its reach is limited.

When considered in the larger context of national energy generation and concerted, committed global adoption of renewable power technologies, CO_2 offsets are troubling. Continuing to release carbon with the expectation that it will be balanced out, or even erased, at some other time in some other place is a dubious enterprise. Once carbon is emitted, it contributes to global warming today; projects that might compensate indirectly and decades from now are no substitute for a committed program to reduce greenhouse gases in the first place. Offset projects and CO_2 credit-generation ventures, meant to spur the shift to clean energy in developing countries, might just be inhibiting authentic long-term planning and construction of coordinated renewable energy systems. Relying on CO_2 credit trading and offsets to smooth a transition to a low-carbon future is unwise. Unfortunately, the successor agreement to the Kyoto Protocol and U.S. cap-and-trade legislation both lean heavily on these mechanisms.

What I learned is that the outcome of industrial organic, commodity biofuels, and CO_2 offsetting isn't authentic protection and stewardship of the environment. What's transpiring is a tailoring of environmental crises so they can be dealt with in ways today's economic and political structures deem least threatening to the status quo.

Fortunately, some solutions have real potential to work, provided they're given adequate backing. The small local farms I visited raise crops and animals without chemicals, cultivate nutritive soil, and foster biologically rich ecosystems. Against all odds they have forged a way of growing food to get what we need without stripping the biosphere of its life. Similar to how Dayaks on Borneo practice agroforestry, these beyond-organic farmers have tapped into a wealth of knowledge that stretches back well before factory farming. Dayaks as well as the New York growers base their methods neither on abstention from extracting resources, nor on a leveling and remaking of entire ecosystems to suit the mechanisms of mass production. They work based on formulating and maintaining farming methods and the social infrastructure needed to care for the environment, raise healthy food, and get it to people.

We tend to oversimplify the way deeper change is made, however. Since these farmers are the ones bucking the industrial food behemoth, the thinking goes, all we need to do is buy their produce. But even when we purchase their greens, eggs, and chops, I found, many of them are still struggling to get by. I didn't meet a single farmer who said, "Oh, yeah, business is booming, everything's great!" Business was booming, but no one was earning a living wage from farming alone. The obstacles and barriers were many, including the burdensome debt of mortgages, ever-increasing local taxes, lack of access to processing and distribution, and little to no cooperation from government agencies such as the USDA. Without a greater support structure, these producers will remain relegated to a high-end niche market, and many may go out of business. In the final stages of writing this book, I send Morse Pitts an e-mail with a few follow-up questions. He's already told me he hasn't found a new location for Windfall, two years after I first visited the place. In response to my questions he sends a text message explaining that he sees no other option than to sell his land and transition to something else. "Turns out my dream of leaving a farm for the next farmer was kind of silly." Just because their cultivation methods may be ecologically superior to industrial organic growers—who often abide by the lowest standards possible—doesn't mean beyond-organic farmers will prevail. The rules of the marketplace support the big guys; small farmers typically can't make a larger environmental impact because our political and economic system won't let them.

In London and Freiburg I saw that ecologically advantageous housing is up and running, and it works. By living in a super-low-energy apartment I experienced that this type of architecture isn't culturally exclusive or unfamiliar, nor is it awkward or uncomfortable. I went to places where thousands of regular people occupy these green homes, raising their families and leading utterly normal lives. Even amid this success, the impediment of cost persists. Primarily, not everyone can afford to build a new house, and because existing structures account for the great majority of all dwellings, new construction is only a small part of the picture, even in Freiburg. Retrofitting buildings to be more energy-sparing is often seen as an unnecessary expense, a cost beyond the reach of the home-owner, even if it will pay for itself over the long run. From these projects I also learned that a lack of technology or know-how isn't what's keeping energy-efficient architecture from widespread adoption in countries besides Germany. According to how value is allocated in the current economic framework, renewable energy and low-pollution buildings come with higher price tags, which keep them from being more widely accessible. That doesn't have to remain the case; as Freiburg demonstrates, political and economic obstructions to greener energy and homes can be challenged and overcome.

As for what we drive, the first eco-car to make it to the mainstream was Toyota's gas-electric hybrid Prius. But even as waiting lists for the Prius grew longer and demand for smaller, less polluting cars shot up, U.S. auto firms continued to lag. When I went to Detroit, I discovered that the world's top manufacturers haven't meaningfully produced green cars because these vehicles don't make them as much money as the gas hogs. As with superefficient architecture, the right equipment and engineering for fuel-sipping rides already exists. The holdup isn't for technology that produces fewer greenhouse gases, but for the auto firms to figure out how to squeeze higher margins from it. Even as the big automakers mass-produce eco-friendlier machines, this fundamental logic remains unchanged. That means technologies that are least profitable, whether they're environmentally sound or not, will have to wait.

Only when their economic and political options began to run out did the U.S. auto majors start dedicating serious resources to greener vehicles. But the efficacy of their domestic efforts remains to be seen. GM's much vaunted plug-in hybrid, the Chevy Volt, seems to be the most promising green tech on the road in the United States. Yet only a few hundred are slated to go on sale this year, and they come with a higher sticker price than nonhybrids. Left to the market, it will take decades for car owners to replace higher-emission vehicles with more efficient rides. Even when that happens, triple-digit mpg, as GM promises with the Volt, is not guaranteed. Additionally, with plug-in hybrids as well as full electrics, it is imprudent to place our transportation future on juice from coal-burning power plants since generating electricity is the most CO_2-intensive endeavor in the United States today.

One remedy is tighter rules on emissions and mpg, as in the form of a carbon tax, which could be levied on transportation fuels as well as power plants. The key with a carbon tax is that the revenue must be invested in developing renewable, clean energy. If the money is spent otherwise, say, as giveaways to industry to soften the blow, such a program will prove fruitless. In Europe, where taxes on gas and diesel are much higher than in the United States, companies including Ford and GM manufacture and profitably sell superefficient vehicles. To cut greenhouse gases Americans—the world's biggest polluters—must have affordable access to far less wasteful cars. We must also have fine-tuned mass transit and truly safe roadways for bicycles. The market's inability to deliver these choices is a strong signal that the system isn't working.

In researching this book I kept coming across third-party certification outfits, including Quality Assurance International for organic food, the Roundtable on Sustainable Palm Oil (RSPO) in Southeast Asia, and the Gold Standard for CO_2 offsets globally. These types of bodies are ostensibly formed to ensure consumers are getting what they pay for by keeping producers honest, and in response to outcry from environmental and social NGOs over destructive practices. But the role they play isn't so straightforward.

The RSPO was established by the World Wildlife Fund with Unilever (because palm oil is used in many processed foods), a handful of European food manufacturers, and Southeast Asian oil palm firms, in the midst of activist campaigns in the EU drawing attention to the crop's extravagant ecological and social costs. Today the RSPO counts the agribusiness giants Archer Daniels Midland and Cargill, the dominant palm oil producer Wilmar, and the World Bank's International Finance Corporation among its members. The RSPO presents itself as a legitimate overseer that encourages sustainable cultivation practices. However, on Borneo the RSPO seems either impotent or acquiescent in the face of its members' continuing to clear-cut and burn the rain forest while displacing indigenous and peasant communities.

This can happen because most of these oversight bodies are essentially accountable to no one. Even when they are, as with organic certification in the United States, a paucity of enforcement exists. Consequently, companies such as AZPA in Paraguay and Wilmar in Indonesia can carry on selling purportedly eco-friendly goods grown where diverse native ecosystems once stood, and carbon offsetters, including Myclimate, can continue selling credits for problematic projects. A third-party certifier's "trust mark" can soothe a nervous public by communicating that ecosystems are being taken care of even if they're not. Growers, food processors, builders, and carbon offsetters have access to a host of certifications, and we consumers can buy an increasing range of products bearing these logos, but none of it matters if real changes aren't being made on the ground.

Some certification programs, especially those that are community-based, may be more effective than what I found, but third-party certification often serves to patch the cracks in the dam rather than deal with the underlying forces that are driving ecological decline. Certification as practiced by most licensing bodies today can't truly deliver cleaner, greener goods because the system focuses on symptoms instead of causes of ecological harm. The only way to successfully take care of the environment is to remove the motivation to destroy it. This can't be achieved through current forms of monitoring because the incentives to exploit nature remain in place. If profits result most readily from pillaging ecosystems, then the destruction will continue. Therefore we must reconsider how we define profitability. By telling ourselves that certification bodies and their seals can and will defend the biosphere, we forfeit the chance to establish real solutions to environmental disaster.

All the billboards, T-shirts, logos, and ads that declare buying this brand at that store will help save the environment can persuade us that it's possible to shop our way out of global warming—and it brings a sense of relief because doable solutions exist! But many of us know, or at least suspect, that purchasing the "right" goods isn't enough, even if we're too freaked out to admit it. In reality much of what manufacturers tell us about the provenance of the items we buy is more akin to ad copy than honest information. We would be well served to consider that all those messages of doing right by the planet, and all those eco-products on sale that are supposed to get us to a bright green future, might just be a form of appeasement.

When I went to the places where green products are made, I encountered industries with an insatiable appetite for raw materials. I saw corporations collaborating with government officials who abused their power to facilitate unfettered resource extraction that also mauled indigenous and peasant communities. I witnessed the unremitting evisceration of native forestlands, and the broadsiding of successful solutions such as beyond-organic farming and low-emissions vehicles. While in developing countries, I glimpsed how plundering ecosystems continues to make perfect economic sense, even for businesses that are green. Environmental responsibility practiced this way looks more like camouflage to enable ongoing destructive practices rather than a break from the toxic past.

The dysfunctional medical apparatus in the United States offers an illuminating parallel to our system's inability to implement solutions that work. Quality health care exists, and tremendous breakthroughs happen all the time. But lifesaving treatments remain inaccessible to tens of millions in America, and hundreds of millions worldwide, because people can't afford them. As a result in the United States, families needlessly go bankrupt, the sick unnecessarily endure physical pain, and, in the worst cases, people die. Correspondingly, in developing countries, millions of pointless deaths from easily curable diseases such as malaria and diarrhea, as well as senseless suffering from incurable but treatable illnesses such as AIDS, persisted for years and in some places still does because pharmaceutical companies resist any lowering of profits. Confining treatment to those who can afford it makes economic sense, but it's brutally irrational based on measures that put human health before profits.

The 2008–9 economic meltdown provides another useful analogy, this time relating to the effectiveness of current solutions to ecological destruction. The seeds of the financial crisis were sown when banks began issuing what are called subprime home mortgages, loans given on onerous terms often to borrowers who could not possibly pay them back. The debts were then bundled and sold in financial markets, where respected rating agencies consistently gave them top scores, signaling nice returns with relatively low risk. This triggered a frenzy of investing that sent money gushing into Wall Street. When, after years of booming returns, investors started cashing in their bets, the most elite financial firms were so spectacularly overleveraged that the whole system came crashing down. Hundreds of billions of dollars that industry experts assured investors were stable simply didn't exist. Now the world is wracked with financial hardship and incomprehensible debt.

You could say we're similarly leveraged on greenhouse gases. Although catastrophic levels of toxic emissions have already been released, we're at the point where we can still get away with polluting and convincing ourselves that things will be fine. Depicting the economy as secure was politically and socially feasible right up until we were thrown into the full impact of the crash. The market and its regulatory lapdogs failed to contain predatory profit seeking in large part because the most powerful interests were making a killing. For similar reasons regulatory forces that lack real independence are incapable of quelling the ravaging of nature because it's so lucrative. As for the rest of us, with so many political, busi-

188 GREEN GONE WRONG

ness, and industry leaders, and, of course, celebrities, claiming that we're saving the planet, we can more easily let ourselves believe. But if emissions reductions are fabricated, as was true of so much wealth in the precrash stock market, then as our global-warming debt comes due, we will suffer all the more cruelly. If we've made our environmental investments in false solutions, we will lose, big-time.

CAPITALISM'S NATURE

Much of the thinking behind current solutions to environmental crisis is the philosophy that's referred to as natural, or green, capitalism. Embraced—consciously or not—by many nonprofit groups, businesses, and some in government, natural capitalism says we can use the levers of the market to fix ecological breakdown. According to natural capitalism, going green by saving energy, cutting out waste, and using more sustainable materials and methods will give companies an edge on their rivals as natural resources inevitably dwindle. This approach likely informs Barack Obama's moves toward creating green jobs, encouraging energy conservation, and investing in renewable power. While visionaries have called for getting away from ecologically destructive practices for generations, over the past ten to fifteen years more people have embraced natural capitalism as the best, most realistic way to set things right.

Popularized by Amory Lovins and L. Hunter Lovins, founders of the resource policy center the Rocky Mountain Institute, and entrepreneur and writer Paul Hawken in their widely read 1999 book, *Natural Capitalism: Creating the Next Industrial Revolution,* the philosophy entreats business owners and CEOs to align their firms' goals with the well-being of the planet. Expanding the concept of socially responsible business, natural capitalism promotes what's called the "triple bottom line," a form of accounting that prioritizes not only profits, but also people and the planet. Other treatises have appeared in recent years including Thomas Friedman's *Hot, Flat, and Crowded*; *Cradle to Cradle* by Michael Braungart and William McDonough (who's responsible for the Ford Rouge renovation); and *Green to Gold* by business writers Daniel C. Esty and Andrew S. Winston. These books argue that, counter to common assumptions, profits won't suffer but will flourish by adopting greener practices. And, vitally, companies and countries that take an eco-friendly route will gain competitive advantage. Natural capitalism promises big wins to those who make the change because, according to its calculus, what's good for the environment is good for business.

Since the inception of industrial production, companies have regularly sought cost savings by streamlining manufacturing, but natural capitalism takes such improvements a step further. In addition to basic efficiency upgrades, natural capitalism advises redesigning products and processes to copy nature's ingeniously waste-free, energy-saving ways, a concept known as biomimicry. Consider the spiderweb. The silk of arachnids is tougher than Kevlar, a synthetic fiber used in military body armor. And, while spiders spin their webs from digested flies and other insects, making petroleum-based Kevlar requires high levels of energy and hazardous chemicals. Biomimicry is meant to push industrial production in a more biological direction.

Natural capitalism also promotes compelling ideas about the "flow" of goods. Centrally, instead of buying, we could lease products we need, such as refrigerators or cell phones, for the service they offer—in this case keeping our food cold and allowing us to stay in touch. When these devices break, the manufacturer repairs or replaces them, and when they die, the company takes them back to either reuse the parts in new machines or recycle the materials. Xerox does this type of "service leasing" with its Document Centre line of digital copiers. Such a program allows a company to scale back product obsolescence by expanding serviceability and remanufacturing using salvaged components. Consequently, profitability hinges less on getting consumers to keep buying ever-newer units and chucking the ones they have, and more on delivering the needed service.

Business as usual isn't working, Hawken and the Lovinses rightly observe. This is so because, as they state, "[industrial capitalism] neglects to assign any value to the largest stocks of capital it employs—the natural resources and living systems, as well as the social and cultural systems that are the basis of human capital." This allows for what economists refer to as the externalization of costs onto the environment and the future, whereby businesses cash in the store of nature's wealth for themselves today. Hawken and the Lovinses explain the result is a gravely malfunctioning market. Due to distortions from perverse government subsidies and trade policies skewed in favor of the biggest corporate polluters, the authors contend, it's impossible for consumers to have what economists beginning with Adam Smith call full information. We often don't realize the limits of nature because low prices and abundant supplies—our grocery stores are packed to the gills, clean water flows from our taps, and the lights come on when we flick the switch—mask this reality. Consequently, we lack full information when we choose what food to eat, what house to buy, and which mode of transportation we'll take.

In previous writings, Hawken has argued that "cost/price integration"—referred to by many in environmental circles as true cost pricing—can remedy this core problem. With such accounting, the price tag on consumer goods would reflect the full cost of the resources that went into their manufacture, distribution, and disposal. Natural capitalism contends that creating such integration, which will require government intervention and regulation, will at last let markets work properly. When external costs are added into the price of food, fuel, and fiber, people will have full information and so will buy ecologically responsible goods because those will be the least expensive. When consumers demand more eco-friendly goods, due to market competition companies will have no choice but to oblige.

While it may seem straightforward, cost/price integration is tricky. Consider, say, a bag of potato chips. Do we begin this accounting in the factory, or the potato field with the fertilizer and the pesticides, or perhaps the farmer's tractor? Or do we go back further, to the mining of the metals to make the tractor? How do we value the suffering of people whose drinking water is polluted by the mine, or the asthma cases in neighborhoods near the steel plant? And how do we integrate the environmental and social costs of extracting the coal and oil needed for producing a bag of potato chips? If we truly factored in these elements, the market as we know it would seize up; almost everything would become impossibly expensive. Also, cost/price integration would need to happen on a global scale for economic and geopolitical reasons. If, say, the United States required its companies to internalize costs but the EU or Russia didn't, American firms would be driven out of business because they couldn't compete. Cost/price integration is an important concept that is useful to highlight our current, criminally negligent accounting system. It can lead us into the crucial discussion of where goods come from and how we determine prices—and wages. But we need to push the discussion further to include a questioning of the limits of market mechanisms as tools for curing environmental ills.

Another key aspect of natural capitalism as laid out by Hawken and the Lovinses is the idea that we can flip the economic equation so that business growth can be achieved by using *less* from the biosphere. As an example of how natural capitalism can work, in their book Hawken and the Lovinses point to the chemical company DuPont. In line with the goals of the Kyoto Protocol, in the late 1990s DuPont pledged to cut its greenhouse gas emissions to less than half its 1991 levels. Doing so was a smart move since for each ton of CO_2 the company said it was saving $6 in net costs. The authors explain this is the two-for-one we should be seeking. However, when a firm such as DuPont saves billions by reducing its energy footprint, it will funnel much of that money right back into making more goods to sell to more clients. Staying competitive demands ongoing expansion, so even though the energy *intensity* of a company's production may go down, its *scale* of production will continue to escalate. As such, natural capitalism is misleading. Hawken and the Lovinses tell us, "America could shed $300 billion a year from its energy bills using existing technologies. . . . The earth's climate can thus be protected *not at a cost but at a profit.*" When that profit gets channeled back into polluting processes and products to keep a company financially fit, the larger environmental upsides the authors predict fail to materialize and the situation gets worse. This backfiring is known as the Jevons Paradox—a concept forged in the mid-nineteenth century by the economist William Stanley Jevons—whereby greater efficiencies lead to greater resource use rather than less. In a recent interview, Wes Jackson, a plant geneticist and president of the Land Institute, said, "When the Wal-Marts of the world say they're going to put in different lightbulbs and get their trucks to get by on half the fuel, what are they going to do with that savings? They're going to open up another box store somewhere. It's just nuts."

We would be well served to ask after the deeper reasons why our system functions this way, especially if we do so without reciting the well-worn lines that we as individuals are greedy and can't control ourselves. To be sure, humans seek material pleasures that give us satisfaction, but the quantity and toxicity of waste Westerners produce today is in no way normal or natural. We've had to learn to be like this, and companies looking to expand their market share have delighted in schooling us. For over half a century industry and commerce have unleashed their PR and marketing machines on the public with the explicit intention of teaching and encouraging us to burn through consumer goods (i.e., natural resources) with abandon. This is true for the simple reason that the more we consume, the higher the profits.

Or, to get some relief from the guilt of personal responsibility, our society tells itself that we're here because we believed—through stubbornness, ignorance, or wishful thinking—that the world's systems would always provide. For so long, the narrative goes, we thought we could dump pollution into the water, pour emissions into the sky, and pull raw materials from forests, mountains, and beneath the earth's crust. And now we're experiencing the rudest of awakenings.

Far from being unaware, however, people, including highly influential leaders, have for a long time understood that the earth can't give indefinitely. Amid periodic famines, eighteenth-century classical economists, namely Thomas Malthus, concerned themselves with the question of resource scarcity. Theodore Roosevelt, when he was president in the opening decade of the twentieth century, institutionalized resource and land conservation to restrain the exploitation of natural systems. Less grandiose expressions of this awareness existed at the time as well. In 1913 the popular magazine *Scientific American* published an issue on energy problems that observed, "The question of the possible exhaustion of the world's oil supply deserves the gravest consideration. There is every indication that we are face to face with this possibility." Other articles in the issue delved into technologies to capture the power of the sun, the wind, the tide, and even the earth's rotation. What's more, eighty years ago the godfather of electricity-intensive living—of all people—Thomas Edison told his friends Henry Ford and Harvey Firestone, "I'd put my money on the sun and solar energy. What a source of power! I hope we don't have to wait until oil and coal run out before we tackle that."

The obstacles to applying effective solutions to ecological degradation can be overcome, but we will fall short if we get stuck focusing on human nature as a prime barrier. As the stories in this book reveal, we will make headway only in the symbolic realm if we seek what George Orwell has called "a change of spirit rather than a change in structure." Even with greater public awareness, some pro-environment legislation (mostly in European countries), and the involvement of third-party certifiers, we're still operating under free market capitalism. In this economic setup, it continues to be highly profitable to strip natural systems of their resources, kick people out of their forests, and sell the world's wealthiest consumers endless streams of goods that in short order end up in the landfill.

When companies achieve greater efficiencies, those savings aren't retired, leaving an equivalent portion of natural resources untouched. While efficiency is crucial to saving the planet, it isn't enough on its own. The only way we can have any semblance of cost/price integration, and any way of keeping money from seeking out carbon dioxide, which it almost inevitably does, is through more comprehensive regulation of industry and a major rethinking of our political and economic structures. Otherwise, while there may be gradual shifts, we'll continue getting outcomes such as those I found in my research.

As negotiations for a successor agreement to the Kyoto Protocol, the current phase of which ends in 2012, grind on, powerful interests are lobbying hard for provisions that leave much control over greenhouse gas emissions to market forces. Most of the projects I saw in researching this book were born out of letting the market take the lead in solving ecological crisis, and they aren't working. Waiting to implement solutions to global warming and other major environmental troubles until these technologies and systems are profitable enough is reckless and bizarre in the extreme. Seeing our options through the lens of consumption, even when it's well intentioned, is keeping us from using tools we already have to protect the ecosystems everyone needs. "We have to ask ourselves, who are we as a society and what are the limits of the free market?" economist Frank Ackerman tells me. "What do we owe to nature and human health? You can't deduce it from the market. You have to come to the table with moral statements. These are not economic truths, they're pre-economic assumptions." We need to do this because, he explains, despite what many believe today, the market isn't able to adequately value environmental health. "The fascination with the market—and it is a fascinating thing—has run wild in society," Ackerman observes. "People imagine it can do much more than it can."

Shopping green is alluring in part because it is simple (albeit often expensive), unlike the messy business of working toward systemic change. But consumption as politics bypasses pushing for action that might bring substantive shifts, such as meaningful controls on greenhouse gas emissions, comprehensive programs that sustain holistic farming and food, support for establishing and distributing solar, wind, geothermal, and tide-based energy to power buildings and vehicles, major investments in mass transit, and undoing the economic incentives that encourage native-ecosystem destruction. Even when back-end remedies work—say, reforesting a stretch of land in Costa Rica—they simply can't keep pace with the degradation the current growth-based economic system leaves in its wake.

If improvements to the biosphere are based on the needs and caprices of corporations, financial market bubbles, and wrongheaded government policies, then global warming, dying oceans, and biodiversity loss will continue. As the notion of cost/price integration indicates, the way we currently assign value sets us up for ecological failure. To change course, we must create a new notion of growth, where personal gratification in terms of achievement and desire can be met, and where the security that money offers can be attained in ways other than liquidating nature and exploiting people. Meaningful transformation requires not just unconventional products, but the creation of an alternative logic, where consuming less would *improve* the standard of living and where success was defined quite differently. We live in a time of curtailed democracy in which average citizens are implored to "Vote with your wallet" rather than truly participate in the process of being citizens. This will work, we're told by today's eco-friendly marketplace, because supply and demand and market incentives are the most effective means of saving the planet. In the United States the top 20 percent of Americans own 85 percent of the wealth, and globally the scales are tipped even further. So we can vote with our wallets all we want, but the people with the most money—precisely those who lavishly benefit from a system built on ransacking nature—will inevitably control the most votes. Only when we rethink how and what we value—so that we no longer base well-being and quality of life on excess production, consumption, and wasting—will we truly be able to address global warming and other forms of ecological ruin.

Notes on the Possible

The Dayak community I visited in Pareh, like many others on Borneo, practices agroforestry, a complex system of cultivating crops for food, fuel, construction, medicine, and income within the existing forest. The goal of this farming method is to raise what the people need while maintaining the diverse biological web that supports the rain forest's bounty into the future. When I was in Pareh, Margareta and Momonus fed us mostly food either gathered from within the trees or picked from their garden; we also ate eggs from their chickens, plus one can of sardines. This is how the others in the village eat as well, primarily relying on farming and hunting methods that coexist with the native ecosystem. My guide from Walhí explained to me that during the Asian economic crisis of the late 1990s, many of the poorest city dwellers returned to their families in the rain forests, such as those on Borneo. "This was an important reason Indonesia could survive the crisis," he told me. "Out here there was plenty to eat, the forest was a safety net." No doubt the same safety net is being utilized as the current global recession wears on.

Cultivating biodiversity is just as central to this agricultural practice as cultivating food. Integral to the holistic farming of the Dayaks of Pareh is land management in which the forest at once belongs to everyone and no one. No individuals "own" specific plots, but each family has discrete parcels. Sharing the land—while maintaining boundaries between each other's crops within that arrangement—facilitates getting everyone fed while keeping the forest fertile and strong. When the soil grows depleted, typically after about three years, the community relocates their plots to a more nutritive area, letting the vacated land sit fallow to regenerate. This can take as long as fifteen years, after which point it can again be used to grow on. The vast majority of the forest remains open for hunting and gathering. Agroforestry as practiced by Dayaks on Borneo is so effective that for centuries it provided for many of their needs without tipping the rain forest's fragile balance.

A major argument against integrated methods such as those of the Dayaks is that they don't use land efficiently enough. With an exploding global population, common sense says, we need to produce as much per acre as possible. Following this logic, it's a waste of resources to let only a few hundred people use a relatively large swath of forest to meet their needs when that land could be producing high-yield crops to feed thousands. According to the calculations of Thomas Malthus, the eighteenth-century economist, the earth has a limited carrying capacity while humans have a relatively unrestrained ability to procreate. As a result, he predicted, we were on a collision course with scarcity. The threat of overpopulation was amplified in the late 1960s by Paul Ehrlich's bestseller *The Population Bomb,* in which he foresaw widespread human die-off from starvation. At the time this sentiment gained credence among prominent environmentalists and thinkers. Ehrlich's Malthusian argument has made a comeback in recent years, holding sway in much of today's analysis of ecosystem breakdown.

The question of population control is complex and can quickly veer onto racist ground. (*They* need to stop having so many babies.) In thinking about the possibilities perhaps we could allow ourselves to see other perspectives on the problem of meeting human wants and needs using the biosphere that we have. The planet has a lot of people, but a lot in relation to what? According to overpopulation theories, the problem is *that* we consume; the more of us there are, the scarcer resources will become. However, this approach fails to consider the more central question of *how* we consume. According to the World Resources Institute, the average American "consumes around twenty times more meat and fish and sixty times more paper, gasoline and diesel than the average Indian." The difference between wealthy countries and the very poorest, such as those in Africa, is even more extreme. Shocking as these numbers are, the point isn't simply that Westerners consume in such higher quantities than people in less developed countries. The point is that our economic and political system blocks the resources that exist from getting to the people who need them.

According to the Food Ethics Council, the fruits, vegetables, grains, meat, and other edibles that Europeans and North Americans throw away is enough to feed the world's 1 billion hungry people. The United Nations

Food and Agriculture Organization has reported that the primary reasons for food scarcity are not supply, but rather economic and political. In other words, the problem isn't a shortage of food, it's a shortage of money to buy it. The global food crisis of 2007–8 was linked to the diversion of edible crops for biofuels, but, we now know, the real problem wasn't a lack of supply, it was ever-skyrocketing prices. When we limit our options to technological fixes, such as agrochemical factory farming, and steer clear of the structural dimension, we undercut our ability to truly solve ecological and social crises. To feed a growing population, we can continue expanding an agricultural system that we know adds to greenhouse gas emissions, depletes soil, spoils rivers and oceans, and devours huge quantities of water and fossil fuels. Or we can more fully engage with our political and economic structures to deliver the food we already produce to the people who need it. This engagement gives us the opportunity to reorganize the model so that we can grow food—and build houses and transportation systems—in ways that foster biodiverse ecosystems and are inherently socially just. Today's environmental revolution does depend on technology to be successful; sophisticated farming and manufacturing methods and tools—a mix of old and new—are crucial. But the changes we need to make are absolutely reliant on how we as neighbors, community members, citizens, and humans put those technologies to work.

The holistic land stewardship that's employed by countless indigenous groups in a range of ecosystems helps demonstrate an alternative range of possibilities. This chapter considers options to what was investigated in the previous pages, offering solutions that allow us to see ourselves as more than just right-minded consumers. Below are examples of sustainable cultivation practices that can produce bountiful harvests and a good standard of living while attending to the biodiversity necessary for robust ecosystems. In addition, and crucially, these answers acknowledge the economic and political underpinnings of environmental degradation. Such possibilities begin to point to a more substantive and appropriate way forward and might provide a framework that could be applied in various global regions as well as in the spheres of shelter and transportation.

A balanced ecosystem can be achieved by understanding farmland as a complex bionetwork in constant interaction with human activity. Referred to as agroecology, this approach values not only the crops produced, but also the silent workings of nutrient-building life within the soil, the role of bugs, weeds, and animals, and the contribution of humans. Miguel Altieri, a leading figure in the field of agroecology and a professor of entomology at the University of California at Berkeley, draws the connection between socially just practices and a thriving agriculture. This dynamic view of raising crops is not just about chemical-free or locally grown food. As Altieri has written, "Agroecosystems are communities of plants and animals interacting with their physical and chemical environments that have been modified by people to produce food, fibre, fuel and other products for human consumption and processing." Agroecology sees farmland not as a homogenized, sterilized site of production, but as a place where natural processes continue to occur and cultivation becomes part of larger biological cycles. By practicing farming as such, Altieri's research has shown, productivity is markedly increased and sustains itself over time with fewer and far less toxic external inputs than are required by conventional methods. Agroecology debunks the claim that industrial farming is the only way to meet the needs of the planet's 6 billion people. By practicing agroecological methods, Altieri says, productivity of organic crops can be doubled, making them competitive with those grown with conventional, chemical-reliant techniques.

If agroecological methods can protect the environment while putting out enough produce to meet global demand, the question then follows, can this be done on sustainable economic terms? As we saw in New York State, many holistic farmers are unable to earn an adequate wage, let alone sell their goods to consumers outside an upper-end niche market. Agroecological methods include addressing the need for functional, affordable processing and distribution networks. And, in some places, agroecology includes the participation of consumers, ensuring their input on farming practices and food prices. Owing to agroecology's efficiency gains, the method also has the potential to outperform spurious large-scale "organic" farming such as what I found in Paraguay. Some examples of programs conducted over recent decades in Central America, and a current project in Brazil, help flesh out what alternatives might look like.

In Peru beginning in the early 1980s a group of anthropologists collaborated with local communities of the Andean plains to revive a lost form of agriculture. The ancient farming system, called Waru-Warus, or Waru-Warns in the Quechua language, is believed to have evolved three thousand years ago, although its exact age is uncertain. When the project started, traces of old Waru-Warus fields could be seen scattered across the plains. The practice had long been abandoned, first because of a centuries-long drought, then, in the mid-to-late twentieth century, due to agrochemical farming. The researchers and some of the villagers wanted to learn more about how the pre-Columbian system worked, so, using traditional farming implements including Andean foot plows, they began rebuilding the ancient croplands. Once harvest season rolled around, the farmers discovered a dramatic jump in yields compared to their conventionally raised plots; in some cases productivity doubled, in others it shot up as much as fourteenfold.

Waru-Warus consist of platform fields that are typically one yard high and can stretch up to a hundred yards long and ten yards wide. These beds are surrounded by canals, which harvest rainwater and are used for "splash irrigation." Farmers can recharge their soil with nutrients in the form of algae, which is easily collected from that growing in the canals. The raised fields bounded by waterways protects against harsh weather, curbing the effects of floods and droughts while maintaining warmer soil temperatures during the nighttime cold snaps common in the 12,500-foot-high altiplano. With such impressive results, the Peruvian government and several NGOs joined the program. For the ensuing twenty years these efforts fostered the reestablishment of Waru-Warus across the plains, much of which continues today. In bringing nontoxic, regenerative farming to the region, this project also helped increase farmers' livelihoods through greater social engagement. Without the social infrastructure formed by the participation of residents, government, the anthropologists, and NGOs, such a project would be much harder to sustain. By contrast, just across the border in Bolivia, where farming conditions are identical, Waru-Warus test plots were initiated, but neither the government nor private groups took up the venture. Today the fields are derelict.

Another government-NGO collaboration with Peruvian farmers entailed a restoration of ancient terraced fields. Their efforts led to an increase in yields of potato and oca (a tuber) by more than 50 percent. Over ten years this higher productivity boosted annual incomes from about $100 to $500. Farmers in Honduras had similar outcomes from a program to control erosion and reinvigorate depleted soils by using organic fertilization and by intermingling various crops. Consequently yields tripled, and in some cases quadrupled. Families shifted from subsistence farming to selling produce at local markets. Landless fieldworkers' income also went up by 50 percent, and dozens of jobs were created as villagers became extension workers teaching agroecological methods. Consequently, outmigration to urban slums reversed as people repopulated the countryside, restoring abandoned farms to take advantage of the earning potential. The social benefits of these projects aren't possible without the ecological improvements. And those wouldn't happen without the larger support and involvement of state agencies, environmental and social justice NGOs, and, of course, the farmers themselves.

Currently a similar movement is happening in the farming regions of southern Brazil, spearheaded by the Rede Ecovida de Agroecologia (Ecovida Agroecology Network), or Ecovida for short. Ecovida is a partnership of farmers, government bodies, scientists, environmental organizations, and the public that is building a community-based agroecological system. In the 1980s, Brazil's southernmost states of Paraná, Rio Grande do Sul, and Santa Catarina began shifting to alternative cultivation methods in reaction to the country's increasingly industrial agricultural policies. Underpinning those commercially oriented policies was a set of technologies pioneered in the United States and exported to developing countries known as the green revolution. These new practices primarily entailed increased application of large-scale monoculture farming that regarded the earth as a medium through which crops could be grown using chemical inputs; the very idea was to make soil health irrelevant. Abandoning this form of agriculture was supported by strains in the Catholic and Lutheran churches, trade unions, rural workers, and environmental groups. Ecovida is a product of this movement and was established in 1998.

Ecovida's purpose is to continue steering farming away from the rainforest-leveling, monocropping, petrochemical-doused, export-driven ways of agribusiness, and toward an integrated social-ecological system that serves the people of the region. Today the organization is set up as a network connecting fifteen hundred family farms with their wider community. Taking the process one step further, the state apparatus in Rio Grande do Sul has adopted a number of supports to help this biodiverse, socially integrated method of cultivation flourish.

A key component of Ecovida's work is its Association of Participatory Certification, which grants the group's organic seal. To earn the label, Ecovida farmers must follow their country's official organic standards, as in the United States. But these growers must also adhere to a set of operational and production principles established and managed by representatives of Ecovida's members—peer farmers, NGOs doing agro-ecology-related work, professional agroecologists, unconventional food processors and marketers, and consumers. So instead of securing certification through a U.S.-style system freighted with conflicts of interest, the Ecovida program convenes an association of the various participants to review farmers' practices. This process fosters an ongoing exchange of cultivation techniques and feedback on their efficacy among growers as well as with experts. After review of a farm, the Ecovida certification body grants its approval or offers recommendations on how to improve or, when a grower continually fails to comply, takes disciplinary action, which farmers can appeal. Another important aspect of the Ecovida project is local distribution of its members' produce at an affordable price.

Working in a smaller geographical area allows for the various parties to be involved, sealing the social component. Aligning with Altieri's explanation of agroecology, Ecovida's approach integrates the ecological with the social and technological. In doing so, the participating Brazilian farmers and processors are less likely to take up the unseemly and at times fraudulent maneuvers U.S. and EU certification programs lend themselves to. Unlike the Western focus on organic *products,* Ecovida's approach, and agroecology in general, treats farming as a dynamic, culturally and biologically diverse *process.*

In the United States, related movements are happening that include more accountable certification bodies that differ sharply from the private inspection and licensing methods under USDA standards. Likewise, business models that allow companies to operate with greater ecological integrity are also in use and reaping benefits.

Certified Naturally Grown, or CNG, is a peer-led program that, similar to Ecovida, bases itself on a combination of environmental and social practices that foster deeper stewardship of natural resources. CNG was started by a group of farmers led by Ron Khosla in response to the institution of the 2002 official USDA organic standards. These growers were distressed by what they saw as the inadequacy of the new rules. If farmers can't afford the inspection fees or the time to maintain the excessive documentation, and they decide not to risk ruining their soils by following the USDA's homogenized guidelines that aren't appropriate for every ecosystem, then they can't label their goods organic, whether they grow organically or not.

Tailored to unconventional farmers who don't fit the USDA's idea of organic, CNG requires its participants to follow a more holistic methodology in their fields. Earning the seal costs between $50 and $175, as opposed to official organic fees that can easily crest $1,000, and calls for documentation better suited to smaller operations. Working as volunteers under safeguards to maintain the system's integrity, groups of farmers—not lone outsiders—inspect the operations of other farmers. CNG isn't just about keeping growers honest; it also aims to nurture the culture and community of local farmers. According to Khosla, CNG outfits have sprung up in all fifty U.S. states, as well as overseas.

Organic Valley, the largest farmer-owned cooperative in the United States, provides another glimpse at our options. Established in 1988 with just seven farmers, the co-op has expanded to include thirteen hundred members that produce milk, cheese, eggs, and more. Organic Valley supplies its small farmers with a range of supports including training and help transitioning to organic methods. The co-op's network of farmers stretches across thirty-two U.S. states, and their products are offered countrywide; the company did over $500 million in sales in 2008. Calling itself the "uncorporation," Organic Valley has a structure whereby management and member farmers have equal say in much of the decision-making. This setup of accountability seems to be effective, as two recent episodes reveal.

In 2004 Organic Valley canceled shipments to Wal-Mart at the behest of its farmers. The powerful discount retailer was pressuring the co-op to bump up production and do so for less money. Organic Valley's members decided that would drive the co-op toward the very factory processes they opposed. So Organic Valley ditched the deal. A few years later, the cooperative structure allowed the farmer-owners to block another attempt to erode its ecologically sound practices. But this time the pressure to compromise was coming from Organic Valley's own management. In 2008 the Cornucopia Institute busted the company for "quietly" buying milk from a seven-thousand-head factory dairy that had earned the organic seal even though it was using some industrial-feedlot methods. When the story broke, Organic Valley management refused to stop buying milk from the Texas dairy, saying it needed to augment supplies. When the member farmers got word, they forced Organic Valley to pull out of its contract with the operation. This decision didn't serve the bottom line— any corporation would have balked at such a move. But the accountability inherent in the cooperative structure enabled the farmers to valorize other aims, such as ecological well-being. Kevin Engelbert, an Organic Valley member farmer, commented at the time, "The farmers who own the co-op are the ultimate watchdogs."

In buying milk from the industrial dairy, Organic Valley was caving in to the growth imperative intrinsic to capitalism; the company needed to get bigger or it would lose customers to rivals. This economic force inevitably pushes producers to tend the balance sheet more diligently than the natural systems we all need. If Organic Valley doesn't have enough farmers who want to do the right thing, the company could easily slide into barely organic practices because that pressure is always there. The cooperative dairy owners are willing to stay involved and forgo some portion of potential profits to maintain ecological and social standards. In other words, they are creating a different economic logic. Ultimately, as agroecology in Latin America, participatory certification efforts such as Ecovida and Certified Naturally Grown, and the cooperative structure of Organic Valley show, a healthy biosphere is achievable. But to get there we can't simply turn our agency over to the market. Nor can we assign responsibility for environmental disaster, or health, to the actions and choices of individual consumers. Flourishing ecosystems will be the result of social structures that address a pillaged and polluted environment through an economic and political set of solutions.

Systemic approaches such as those described above can seem unfamiliar, or too complicated and unrealistic, but they don't have to be. Delineating some shifts that could take place in the current U.S. food system might make these ideas more concrete. Continuing in the sphere of agriculture, we could have greater ecological and economic efficiency by applying readily available solutions. Building and streamlining distribution for unconventional and organic local produce would allow farmers to get their goods to consumers at a lower cost and with a smaller environmental footprint. Likewise, reinventing food-safety rules so they're appropriate for, indeed encourage, small farmers and processors would give eaters greater access to affordable, ecologically healthy food. On their own such changes cannot undo the large-scale environmental destruction caused by a system that needs unfettered access to natural resources, but these alternatives can begin to lead us in a more generative direction.

Distribution is a major struggle for countless unconventional and organic growers and animal farmers today. It's tough finding and keeping channels that run from field to fork. Processors such as General Mills and retailers ranging from Wal-Mart to Whole Foods and the British supermarket chain Tesco prefer to work with one supplier rather than many small farmers because it's more cost-effective. Also these stores need consistent quantity and quality and won't risk what might be less uniform produce from a collection of small growers. An appropriate distribution system would begin to pry open the current arrangement that excludes small producers, denying them meaningful access to consumers. Keeping local unconventional farmers out of larger markets confines them to servicing the affluent and facilitates growers with less stringent methods in flooding the mainstream organic supply chains. Creating and supporting a system that helps local unconventional producers become even more ecologically sound, through coordinating the transportation of their goods, while maintaining a fair price, is a crucial component of environmental stewardship.

Another important step forward is to renovate food-safety rules to accommodate small growers and processors, and not just the big guys. This would make services that are often inaccessible, such as slaughtering, available and affordable to local all-natural farmers. Ironically enough, increased safety standards to minimize contaminants such as *E. coli* have eased the massive consolidation in U.S. meat processing. Such lethal contaminants weren't a serious problem before food began rolling down factory-farm assembly lines. Regardless, small slaughterhouses are now bound to identical rules to those of the majors; they must file all the same costly and complicated paperwork and buy expensive equipment that's excessive for their needs. These locally owned processors often can't afford to meet such demands and are forced to close. According to a 2009 story in *Mother Jones,* it costs on average $2 million more for a locally owned abattoir to build to USDA standards. This is a drop in the bucket for a Tyson or a Perdue, but a killer for any mom-and-pop. Implementing and overseeing a different system for small operators will increase administrative costs for the USDA, which will have to budget for more inspectors. But this seems justifiable as a responsible investment in ecologically and socially valuable farming, not to mention food security.

Additionally, as many others have pointed out, the U.S. farm bill, which is updated every five years, could start kicking in real support for organic and beyond-organic cultivation. Serious subsidies for research and development could foster a dynamic agroecological movement in the United

States, with a force of extension workers well trained in unconventional methods and the latest breakthroughs. The bill could also contain aid for first-time farmers to buy land, and low-interest loans for existing alternative growers forced to relocate due to exurban sprawl. Also vital are ongoing assistance in education, creating networks to foster social and environmental responsibility, as well as tax breaks and other economic incentives for established unconventional farmers—and not just those certified as organic. These changes could also include enticements to build and maintain effective and efficient distribution networks for alternative growers.

All these efforts involve a cast of players including individuals, community organizations, NGOs, social and environmental activists, researchers, academics, scientists, politicians, businesses, and, yes, consumers. We must consume, and that inescapably requires resources. But we can meet our needs in ways that are far less damaging, and at times even advantageous, to ecosystems. And we can readjust our conception that a high standard of living necessarily produces high levels of waste and pollution. To do right by the planet we're obliged to reflect on the ecological impacts of our food, shelter, and transportation, but not just as the result of individual choices. The quality and quantity we consume is a cultural practice, the outcome of our specific historical conditions. It isn't inherently human; it is learned behavior that we can change by adopting new behaviors.

Taking a socioecological approach asks us to more fully participate in our societies, to experience ourselves as actors in political life. It would be a major relief if we could buy our way out of global warming. When we try to do that, however, we get clear-cut rain forests for biofuels, organic food grown on vast stretches of monoculture where native ecosystems once flourished, and machinations such as carbon offsetting that cannot wipe out CO_2. Greater engagement can seem daunting, to be sure. Getting involved isn't nearly as accessible as buying something at the store. With all those green products and the resulting notions about how we've become more responsible, it's easy to be lulled into thinking we don't really need to do more.

When I was on Borneo, I met an anthropology Ph.D. student who was doing her fieldwork. She was on her second long-term stay in a Dayak village and was in Pontianak, the main town in western Borneo, for a week-end break. She told me that in her village an oil palm plantation was trying to break the community to get their land. One by one the villagers began making deals. Those who didn't want the plantation were rapidly being outnumbered as deception ripped through the families. The anthropology student said one reason so many people were taking the plantation's money was because the Dayaks of that village couldn't imagine that the forest wouldn't be there in the future. They see it as a place they can always go back to, she said, even if for now it will be used for oil palm. The rain forest's history is ancient, and it has always served the Dayaks. So even though the community knows the oil palm estate will level the native ecosystem, many believe they'll be able to return to the forest, that its abundance will never actually run out.

I later realized (while watching a documentary featuring the philosopher Slavoj Zizek) that in many ways Westerners aren't so different in how we regard the natural systems we need. Imagining life carrying on as we know it comes easily. But visualizing our quotidian environments wiped out, or eroded by the effects of global warming, is almost impossible; that level of disaster is still too abstract. Based on an evacuation map that the city of New York sent out not long after Hurricane Katrina, my house in Brooklyn will be among the first to go underwater if a hurricane hits, or, presumably, as sea levels rise. Not long after the city mailed out the map, the owners of the butcher shop around the corner told me their insurance company revoked the building's policy because of the newly assessed flood potential. Neither of us is leaving, though, because somehow such a catastrophe continues to seem profoundly unreal. Even though we hear the steady stream of reports about the latest ecological disasters, my neighbors and I wake up every morning to find the birds chirping, trees swaying in the breeze, people rushing down the sidewalks. Perhaps we share with the Dayak villagers an inability to comprehend the loss of the environment we live with every day.

Governments and major corporations in the most developed economies are fully apprised of the findings of the world's top climate scientists. Regardless, the majority of leaders continue with policies and practices that so obviously exacerbate the situation, including promoting ecologically themed but ineffective products. By accepting green consumer goods as a way out, we consent. Compared to the scale of the disaster, such solutions are extraordinarily inadequate—akin to a cancer patient fussing over a hangnail. Perhaps we are like the Dayaks in this regard as well. The community I met in Pareh believes it can use the chain saws it confiscated from the clear-cutting crews as leverage against the oil palm plantation and its multinational corporate partners. The feebleness of this strategy, however earnest, is not so different from Westerners' embrace of green goods as a way out of ecological calamity. But we can do things differently. Viable solutions in all realms are out there. We suffer no shortage of knowledge or ideas, no dearth of entirely levelheaded and realistic possibilities that aren't just a new range of products to buy.

Part of what's holding us back is a lack of political will. When that expression is used, it often evokes leaders who don't have the guts to stand up to the moneyed interests they rely on to get elected. However true this may be, political will comes not just from leaders. It also originates with a public that has the determination to push for fundamental transformation that can lead to real solutions. A crucial step in getting there is informing ourselves about what options exist. Industries such as oil, coal, automotive, agribusiness, and manufacturing and their friends in government have a lot to lose if things change too much. So, directly and indirectly, these powerful interests marginalize and muffle genuinely greener efforts. Perhaps practicing environmental responsibility means granting ourselves the time to find out who's doing what to help the planet, and if we want to participate, or study up on it, or create something of our own. The following appendix lists organizations and projects that I came across in writing this book. In no way is it a complete survey of what's out there—consider it a small contribution to the growing list. The current moment of environmental awareness, and people's excitement about finding answers to global warming and ecological degradation, is unprecedented, and because of that it is precious and must not be squandered. The solutions we seek today will have profound and lasting consequences for generations; let's make them good ones.

Afterword

I n this book I have presented information and stories that illustrate the pitfalls of trying to spruce up an economic system that must keep burning through natural resources because it must grow. I have said we must decouple development from economic expansion so as many people as possible can have a good standard of living without overtaxing air, water, and soil. I have also said that to do this we must experience ourselves as political actors. So, what do I mean when I say we need to separate growth from development? Is this possible? And what do I mean when I say we should participate? I think these are valuable ideas, but as I have presented them, I now see, two years later, they are too vague. Much Left political economic discourse says social change will be triggered by a breakdown in the system—a crisis. But change doesn't always work that way. More often, the process happens unevenly, at varying paces, and it is more mundane than the revolution often envisioned. It involves women and men pouring over books and reports and studies. It involves dialog and collaboration, friction and history and experimentation. It involves people living in unexpected ways, taking over physical and intellectual and political space. Of course, this process is under way—indeed is ongoing.

I do not have an answer; there are no ready-made models we can snap into place. But I know we can discuss specific ideas. Here I will present other people's visions of how we could live differently in a system that doesn't trash the planet. I will primarily focus on participatory economics and what's called a steady-state model, and will touch on ecosocialism. This is by no means an exhaustive survey of the literature, but an effort to entertain some ideas and to examine them. I am doing this because I want to know details. I want to try to imagine myself there, in this alternative reality. How else does the political imagination work? If I tell you theories, you get bored; the life they have often seems faint. If I give you findings from research studies you might be impressed. But then what? The theories are still intangible. How do they apply to life in your neighborhood? Where will the meetings be held? How will we get people to come? Will people feud over the decisions? What about corruption? Do we hold each other accountable through compassion or shame? If we can continue mapping these systems, if we can see their features and functions more clearly, then new options might begin to seem realistic.

DO IT YOURSELF

Participatory economics was developed over twenty years ago by economist Robin Hahnel and writer Michael Albert. Their 1991 book, *The Political Economy of Participatory Economics*, explains how everyone can take part in deciding what and how much gets manufactured and consumed. Sitting at my kitchen table, I try to imagine it: Along with my neighbors, I would go to our consumers' council meeting, which would happen at the same time each year. Everyone would arrive with lists of what they think they'd need in the coming twelve months, including clothing, food, electronics—everything. Before the meeting I would walk around my apartment tallying what I should ask for. I'd figure how much toilet paper I use each week, then multiply that by fifty-two. I would rustle through my closet and look at the soles of my shoes—will I need new ones? How many books will I read this year? How many eggs will I eat? How many batteries and light bulbs and sponges will I go through? Will my computer last another year? I bought a box of two hundred coffee filters a year ago and there are some left. Should I finger each thin filter, counting what I've used? If I drink more coffee in the coming year, or have more houseguests who do, I'll need more. Algebra: if X then Y.

The meeting, I imagine, would happen down the street at what is now a Community Board office, in its stuffy fluorescent-lit back room. I would come, list in hand. My neighbors would be there; some would be friends, others I would have never met before. My landlords—three adult brothers who live in my building—would be there, along with the butcher from around the corner and the woman who works at the Laundromat across the street. The discussion would be a comprehensive assessment of all our lists. What did each of us want and why? We would refer to the pamphlets we'd been sent, which give not only a price in dollars for each product but also a detailed description of its ecological and social costs. For smart phones, say, the price would factor in the pollution created by drilling and refining petroleum for the plastics and by the mining of rare earth metals. The price would reflect the impact of conditions on workers, such as exposure to toxic substances. Our choices would also be governed by energy use, which would be limited in order to meet ecological standards. We would make our decisions using far more comprehensive information than we have under a market system. What if we looked at products and could immediately see the life—human and ecological—that went into making them? (How different our existence would be if we consumed according to what we wanted instead of being cultivated as consumers by corporations. We would leave behind the *Hey you! Buy this! You won't be happy without it!* We might achieve new levels of self-determination.)

Our neighborhood consumers' council would submit its request, as would all the other consumers' councils around the country, and according to Hahnel and Albert's proposal, the lists would converge at a central computer. Using a special algorithm, the computer would decipher what kinds and quantities of raw materials and energy would be required to make everything we needed. (This automated method seems to be an attempt to bypass the concentration of power that has resulted from centralized planned economies.)

Factories would receive the processed orders for the coming year. Restaurants and shops would be told how many customers to expect in the next twelve months. Each factory would have workers' councils that would democratically decide how much to produce given the amount of materials, energy, labor power, and the capacity of the equipment at their disposal. Could they increase production to meet a higher demand for a certain product, or must they cut back because of low demand or too few supplies? Maybe there wasn't sufficient cotton grown that season to make enough fabric for all the jeans and t-shirts people wanted. Perhaps there was a glut of sneakers from last year so people could have more than they'd requested. After the workers' councils reviewed the orders, they would be sent back to the consumers' councils and revised. This process could go back and forth as many as five times, Hahnel and Albert say, until a final plan was reached.

So, this is how we might meet our needs without a competitive market economy. We'd work out what we needed ahead of time, program in the demand and calibrate supply. Everyone would ultimately agree to agree, but we get choices, Hahnel and Albert assure. I'll take this; you take that. And so we enter the year with our negotiated wants registered, and the factories and farms and timber and mining and energy and transportation outfits get to work. I imagine as the year wore on we would use the Internet to send for replenishments from our "shopping cart," like on Amazon.

Under participatory economics, the workplace would change in other ways, too. It would become less alienating, more democratic, Hahnel and Albert say. The system would involve a balancing of tedious, rote labor with intellectual labor. Surgeons would wield the scalpel, but would also change bedpans; bankers would oversee accounts, but would also sweep floors. Through their councils, workers would engage in management and decision-making. In a democratic way, sometimes using consensus, other times majority vote, workers would resolve all aspects of operations. And then everyone would engage in the hands-on labor. If a worker wanted to earn more money, she could put in more hours; if instead she wished more leisure time, she could have a shorter workweek and correspondingly lower wages. I think of the years I've spent waitressing and how different that job would have been had we all been equal—waitresses, bartenders, bussers, dishwashers, cooks, managers, the owner. I would have felt more dignity, and I would have been more engaged. The Nobel laureate economist Elinor Ostrom has shown that equality is crucial to participation because if people don't have a fair say in decisions, they are far less likely to take part and less likely to care about long-term outcomes.

One evening I sit across the dinner table from a good friend, who is also my next-door neighbor, at a local restaurant. I tell her about the consumers' councils I've been reading about. If we had one, we would discuss our individual wants and needs as a community, and we would revise our lists over the ensuing meetings so that production and consumption would align. She looks up from the bread she's nibbling. "What if someone takes anti-depressants?" she says. "Everyone on the block doesn't need to know that." The waiter delivers our fish. (We would have had to request this dinner sometime in January and it is now March. Three months ago I didn't know we would be sitting here, on a Sunday evening, eating fish.) We talk about our landlords, the three brothers, who are all right-wingers. They don't like Barack Obama, but they do like the free market. This is a working-class enclave of Brooklyn whose old-timers identify with evangelical Republicans and often distrust people of color. What if we had to discuss what we needed for the year with people of very different mind-sets? There are details about them I don't want to know, and plenty I don't want my neighbors to know about me.

If I were pursuing this project with friends with whom I shared beliefs, I might feel more comfortable. But I don't want to cloister myself; I don't want to be surrounded by people I agree with all the time.

The idea of neighborhood councils and holding each other account-able sounds good in the abstract, but when it gets more concrete I feel resistant. Sitting in the restaurant eating our fish, my friend and I wonder aloud: What if people refuse to participate? This system is, after all, par-ticipatory, not mandatory. Will they consume for the year what our group decides they should? Will dissenters start rival councils? Black markets? Just because participatory economics might be more equitable and better for the environment doesn't guarantee support.

Still, what would it be like to live in a more egalitarian, participatory society? We have few models. Denmark is one. It has among the most equal distributions of wealth in the world; it also has had one of the fastest-growing economies in Europe. And consider Cuba. There is little income disparity among the population; everyone is poor. I imagine living under a new economic system would be like living in a foreign country. There would be people you could relate to in the most fundamental ways. But their practices and values, their food and clothes, the way they keep house, all of that would seem disjointed. The smallest exchanges could feel off, unclear, uncomfortable. Attempting to communicate without speaking the language would take courage. But then you would begin to learn your way around, make friends and find patterns. You would learn how to cook the food raised there. You would learn how to use the transportation sys-tem and the toilets and how to wash your clothes they way they do. Deep changes might seem to bring instability, but they might create greater security than we currently have.

One of Ostrom's findings is that people take better care of natural resources when they work together in a community than when resources are owned and run by governments or private entities alone. She has upended the fallacy of the "tragedy of the commons"—that communities with free access to natural resources will necessarily deplete and destroy them. She has overturned the conclusion that resources must be taken from communities and placed in the hands of responsible owners. When people are in groups with high levels of communication—"feedback"—

they are more likely to keep track of each other. She's proven this over and over in studying forest dwellers and fishing communities in underdeveloped countries. If someone is gathering food in the forest on a day when it's prohibited and a community member says, "Hey, you're not supposed to be out here," then the system can work. You don't have powerful interests restricting access. People can cooperate to figure out how to best use and manage resources. They feel a sense of shared responsibility because they answer to each other. Ostrum has shown that this brings out the best in people. When I talk to her on the phone, she says she wishes there were neighborhood governments so that we could make decisions on that kind of granular level. She wants metropolitan areas essentially to comprise small towns and villages—communities of communities. Then life would happen on a human scale. Decisions would be made by people we knew. We would understand why *this* happened and not *that*. We would feel a connection to the future and, Ostrum says, that's one of the surest ways to foster a sense of responsibility.

DOLLAR SIGNS

I want to take a moment to praise the price signal, as it is referred to by economists. This mechanism—the price of a product or service—is an incredibly efficient mode of communication. It simply, and rapidly, tells companies extracting raw materials, and manufacturers turning those into goods, and consumers buying them, when to ramp up and when to slow down. If there is a shortage of, say, steel, prices crest; shipbuilders, automakers, and large construction firms scale back. Then over time, steelmakers, incentivized by the ability to charge higher prices, boost production and supplies even out. Prices go down on related goods and consumers start buying again.

The price signal, a key feature of a market economy, allows all of this to happen in the span of hours or days. Under a planned economy—one based on a predetermined distribution of resources—information about shortages or gluts might not be understood for weeks or months. Friedrich von Hayek, the grandfather of neoclassical economics, in his 1944 book *The Road to Serfdom* says a state-run economy could never achieve greater efficiency in resource allocation than a capitalist one.

In the fall of 2011, as the Occupy Wall Street protests are unfolding across the country, I hear a radio interview with Hahnel about his work. The journalist asks what would happen if an unexpected frost in Florida killed the orange crop. Hahnel admits that's where his system is weakest: participatory economics can't respond to abrupt changes in conditions. Hahnel and Albert's plan allows for revising demand—what individuals or families have requested for the year if, say, someone gets pregnant or loses a job, or gets a better job that pays more. Absent the price signal, though, there is no equivalent tool to address sudden shifts in supply. And that inhibits the swift action companies could take to stay in business and stem jobs losses, or even keep entire industries from being made vulnerable.

To be sure, the price signal can do a lot. But, as the story of ecological strife reveals, it can't do everything. Prices don't convey information about the social and economic impact of clearing the forests on Borneo, or of asthma among inner-city children caused by air pollution, or the toll extreme weather takes on animals and plants—because prices don't have to. Neva Goodwin, an economist and co-director of the Global Development and Environment Institute at Tufts University, notes in a 2005 paper, "Markets are sensitive only to benefits or costs that can be translated into willingness to pay on the part of buyers, or into costs incurred by sellers." In other words, if in a city such as New York the children in heavily trafficked neighborhoods have asthma but everyone still buys goods hauled in on eighteen-wheelers, then the market sees no problem.

As noted earlier in this book, economists refer to deleterious outcomes as negative externalities. Goodwin defines an externality as the outcome of "an economic choice or action by one economic actor that affects the welfare of others who are not involved in that choice or action." Markets simply cannot register the larger effects of choices made by economic decision makers—be they major industries such as mining, energy, and manufacturing, or shoppers buying organic sugar at Whole Foods in the hope of protecting the environment.

But some economists believe this fault with pricing can be fixed. Robert O. Mendelsohn has spent his academic career trying to calculate the monetary value of ecosystems and pollution. He is Edwin Weyerhauser Davis professor of forest policy at Yale, where he also teaches economics. I read a paper he cowrote in 2009, "Environmental Accounting for Pollution." In addition to laying out various methodologies for establishing value, the paper considers the cost of air pollution on a human life. The authors seek a price to express the risk of premature loss of life among people who are exposed daily to air pollution. So they analyze studies comparing wages for high-risk manual jobs and those considered safe. They also look at studies asking people how much they would pay to keep their lives from being cut short. I find a radio interview with Mendelsohn where he discusses the report's findings. "It turns out that if you talk about a very small incremental risk, something like one in one hundred thousand that you might die this year," Medelsohn says, "that's worth about $60." I scroll the player back so I can hear it again: $60.

There are profound questions involved in assigning a price to destruction, human and otherwise. In her 2005 paper Goodwin asks, "Who is in a position to perform such calculations? Whose figures can be trusted?" She notes that analyses can be "marred by data inconsistency, by difficulties in quantifying values that may be unquantifiable (such as the value of a life), and by the motivations of those collecting and evaluating the data."

When I reach her on the phone, Goodwin questions the overall relevance of trying to internalize costs. "In theory you can find these kinds of prices. But if a huge portion of the earth becomes uninhabitable—rising sea levels, increases of heat, of floods—how do we put a price on that? It's totally meaningless," she says.

STEADY AS YOU GO

What if we had an economy that didn't rely on markets and pricing? What if it wasn't based on growth? Would it be possible to achieve and maintain a high standard of living without economic expansion? Herman Daly thinks so. He's an economist and pioneer of a forty-year-old theory known as ecological economics (to which Mendelsohn subscribes). Unlike many of today's ecological economists, however, Daly believes we can never truly count the costs of a growth-based economy. Instead, he seeks a shift away from the anthropocentric, the assumption that the world's resources exist for human use, to the "biocentric," the notion that humans are just one part of a much larger biological network. To get to there, Daly recommends we abandon growth and take up what's called steady-state economics—an economy that reaches a level of development and then enters a holding pattern. This system turns an airplane, Daly likes to say, into a helicopter. A steady-state system is a machine capable of both moving and maintaining its position without crashing. Airplanes can't do that. Capitalism is an airplane.

In the 1989 book *For the Common Good*, which Daly cowrote with John B. Cobb Jr., the authors outline policies, structures, and specific prescriptions that cover the most fundamental aspects of social and economic life: trade, land use, agriculture, labor, industry, taxes, and national security. They propose making the United States as self-sufficient as possible; in their vision, other countries would do the same. The purpose of this form of nationalism is to appropriately scale the economy according to what we have and what we need. Assessing our resources based on what which is within our national boundaries could be considered arbitrary because borders are arbitrary, but it provides a discrete set. The authors see this squaring of ecological accounts through geography as a more straightforward way of delinking prosperity from economic growth.

First, the United States would become largely self-sufficient. We would make our own clothes and shoes and computers and grow almost all our own food. We would provide our own minerals and metals and fuels. Each year we would, as a country, decide what percentage of non-renewable resources could be extracted domestically: how much oil we'd drill, how much natural gas, how much copper we'd mine, how much coal. (*For the Common Good* doesn't offer specifics on exactly who decides and how.) Logging, mining, and drilling would continue, but within limits, the authors say, enforced by import permits and export tariffs. Both domestic production and trade would be based on public needs in conjunction with ecosystem needs, and this would determine the size of the U.S. economy.

Needless to say, trade would drop dramatically. Indeed, the authors call for *balanced* trade as opposed to free trade; the country couldn't import more than it could expect to export, in terms of value. Re-conceptualizing trade is critical because of the globalized economy. Scaling back production at home while increasing imports would defeat the purpose of a steady-state system.

As a result, employment in shipping would decline, as it would in retail and the extractive industries. At the same time, manufacturing jobs would increase. For example, the largely dormant factories in upstate New York that used to make train cars could ramp up production—since oil supplies would be sharply cut, mass transit would likely take off. I imagine we would reinvent our manufacturing base to turn out higher-quality goods designed for durability, as opposed to products designed to be used and thrown away. There would be, as Daly has noted, a shift from ever more stuff to a smaller amount of better stuff. We might see more of what's happening in Brooklyn, the borough where I live. This is a hive of artisanal, handcrafted, higher-cost consumer items—specialty pickles, hand-tooled bicycles, and locally cobbled shoes. These endeavors are compatible with a steady-state system because while they are more labor-intensive, they are less energy- and raw-material intensive. In this system, people would either have to pay more for what they consumed or they would have to consume less.

No doubt you'd need a good wage to live in a steady-state economy. Will the workers in the train factories be paid enough to buy the hand-made shoes? Will schoolteachers be able to afford the locally grown food? What will be sacrificed when those lacking sufficient disposable income have to go without? On my block probably every apartment has a computer, not to mention televisions and refrigerators and stoves and everything else a house requires. Who will and won't be able to have those goods? And will these things also be manufactured in Brooklyn? Will the artists' lofts be turned back into factories, say, to assemble laptops?

Daly and Cobb don't talk about where the factories would be, but they do talk about land use. Under a steady-state framework, rural areas would be transformed. The authors say that to boost ecological wellbeing, we should vacate much of the country's land. They recommend expanding wilderness zones, reducing grazing in national forests, a government buy-back of rangeland in the West, and raising the price of water to get farmers off acreage unsuitable for agriculture. Daly and Cobb propose the elimination of subsidies for industrial agriculture and a tax structure for cropland that would drive investors and speculators away: land would be valued for its use, not its potential to earn money for landlords. Sustainable farmers who nurtured soil and biodiversity would get generous tax credits. These changes would encourage new farmers, a rarity today due to high upfront costs, primarily for acreage. Ultimately, Daly and Cobb say, half of all land in the United States could be freed from human settlement and agriculture. The nation's farming infrastructure would be reconfigured; growers with hundreds or thousands of acres who raise corn for cows and commodity crops for export would give way to networks of small farms that would grow food for people in nearby cities and towns.

Daly and Cobb also talk about resource supplies. With restrictions on raw materials extraction, it might be decided that next year we would pump 2 percent of our oil reserves and no more. Maybe that would mean gasoline would be rationed—you can fill your tank, but only twice a month. If gasoline were more efficiently put to use powering hybrid electric buses, then ridership would likely go up. Maybe this would lead to superefficient networks of public transit. Maybe it would lead to cars that got 100 mpg, and safe, ubiquitous bike lanes. But, I think to myself, in extreme cases, this could also lead to uprising and rebellion. It strikes me that the models I am reading about don't account for complex social forces. They assume that most people will be won over and stay on side. Just as neoclassical economists suffer from basing their analyses on "perfect markets," many alternative economists succumb to idealizing their own models. Participation can take many forms—it might mean enthusiasm and dedication. But it might mean resistance. I try to imagine telling my neighbors about this plan.

"We would get jobs in factories—maybe they would be worker-owned," I'd say.

"I slaved in a factory over in Greenpoint all my life and I wouldn't wish that on anyone," the retiree who lives two doors down might say.

"But can you imagine these jobs not being so tedious, so backbreaking?" I, who have never worked in a mill, would say.

"Ha!"

My musings bring clarity: this is not a dream we all share. Do we—can we—ignore those who disagree? These alternative models shouldn't have to answer every question regarding practicability, and yet it is precisely the lack of answers to these basic questions that casts such ideas as naïve, even delusional. I can see how dramatically curtailing trade and capping raw materials extraction would make little sense to people hoping today's economy will recover, hoping to get their jobs back. I can understand how a steady-state system could seem foolish when it is so plain that capitalism, based as it is on economic growth, has dramatically improved so many people's livelihoods. But I cannot understand the math that ignores the costs paid by the world's ecosystems and many of the world's poorest, millions of Americans among them, for what in reality is an uneven amassing of wealth.

On the phone, I ask Goodwin her thoughts on the matter. "That capitalism has delivered the highest standard of living to the most people is absolutely true," she says. But she advises me to look back to when poverty was rampant in western countries, to, say, 1800, when there were about a billion people alive. "There are a billion people alive today who are living in as bad or worse conditions as those billion people," Goodwin notes. "The population has grown, and we've managed to deliver better lives to a lot of people, but all this inequality has a great downside."

ALL NATURAL

Ecosocialism is a lesser-known theory, both in popular discourse and in the academy. One of its originators and proponents is the author and academic Joel Kovel. His book *The Enemy of Nature*, first out in 2002 and updated five years later, paints a picture of a new society that shuns the market altogether, since the market is where the value of what we need and use gets disconnected from its intrinsic worth. We are of nature and in nature, Kovel says. If that is so, then categories that exist today, such as "the environment," cease to make sense. Ecosocialism is a more ephemeral theory than either the participatory or steady-state models. It exists as a string of ideas; as a reality, it is a lyric. The concept is that the state would take ownership of the means of production and give the tending to workers. No one would own land or buildings or machines—we would have personal property, not private property. I don't have enough to go on, though; Kovel focuses primarily on critiquing other options as inadequate to address ecological crisis. In the book, his ideas are largely concerned with salvaging socialism from its twentieth-century wreckage, and therefore they gloss over how ecosocialism would function in practice. His ideas are so rooted in being correct that I don't want to cross them; they impinge on my imagination. In a more general sense, though, he offers inspiration. We must value the use of water and timber and minerals, as well as finished consumer goods, over what we can earn by selling them. We must cease selling our labor, and instead freely give and receive. There is something beautiful, even spiritual, about ecosocialism as Kovel presents it: "Ecosocialist society is defined by *being*, achieved by giving oneself to others and restoring a receptive relation to nature."

I am looking for something else; again, I want details. I recall my conversation with Goodwin. On the phone she explained her idea of contextual economics. To her, economics exists within a specific political, social, and ecological context, and this must be acknowledged; something neoclassical economics doesn't do. (Most glaringly, it fails to contextualize Adam Smith's notion of smallholders competing with each other to everyone's benefit. Von Hayek and his neoclassical acolytes overlook the fact Smith was writing before the steam engine, before the intensification of production, before economies of scale, before the concentration of wealth through industrial capitalism.) Goodwin's is not a discrete theory, but rather a theory of theories. A good way forward is to take from all that is out there and use what works, her theory says. Piece together a new system from the old, the existing, and the imagined. Can you have growth without development? "Certain kinds of growth—in which the quality of goods and services increases without increasing resource and energy use," she said on the phone. I think of the handcrafted products made in Brooklyn. "But that can go on for only so long. Eventually we will reach ecological limits. So no, we can't indefinitely have economic growth."

Can we separate economic growth from development? "Yes," she replied. "We must do this in the most advanced economies, but not in the poorest countries. They need economic expansion. If they don't have enough food, they need to grow more crops; if they don't have schools, houses, hospitals, they need to build them. If they want education, they need energy." Advanced economies don't need economic growth; they need to redefine what they mean by human development. What are our criteria for well-being? We must identify these for ourselves as individuals within communities, and not based on what she calls the "misinformation of advertising and marketing." Goodwin eschews easy answers. She appreciates the notion of "small is beautiful" but sees it as overly romanticized. She says the happiness index some economists are developing can be useful, but can easily oversimplify matters. "You could have a very happy group of people who are all stoned," she told me. "That's a very happy group of people who are not taking care of the future."

I know that if the profit motive stays in place economic growth in all its destructiveness will continue apace. But I don't believe we must choose between ecosocialism, participatory economics, a steady-state system, or any of the other options out there. Like Goodwin, I want to take what works from all we have. And I don't want to be correct. No economic system can be implemented and maintained through piousness or be entirely utilitarian. History makes this clear. When I encounter various models in the pages of books and in public talks, the thinkers and writers describing them present systems that, once established, will be virtually free from struggle. There will be no opponents, no dissent; ecocentrism will ring true across society. Perhaps this is merely a flaw in presentation and not in logic, but if we don't treat their ideas as "actually existing"—as in "actually existing socialism" isn't really socialism—as messy, then we can't fully engage in debates and attempts to put these theories into practice. A system prioritizing ecological and human health is not and will not be perfect; it is and will continue to be shaped by myriad forces, some supportive, some undermining, some ambivalent or disinterested, and still others inspired and empowering.

Heather Rogers
October 2012

Acknowledgments

To come to fruition, all books require a host of people. Even though we writers spend so much time by ourselves at our desks, we cannot do this job alone. The scope of travel for reporting *Green Gone Wrong* meant that I relied all the more on support—emotional, intellectual, and financial—from many.

At various, and key, stages along the way Dara Greenwald and Emily DeVoti gave terrific input and cheered me on. Brenda Coughlin, who offered whip-smart contributions throughout the process, has been a wonderful friend and ally. My cousin Charlie generously shared his astute observations of farming and the emergent green economy; our many conversations helped spark important ideas. For his fertile ideas and more general support as I toiled away, I warmly thank Josh MacPhee. I'm also grateful to Anthony Arnove for his incisive feedback on the manuscript and overall enthusiasm for the project and my work more broadly. Patrick Bond provided valuable input that aided me in better understanding the oftentimes convoluted world of carbon offsetting. As the fact checker on the book, Jesse Finfrock was thoughtful, nuanced, and top-notch. Thanks to Elizabeth Hopkins for her attentive research. Having added to this effort in a range of meaningful ways, Meghan McDermott, Maddalena Polletta, Williams Cole, Atticus Cole, Walter Ludwig, Pedro Diez, Kevin Kaplicki, Eric Triantafillou, Igor Vamos, Joachim Koester, Shane McKenna, and Erin Durant are deserving of my appreciation.

I'm grateful to the Investigative Fund of the Nation Institute. Without its generous support most of the foreign reporting for this book would not have been possible. Thanks to Esther Kaplan and Joe Conason at the Investigative Fund and Hamilton Fish at the Nation Institute for their ongoing and crucial backup. Additionally, the Wallace Global

Fund provided substantial support for this project. WGF's contribution was vital as it allowed me the time I needed to do the hard work this book required.

Beth Wareham, Whitney Frick, and the team at Scribner have been great to work with. I appreciate Beth's ability to take up the project midstream with such gusto and interest. Thanks to Colin Robinson, who brought *Green Gone Wrong* to Scribner and was my editor during much of the writing. I'm grateful for his efforts toward getting this book out into the world. I appreciate Amber Husbands's sharp, thoughtful legal review. Mark Ellingham and Duncan Clark gave indispensable feedback on the initial manuscript. The book benefited from their fluency with popular discussions of environmental issues and their international perspective. Thanks to my agent, Andrew Wylie, as well as Rebecca Nagel and James Pullen at the Wylie Agency. Their help in getting this project off the ground and shepherding it along has been key. I'm also grateful for the support of the progressive think tank Demos and the Center for Economic Research and Social Change.

Leo Panitch and Colin Leys at the *Socialist Register* gave me an initial platform for formulating the threads of what developed into *Green Gone Wrong*. In the earliest stages of this project, Jason Schwartz bent the rules at Marlow & Sons, which meant I had enough time to write. Toward the completion of the manuscript, Laura Haber brought me in for a residency at Allen Hall's Unit One program at the University of Illinois, Urbana-Champaign. The stay was productive, giving me the opportunity to present and discuss many of the ideas in this book with an engaged group of students including Sam Siner and Eric Green.

Some parts of this book previously appeared in articles. Much of what came to be chapter 4 was first published as "Slash and Burn: Why Biofuels Are the Rainforest's Worst Enemy" in the March/April 2009 issue of *Mother Jones*. My editors there, Monika Bauerlein and Rachel Morris, took the time to help me articulate the complexities of the situation on Borneo. I learned a lot from them. Fragments that appear in chapter 5 and the "Assessment" were initially published as "Current Thinking: Was Thomas Edison, the godfather of electricity-intensive living, green ahead of his time?" in the June 3, 2007, *New York Times Magazine*. Thanks to Alex Star for his editorial input on that story.

Many people helped me on the ground in the various places I visited. Above all, I'm indebted to the numerous people who told me their stories;

they offered their time, thoughts, opinions, and often their gracious hospitality.

In New York, my multiple conversations with Morse Pitts and Tim Wersan at Windfall Farms, as well as with Ron Khosla of Huguenot Farms and Certified Naturally Grown, were invaluable. I'm also grateful to Jennifer Small and Michael Yezzi of Flying Pigs Farm, and Joshua and Jessica Applestone of Fleischer's Grass-Fed and Organic Meats. I'm fortunate to have had the opportunity to work with Caroline Fidanza, Andrew Tarlow, Tom Mylan, Dave Gould, Sean Rembold, and Mark Firth at Marlow & Sons; their perspectives on and knowledge of food aided me in understanding and appreciating the politics of unconventional farming.

In South America, I'm grateful for the time and insights of Emiliano Ezcurra, who was at Greenpeace Argentina when I was there. Although the reporting I did in Argentina didn't make it into this book, the experience was key in understanding the environmental and social dynamics of native ecosystem destruction. Thanks also to Joseph Huff-Hannon in New York, John Palmer in Tartagal, Argentina, and in Brazil, Osmar Coelho Filho.

In Germany, Elsa Gheziel, Andreas Delleske, Marcus Neumann, Freiburg FuTour, Olaf and Genvieve Zubers, Dr. Clemens Back, Doris Müller, and Achem Hombach were all giving with their time and contacts.

In Indonesia, particularly in Pontianak, several people at community-based and environmental organizations aided me in navigating the complicated geography of deforestation. I'm appreciative of the help extended by Shaban Stiawan, Ari Munir, and Torry Koswardono of Walhi; Lely Khairnur of Lembaga Gemawan; and Julia Kam and John Bamba of Institut Dayakologi. Also deserving of my gratitude are Leila Salazar-Lopez and Brihannala Morgan of the Rainforest Action Network, Elizabeth Linda Yuliani and Budhy Kristanti of the Center for International Forestry Research, as well as Sumi Rae, Adriani Zakaria, Michele Tambunan, and Wira Dinata.

I appreciate the help Dianne Feeley and Bec Young extended while I was in Detroit. Also thanks to Dan Georgakas.

In India, Nirmala Karunan of Greenpeace India was generous with her logistical support. Thanks as well to Leo Saldanha and Bhargavi Rao of the Environmental Support Group in Bangalore. I'm also indebted to Rakesh Kumar, who was a perceptive and adept interpreter and a great partner in the field.

When I was on the road and at home, my family helped me complete this project in myriad ways. I'm grateful to my father, Charlie, my sister, Holli, and my mother, Reese Ludwig, who all made contributions to this book both directly and indirectly. I'm grateful for their abiding encouragement, for keeping in touch when I was in remote places on my own, and offering suggestions, some of which proved extremely useful. My cousin Kelly, ever curious, was a thoughtful and ready sounding board. Last, but not least, I'm indebted to my uncle Mike for coming up with such a great title.

Appendix: Resources

Local Organic

Agroecology and Sustainable Agriculture Program, University of Illinois at Urbana-Champaign, www.asap.sustainability.uiuc.edu

Certified Naturally Grown, Stone Ridge, New York,www.naturallygrown.org

Cornucopia Institute, Cornucopia, Wisconsin, www.cornucopia.org

Fleisher's Grass-Fed and Organic Meat, Kingston, New York, www.grassfedmeat.net

Flying Pigs Farm, Shushan, New York, www.flyingpigsfarm.com

Growing Power Community Food Center, Milwaukee, Wisconsin, www.growingpower.org

Just Food, New York City, www.justfood.org

The Land Institute, Salina, Kansas, www.landinstitute.org

The Leopold Center for Sustainable Agriculture, Ames, Iowa, www.leopold.iastate.edu

National Sustainable Agriculture Coalition, Washington, D.C., www.sustainableagriculture.net

New York City Greenmarket, www.cenyc.org/greenmarket

Rodale Institute, Kutztown, Pennsylvania, www.rodaleinstitute.org

Windfall Farms, Montgomery, New York, www.windfallfarm.blogspot.com

Global Organic

Agroecology in Action, Miguel A. Altieri's website, www.agroeco.org

Alter Vida Centro de Estudios y Formación para el Ecodesarrollo, Asunción, Paraguay, www.altervida.org.py

Chacolinks, Oxford, United Kingdom, www.chacolinks.org.uk

Rede Ecovida de Agroecologia, Brazil,
    www.ifoam.org/about_ifoam/standards/pgs_projects/pgs_projects/15649.php
The Soil Association, London, United Kingdom, www.soilassociation.org

SHELTER

BioRegional, Surrey, United Kingdom, www.bioregional.com

Fraunhofer Institute, Freiburg, Germany, www.ise.fraunhofer.de

Freiburg FuTour, Freiburg, Germany, www.freiburg-futour.de

Passivhaus Institut, Dresden, Germany, www.passiv.de

Rieselfeld, Freiburg, Germany,
    www.freiburg.de/servlet/PB/menu/1179601/index.html

Vauban District, Freiburg, Germany, www.vauban.de/info/abstract.html

Wohnen und Arbeiten (Living and Working *Passivhaus* building), Freiburg,
    Germany, www.passivhaus-vauban.de

TRANSPORTATION

Biofuels

Biofuel Watch, United Kingdom, www.biofuelwatch.org.uk

Center for International Forestry Research, Bogor, Indonesia, www.cifor.cgiar.org

Forest Peoples Programme, United Kingdom, www.forestpeoples.org

Institut Dayakologi, Pontianak, Indonesia, www.dayakology.org

KONTAK Rakyat Borneo, Indonesia, www.kontakrakyatborneo.blogspot.com

Lembaga Gemawan, Pontianak, Indonesia, www.gemawan.org

Milieudefensie (Dutch branch of Friends of the Earth), Amsterdam, The
    Netherlands, www.milieudefensie.nl

Sawit Watch (Oil Palm Watch), Bogor, Indonesia, www.sawitwatch.or.id

Walhí (The Indonesia Forum for Environment, a branch of Friends of the
    Earth), Indonesia, www.walhi.or.id

Green Vehicles

Back Alley Bikes and The Hub of Detroit, Detroit, Michigan,
    www.thehubofdetroit.org

Boggs Center, Detroit, Michigan, www.boggscenter.org

California Air Resources Board, Sacramento, California, www.arb.ca.gov

Oil Change International, Washington, D.C., www.priceofoil.org

Transportation Alternatives, New York, New York, www.transalt.org

Carbon Offsetting

Carbon Trade Watch, Amsterdam, The Netherlands, www.carbontradewatch
.org

The Corner House, United Kingdom, www.thecornerhouse.org.uk

Durban Group for Climate Justice,
www.carbontradewatch.org/durban/index.html

Forests and the European Union Research Network (FERN), Brussels, Belgium,
www.fern.org

SinksWatch, United Kingdom, www.sinkswatch.org

Transnational Institute, Amsterdam, The Netherlands, www.tni.org

University of Oxford Environmental Change Institute, United Kingdom,
www.eci.ox.ac.uk/research/climate/cop07/offsets.php

GENERAL

Environmental Support Group, Bangalore, India, www.esgindia.org

Food First—Institute for Food and Development Policy, Oakland, California,
www.foodfirst.org

Friends of the Earth International, www.foei.org

Greenpeace Argentina, Buenos Aires, www.greenpeace.org/argentina

Greenpeace India, Bangalore, www.greenpeace.org/india

Greenpeace Southeast Asia, Jakarta, Indonesia, www.greenpeace.org/seasia/id

Institute for Local Self-Reliance, Minneapolis, Minnesota, and Washington,
D.C., www.ilsr.org

International Forum on Globalization, San Francisco, California, www.ifg.org

International Rivers, Berkeley, California, www.internationalrivers.org

Mongabay, online environmental magazine, Mongabay.com

Oxfam International's Climate Change Campaign,
www.oxfam.org/en/climatechange

Rainforest Action Network, San Francisco, California, www.ran.org

REDD-Monitor, www.redd-monitor.org

Rising Tide North America, www.risingtidenorthamerica.org

Rising Tide United Kingdom, www.risingtide.org.uk

Via Campesina, Jakarta, Indonesia, www.viacampesina.org

Wetlands International, Ede, The Netherlands, www.wetlands.org

WiserEarth, www.wiserearth.org

Notes

INTRODUCTION:
GREEN DREAMS

1 price freeze on corn: Heather Stewart, "High costs of basics fuels global food fights," *Observer* (UK), February 18, 2007.

1 violent unrest in over thirty countries: Alex Morales, "Argentina, Venezuela, Cuba, criticize UN Food-Summit declaration," Bloomberg, June 6, 2008, http://www.bloomberg.com/apps/news?pid=20601086&sid=aoXaCUUCto yc&refer=latin_america.

1 food prices peaked further still: Food and Agriculture Organization, http://www.fao.org/fileadmin/templates/worldfood/Reports_and_docs/Food_ price_indices_data.xls.

1 half or more of their income to keep their families fed: Paul Krugman, Robin Wells, and Martha Olney, *Essentials of Economics* (New York: Macmillan, 2007), 122.

1 people were killed in Cameroon: Jesse Finfrock and Nichole Wong, "Pouring biofuel on the fire," *Mother Jones,* March/April 2009, 42.

1 prime minister was ousted and at least four rioters were shot and killed: "Food riots turn deadly," BBC, April 5, 2008, http://news.bbc.co.uk/2/hi/ americas/7331921.stm.

2 stampede at a supermarket: Keith Bradsher, "A new, global oil quandary: Costly fuel means costly calories," *New York Times,* January 19, 2008.

2 eliminated by adding household bleach: Interview with Elizabeth Linda Yuliani, ecologist at the Center for International Forestry Research, May 4, 2008.

2 corn ethanol was a net loser: Susan S. Lang, "Cornell ecologist's study finds that producing ethanol and biodiesel from corn and other crops is not worth the energy," Cornell University News Service, July 15, 2005, http://www .news.cornell.edu/stories/july05/ethanol.toocostly.ssl.html.

2 two reports published in early 2008: cited in Elisabeth Rosenthal, "Biofuels deemed a greenhouse threat," *New York Times,* February 8, 2008.

2 deforestation rates in Brazil shot up sharply: Rory Carroll, "Brazilian officials

face charges over Amazon destruction caused by logging," *Guardian* (UK), September 30, 2008.

2 world's third-largest carbon dioxide emitter: *How the Palm Oil Industry Is Cooking the Climate,* Greenpeace International, 2007, 1.

3 likely intensified by the effects of global warming: "Katrina and global warming," Pew Center of Global Climate Change, http://www.pewclimate.org/specialreports/katrina.cfm.

3 industrialized society plays a significant role: *Climate Change 2007: Synthesis report,* Contribution of Working Groups I, II, and III to the Fourth Assessment Report of the Intergovernmental Panel on Climate Change, Core Writing Team, R. K. Pachauri and A. Reisinger, eds. (Geneva, Switzerland: IPCC, 2008), 37.

3 2007 State of the Union address: American Rhetoric, http://www.americanrhetoric.com/speeches/stateoftheunion2007.htm.

4 Whole Foods . . . Wall Street darling: Tradingmarkets.com, http://www.tradingmarkets.com/.site/quotescharts/?qm_page=41537&qm_symbol=WFMI.

4 Wal-Mart . . . top vendor of organic groceries: MSNBC, http://www.msnbc.msn.com/id/11977666/.

4 organic-foods industry expanded: Organic Trade Association, http://www.ota.com/organic/mt/business.html.

4 outstripping conventional food: Elizabeth Brewster, "Tough Times: Stuck in neutral, supermarkets continue to battle other channels for market share," *Refrigerated and Frozen Foods,* June 1, 2004.

5 demand for ecologically astute architecture: Daily Green, http://www.thedailygreen.com/green-homes/latest/2987.

5 real estate market overall is still struggling: "New residential sales in July 2009," press release, U.S. Census Bureau News, August 26, 2009, http://www.census.gov/const/www/newressalesindex.html. Also see "Strong gain in existing-home sales maintains upward trend," press release, National Association of Realtors, August 21, 2009, http://www.realtor.org/press_room/news_releases/2009/08/strong_uptrend.

5 BP has committed over $1.5 billion: Clifford Krauss, "Big oil warms to ethanol and biofuel companies," *New York Times,* May 26, 2009.

5 Keeping drivers on a liquid diet: Clara Jeffrey, "Michael Pollan fixes dinner," *Mother Jones,* March/April 2009, 33.

5 mandates and subsidies in the United Kingdom: Jim Lane, "UK government sets 3.25 percent biofuels mandate from 2009–10, up from expected 3.00 percent," *Biofuels Digest,* February 2, 2009, http://www.biofuelsdigest.com/blog2/2009/02/02/uk-government-sets-325-percent-biofuels-mandate-from-2009-10-up-from-expected-300-percent.

5 parts of China: "China needs new policies to kickstart biofuel sector," Thomson Financial News, http://www.forbes.com/feeds/afx/2008/06/03/afx5073275.html.

5 biofuels are clearly here to stay: *Biofuels for Transportation: Selected trends*

and facts, Worldwatch Institute, June 7, 2006, http://www.worldwatch.org/
node/4081. Also see Sam Nelson, "EPA ruling allays concerns over biofuels
mandates," Reuters, May 5, 2009.

6 a prominent eugenicist: Wikipedia, http://en.wikipedia.org/wiki/Svante_
Arrhenius.

6 "We would then have some right": Ian Sample, "The father of climate change,"
Guardian (UK), June 30, 2005.

6 Hansen told lawmakers: Chris Mooney, "Some like it hot," *Mother Jones,*
May/June 2005, http://www.motherjones.com/environment/2005/05/some-
it-hot.

7 double what it normally is: My typical annual emissions equate to five thousand tons of CO_2.

7 average American spits out almost twice the CO_2: Anja Kollmuss, Helge
Zink, and Clifford Polycarp, *Making Sense of the Voluntary Carbon Offset
Market: A comparison of carbon offset standards,* WWF Germany, March
2008, 41.

7 the world's largest economy: Economy Watch, http://www.economywatch
.com/economies-in-top/.

7 20 percent of the planet's energy: *International Energy Outlook 2009,* Energy
Information Administration, Report # DOE/EIA-0484(2009), May 27, 2009,
http://www.eia.doe.gov/oiaf/ieo/world.html.

7 top emitter of greenhouse gases: "China overtakes U.S. as top CO_2 emitter:
Dutch agency," Reuters, June 20, 2007.

9 world's top organic sugar producers and exporters: Alejandro Sciscioli,
"Sweet experiment with organic sugar," *Tierramérica,* June 13, 2005, http://
www.tierramerica.info/nota.php?lang=eng&idnews=927&olt=137.

10 buildings account for almost 40 percent of CO_2 emissions: U.S. Green Building Council, http://www.usgbc.org/DisplayPage.aspx?CMSPageID=1718.

10 fossil fuels . . . are the top source of greenhouse gases: *Inventory of U.S.
Greenhouse Gas Emissions and Sinks: 1990–2007,* Environmental Protection
Agency, April 15, 2009, ES-8.

10 sole remaining viable habitat for the . . . orangutan: Greenpeace, http://www
.greenpeace.org/usa/news/the-orangutan-s-rainforest-hom/the-orangutan-
under-threat.

11 strengthening fuel economy standards: Saqib Rahim, "White House proposes new, stricter national fuel efficiency standards," *New York Times,* May
19, 2009.

11 perplexingly low 38.3 mpg: John O'Dell, "GM's 230 MPG estimate for Volt
works, or not, depending on the drive," Edmunds.com, August 11, 2009,
http://blogs.edmunds.com/greencaradvisor/2009/08/gms-230-mpg-esti
mate-for-volt-works-or-not-depending-on-the-drive.html.

11 electricity generation accounted for 42 percent: *Inventory of U.S. Greenhouse
Gas Emissions,* EPA, ES-8.

11 India . . . hosts more than 25 percent: United Nations Framework Convention

on Climate Change, Clean Development Mechanism, http://cdm.unfccc.int/
Statistics/Registration/NumOfRegisteredProjByHostPartiesPieChart.html.

12 lifetime of the trees: "Lifespan of common urban trees," CBC News Online,
August 11, 2005, http://www.cbc.ca/news/background/environment/trees_
lifespan.html.

CHAPTER ONE
CLOSE TO HOME: LOCAL ORGANIC

17 one of the biggest such networks: New York State Department of Agriculture and Markets, http://www.agmkt.state.ny.us/AP/CommunityFarmers
Markets.asp.

18 up by more than 150 percent: USDA Agricultural Marketing Service, press
release no. 0488.09, October 2, 2009.

18 topped $1 billion: *USDA National Farmers Market Manager Survey 2006,*
United States Department of Agriculture, Agricultural Marketing Service,
May 2009, 7.

18 exceeded $17 billion: *The Organic Industry,* Organic Trade Association,
2008, 1.

18 organic market was worth $48 billion: "Organic food not healthier, study
finds," Reuters, July 30, 2009, http://www.reuters.com/article/scienceNews/
idUSTRE56S3ZJ 20090730.

18 "70% of human water consumption": "Running dry," *Economist,* September 18, 2008, http://www.economist.com/world/international/displayStory
.cfm?story_id=12260907.

18 fuels rampant algae growth: "Farm runoff worse than thought, study says,"
AP, June 14, 2005, MSNBC, http://www.msnbc.msn.com/id/8214501/.

18 mass underwater "dead zones": Eric Chivian and Aaron Bernstein, "How is
biodiversity threatened by human activity?" in *Sustaining Life: How human
health depends on biodiversity,* ed. Eric Chivian and Aaron Bernstein (New
York: Oxford University Press USA, 2008), 52–53.

18 pesticides also linger as residues on food: Consumers Union, http://www
.consumersunion.org/food/organicsumm.htm.

19 did not factor fertilizer and pesticide residues: Karen McVeigh, "Organic
food not healthier, says FSA," *Guardian* (UK), July 29, 2009.

19 pesticides wreak havoc on human health: U.S. Environmental Protection
Agency, http://www.epa.gov/pesticides/.

19 "Conventional farming is cheaper": Interview with Richard Pirog, August 7,
2007.

20 at around thirty months: Interview with David Huse, July 9, 2007.

20 as young as twelve months: *Fiscal 2008 Fact Book,* Tyson Foods, 7.

21 two thousand and thirty-five hundred other organic farms: Allen Salkin,
"Leaving behind the trucker hat," *New York Times,* March 16, 2008.

22 "I transplanted mint": Interview with Morse Pitts, July 5, 2007.

22 praised by the likes of Alice Waters: Lesley Procelli, "The producers," *Gourmet,* October 2007, 220.

23 No one ever gets more than a week: Interview with Pitts, July 5, 2007.

23 keeps weeds from sprouting: Jill MacKenzie, "Green manure cover crops for Minnesota," University of Minnesota Extension Service, http://www.extension.umn.edu/yardandgarden/ygbriefs/H234greenman.html.

24 known as broadcasting: The One-Straw Revolution, http://www.onestrawrevolution.net/MasanobuFukuoka.htm.

24 "We plant tons of stuff": Interview with Pitts, July 5, 2007.

24 Two years later he died: Interview with Pitts, July 6, 2007.

25 They must keep detailed records: "Certification preamble," *Regulatory Text,* National Organic Program, 1, http://www.ams.usda.gov/AMSv1.0/ams.fetchTemplateData.do?template=TemplateF&navID=RegulationsNOP NationalOrganicProgramHome&rightNav1=RegulationsNOPNationalOr ganicProgramHome&topNav=&leftNav=&page=NOPRegulations&result Type=&acct=noprulemaking.

25 "then you're not growing the food": Interview with Pitts, July 5, 2007.

25 problems with USDA certification: Interview with Ron Khosla, July 17, 2007.

26 require no soil samples or chemical-residue tests: "Certification preamble," National Organic Program, 2.

26 he called Gonzalez to repaint the sign: Interview with Pitts, July 5, 2007.

27 Among the new neighbors: Cardinal Health, http://www.cardinal.com/us/en/aboutus/.

27 warehouse covering twenty-three acres: Google maps, http://maps.google.com/maps?oe=utf-8&rls=org.mozilla:en-US:official&client=firefox-a&um=1&ie=UTF-8&q=%22cardinal+health%22+Montgomery,+ny&fb=1&split=1&gl=us&ei=gcpcSoOuA4v8MM-dsa4C&sa=X&oi=local_group&ct=image&resnum=4.

27 "Farms are just gone from here": Interview with Pitts, July 6, 2007.

28 "If you're going to employ people here": Ibid.

28 "It's not a living, it's a life": Interview with Pitts, July 5, 2007.

29 "It's basically not": Interview with Pitts, July 6, 2007.

29 build a lasting market for humanely raised: http://grassfedmeat.net/about_fleishers.html.

29 trials of being butchers: Interview with Joshua Applestone and Aaron Lenz, September 6, 2007.

30 "If people are under forty": Interview with Eric Shelley, August 31, 2007.

30 top four companies slaughtered: Eric Schlosser, *Fast Food Nation: The dark side of the all-American meal* (New York: Perennial, 2001, 2002), 137–38.

32 fifty different types of grasses: Interview with David Huse, September 6, 2007.

32 Overgrazing has multiple ecological effects: Michael Pollan, *The Omnivore's Dilemma: A natural history of four meals* (New York: Penguin, 2006), 189–90.

32 "The coevolutionary relationship": Ibid., 70.

33 Methane is over twenty times: "Global warming culprits: Cars and cows," ABC News, December 13, 2006, http://abcnews.go.com/Technology/ GlobalWarming/Story?id=2723201&page=1.

33 fifth-largest beef processor: Smithfield News, http://www.smithfieldfoods news.com/VolumeIV_NumberI/index.html.

33 bought out the regional slaughterhouse: Smithfield Foods Company, http:// www.smithfieldfoods.com/our_company/Timeline_Print.aspx.

34 "I'm shipping to one little butcher shop": Interview with Huse.

34 A 2007 study: Ron Strochlic and Luis Sierra, *Conventional, Mixed and "Deregistered" Organic Farmers: Entry barriers and reasons for exiting organic production in California* (California Institute for Rural Studies, February 2007), 22–23.

35 over twenty thousand customers: Reference for Business, http://www.refer enceforbusiness.com/history2/20/United-Natural-Foods-Inc.html.

35 "purchase of the last two natural-food-distribution cooperatives": Samuel Fromartz, *Organic, Inc.: Natural foods and how they grew* (New York: Harcourt, 2006), 189.

36 profile of a farmer named John Wing: Tracy Frisch, "The missing link for locally raised meats?" *Hill Country Observer,* August 2007, 16.

37 "USDA makes it so hard": Interview with Huse.

37 HACCP was adopted and refined: Schlosser, *Fast Food Nation,* 198–99.

37 "The earliest case [of *E. coli*]": Marion Nestle, *Safe Food: Bacteria, biotechnology, and bioterrorism* (Berkeley, Los Angeles, London: University of California Press, 2003), 42.

37 just fourteen meatpacking facilities: Bonnie Azab Powell, "This little piggy goes home," *Mother Jones,* March/April 2009, 39.

38 "because you should leave the earth": Interview with Frank Johnson, July 9, 2007.

38 According to the USDA Economic Research Service: Carol A. Jones, Hisham El-Osta, and Robert Green, *Economic Well-Being of Farm Households* (United States Department of Agriculture Economic Research Service, March 2006), 2.

39 "Nothing," he tells me: Phone call with USDA NOP receptionist, August 23, 2007.

40 key post of head of Compliance and Enforcement sat vacant: Richard H. Mathews, "National Organic Program: Structure, responsibilities, goals," National Organic Program, PowerPoint presentation, November 12, 2008, slide 16.

40 Compliance and Enforcement's stated goals: Ibid.

40 NOP budget: E-mail correspondence with Joan Shaffer, USDA Agriculture Marketing Service Public Affairs, July 20, 2009.

40 all-time high of fourteen: Ibid.

40 farm bill rings in at about $300 billion: Michael Doyle, "When Congress

had a chance, food safety wasn't its choice," *McClatchy,* June 10, 2008, http://www.mcclatchydc.com/227/story/40536.html.

40 fivefold increase: USDA Economic Research Service, http://www.ers.usda.gov/FarmBill/2008/Titles/TitleVIIResearch.htm#organic.

41 Some now criticize Cascadian Farm's: Pollan, *Omnivore's Dilemma,* 161–62.

41 "As the organic industry matures": Kimberly Kindy and Lindsey Layton, "Purity of federal 'organic' label is questioned," *Washington Post,* July 3, 2009.

41 working for the establishment compromises him: Interview with Peter LeCompte, October 16, 2007.

CHAPTER TWO
ALL THE WORLD'S A GARDEN: GLOBAL ORGANIC

43 Paraguay was among the first: Maps of the world, http://www.mapsofworld.com/paraguay/travel/transport.html.

43 among the most biodiverse: "Paraguay: Zero Deforestation Law contributes significantly to the conservation of the Upper Paraná Atlantic Forest," *Leaders for a Living Planet,* World Wildlife Fund, August 30, 2006, 2.

43 home to a wealth of plants: Ibid.

43 soy, wheat, and, increasingly, sugarcane: "Economic sectors: Agriculture country profile select," *Economist Intelligence Unit Ltd.,* April 23, 2008.

43 The native Atlantic Forest once carpeted: USAID, http://paraguay.usaid.gov/environment/forest.html.

43 one of the highest deforestation rates: Ibid.

43 just 8 percent of the primary . . . ecosystem remains: Ibid.

43 slowed the felling of trees: "Paraguay: Zero Deforestation Law," World Wildlife Fund, 1.

44 leading organic sugar producers and exporters: Farm online, http://fw.farmonline.com.au/news/nationalrural/sugar/general/paraguay-the-worlds-largest-organic-cane-sugar-producer/62572.aspx.

44 provides a third of all organic sugar: Interview with Dario Zaldivar, October 30, 2007.

44 subsidiary of Imperial Sugar: Imperial Sugar Annual Report 2007, 7.

44 used by top processors: Interview with Zaldivar, October 29, 2007.

45 consumption of all-natural goods has slowed: Nigel Hunt and Brad Dorfman, "How green is my wallet? Organic food growth slows," Reuters UK, January 28, 2009.

45 continues its ongoing expansion: Organic Trade Association, http://www.organicnewsroom.com/2009/05/us_organic_sales_grow_by_a_who.html.

45 supplies stretched thin: "UK organic food sales soar, supply fails to keep up," Reuters, March 9, 2007.

45 Organic Valley ended its lucrative deal: Kermit Pattison, "Wal-Mart loved

Organic Valley's milk, so why cut off the flow?" *Inc.,* July 1, 2007, http://www
.inc.com/magazine/20070701/casestudy.html.

45   Soil Association reasoned: Caroline Stacey, "Food Miles," BBC Home, http://
www.bbc.co.uk/food/food_matters/foodmiles.shtml#top.

45   divulges the total greenhouse gases: Carbon Label, http://www.carbon-label
.com/individuals/label.html.

45   Participants in the program: John Russell, "Greening the chain—we are all
farmers now," *Ethical Corporation,* May 15, 2009, http://www.wbcsd.org/
plugins/DocSearch/details.asp?type=DocDet&ObjectId=MzQ0NzQ.

46   Versions of the Carbon Reduction Label: CimateChangeCorp, http://www
.climatechangecorp.com/content.asp?ContentID=5828.

47   biggest Paraguayan customers: Interview with Raúl Hoeckle, December 5,
2007.

47   rapidly expanding its operations: Interview with Zaldivar, October 29, 2007.

47   is instead establishing new organic fields: Interview with Hoeckle.

47   his responsibilities are increasing: Interview with Rubén Darío Ayala,
November 3, 2007.

48   To qualify a farm must: Sections 205.205 and 205.206, Electronic Code of
Federal Regulations, http://ecfr.gpoaccess.gov/cgi/t/text/text-idx?type=sim
ple;c=ecfr;cc=ecfr;sid=4163ddc3518c1ffdc539675aed8efe33;region=DIV1
;q1=national%20organic%20program;rgn=div5;view=text;idno=7;node=7
%3A3.1.1.9.31#7:3.1.1.9.31.3.342.6.

48   established in 1989 and owned by: NSF International, http://www.nsf.org/busi
ness/quality_assurance_international/index.asp?program=QualityAsInt.

48   two-thirds of all certified organic food: Bill Alpert, "Ethical consumerism is
in," *Barron's,* November 12, 2007.

49   "Sustainability depends on": Richard P. Tucker, *Insatiable Appetite: The
United States and the ecological degradation of the tropical world* (Berkeley:
University of California Press, 2000), 62.

49   biggest underground stores of freshwater: *Guaraní Aquifer System: Environ-
mental protection and sustainable development of the Guaraní Aquifer System,*
Organization of American States Office for Sustainable Development and
Environment, Water Project Series no. 7, October 2005, 1.

49   legal text that delineates NOP standards: Electronic Code of Federal Regulations.

50   "If you have a requirement": Interview with Luis Brenes, December 17, 2007.

50   "That sounds like a bit of a cop-out": Interview with Jim Riddle, July 28, 2008.

50   NOP regs make no distinction: "Production and handling preamble," *Regulatory Text,* National Organic Program, 3. See USDA Agriculture Marketing Service National Organic Program, http://www.ams.usda.gov/AMSv1.0/
ams.fetchTemplateData.do?template=TemplateF&navID=RegulationsNOP
NationalOrganicProgramHome&rightNav1=RegulationsNOPNational
OrganicProgramHome&topNav=&leftNav=&page=NOPRegulations&result
Type=&acct=noprulemaking.

51 manure from animals fed such substances: E-mail correspondence with Miles McEvoy, deputy administrator, NOP, via Joan Shaffer, October 29, 2009.

51 "What kind of organic farm": Interview with Zaldivar, October 29, 2007.

51 "Organic is becoming exactly": Ibid., October 28, 2007.

51 "I don't do politics anymore": Ibid.

52 "mostly in the last five years": Ibid., October 30, 2007.

52 "Ten years ago": Interview with Avelino Vega, November 4, 2007.

53 "It's very difficult to fight": Interview with Flor Fretes, November 4, 2007.

53 AZPA cultivates twenty-seven thousand acres: "Paraguay introduces new varieties of sweet cane developed in Brazil," Rediex, http://www.rediex.gov.py/index.php?Itemid=190&id=327&option=com_content&task=view.

53 twenty-five thousand acres: Interview with Hoeckle, December 5, 2007.

53 serves at the Network on Investment and Export: "Paraguay introduces new varieties of sweet cane," Rediex.

54 "This is the problem of how farmers interpret": Interview with Salvador Garibay, October 27, 2009.

54 "What incentive do organic producers have to not clear land?": E-mail correspondence with Laura Raynolds, October 28, 2009.

54 QAI is also supposed to inspect: QAI, http://www.qai-inc.com/3_3_0_0.php.

54 "opportunistic ecosystem removal": *D2 Draft Biodiversity and Landscape Standards: Background of the development of draft biodiversity and landscape standards,* International Federation of Organic Agriculture Movements, 3, http://www.google.com/search?hl=en&client=firefox-a&rls=org.mozilla%3Aen-US%3Aofficial&hs=VIV&q=%22opportunistic+ecosystem+removal%22+ifoam&aq=f&oq=&aqi=.

54 "has been an advocate": E-mail correspondence with Jaclyn Bowen, September 22, 2009.

55 farmers pool their money to pay the certifier: *Certifying Operations with Multiple Production Units, Sites and Facilities Under the National Organic Program,* National Organic Standards Board Compliance, Accreditation and Certification Committee, November 19, 2008, 2.

55 their single largest fixed cost: Interview with Zaldivar and Ferriera, October 30, 2007.

56 license belongs to the trader: Interview with Zaldivar, October 30, 2007.

57 Ibarra grows five acres: Interview with Eber Ibarra, November 3, 2007.

57 about $265 per month: *2008 Human Rights Report: Paraguay,* U.S. Department of State, February 2009, http://www.state.gov/g/drl/rls/hrrpt/2008/wha/119169.htm.

57 sometimes collected just two loads: Interview with Ibarra and Luis Gonzalez, November 3, 2007.

58 "I feel like I've been ripped off": Interview with Gonzalez, October 30, 2007.

58 about 70 percent of its members: Interview with Ferriera, October 30, 2007.

58 "AZPA would drop them": Interview with Zaldivar, October 30, 2007.

58 20 percent of their crops: *Shaping Global Partnerships,* FLO International Annual Report 2006/2007, 12.

59 AZPA performs the inspections: *Certifying Operations with Multiple Production Units,* 2.

59 the more money it costs the certifier: Ibid., 7.

60 "arguably the most devastated": Carlos Galindo-Leal and Ibsen de Gusmão Câmara, "Atlantic Forest hotspot status: An overview," in *The Atlantic Forest of South America: Biodiversity status, threats, and outlook,* ed. Galindo-Leal and Câmara (Washington, D.C.: Island Press, 2003), 3.

61 "This land is owned by": Interview with Mariano Martinez, November 4, 2007.

61 "When we started": Interview with Zaldivar, October 29, 2007.

62 an array of directives in a piecemeal system: Organic Trade Association, http://www.ota.com/pp/legislation/backgrounder.html.

62 it issues licenses to private certification companies: USDA Agriculture Marketing Service National Organics Program, http://www.ams.usda.gov/AMSv1.0/nop.

62 QAI is no longer AZPA's certifier: E-mail correspondence with Bowen.

62 AZPA spent about $25,000 annually: Interview with Zaldivar and Ferriera, October 30, 2007.

63 its milk is sold in cartons bearing: Liane Kufchock, "Aurora organic milk class-action suits to be heard in St. Louis," Bloomberg, February 26, 2008.

63 over a dozen "willful violations": USDA, http://www.usda.gov/wps/portal/!ut/p/_s.7_0_A/7_0_1OB?contentidonly=true&contentid=2007/08/0228.xml.

63 According to the investigation: Ibid.

63 it's implausible that QAI could have missed: "USDA finds largest organic dairy perpetrating fraud," press release, Cornucopia Institute, September 13, 2007.

63 QAI spoke in Aurora's defense: "USDA dismisses complaints against Aurora Organic Dairy," press release, Aurora Organic Dairy, August 29, 2007.

63 Aurora signed a consent agreement: USDA, http://www.usda.gov/wps/portal/!ut/p/_s.7_0_A/7_0_1OB?contentidonly=true&contentid=2007/08/0228.xml.

63 "People are really hung up on regulations": Quoted in Kimberly Kindy and Lyndsey Layton, "Purity of federal 'organic' label is questioned," *Washington Post,* July 3, 2009, http://www.washingtonpost.com/wp-dyn/content/article/2009/07/02/AR2009070203365.html?sid=ST2009070203371.

63 "If somebody wants to cheat": Interview with Peter LeCompte, June 19, 2008.

64 "Most consumers are simple minds": Bruno Fischer speaking at BioFach, São Paulo, Brazil, October 16, 2007.

64 "I can't think of the future": Interview with Zaldivar, October 29, 2007.

CHAPTER THREE
THE GREENHOUSE EFFECT: ECO-ARCHITECTURE

69 jobs such as manufacturing or behind clerk's desks: Interview with John Shakespeare, January 9, 2009.

69 BedZED is higher density: Bioregional, http://www.bioregional.com/pro gramme_projects/ecohous_prog/bedzed/bedzed_hpg.htm. Also see Green-roofs, http://www.greenroofs.com/projects/pview.php?id=547.

70 Highgrove sits amid thirty-seven acres: The Prince of Wales, http://www .princeofwales.gov.uk/personalprofiles/residences/highgrove/.

70 radically reconceptualizing home energy: Interview with Jennie Organ, January 9, 2009.

70 40 percent of all carbon dioxide emissions: U.S. Green Building Council, http://www.usgbc.org/DisplayPage.aspx?CMSPageID=1718.

70 36 percent in the European Union: European Commission, http://ec.europa .eu/research/industrial_technologies/lists/energy-efficient-buildings_ en.html#1.

70 half in the United Kingdom: Communities and Local Government, http:// www.communities.gov.uk/planningandbuilding/theenvironment/energy performance/.

71 "living machines," a technology pioneered in the United States: Nancy Jack Todd and John Todd, *From Eco-cities to Living Machines: Principles of eco-logical design* (Berkeley, CA: North Atlantic Books, 1993), xvii.

73 profiles Kathy Baur: Laura Nesbitt, "Earthships offer the ultimate in eco-liv-ing," *Mountain View Telegraph*, January 18, 2009.

73 "When we speak of a good value": LivingHomes, http://www.livinghomes .net/priceValue.html.

73 The company's smallest: Ibid. For lowest-cost home, see http://www.living-homes.net/homesCommunities.html. For highest-priced home, see http:// www.livinghomes.net/budget.html?model=rk1.

74 building systems' design has resulted in: Pelli Clarke Pelli Architects, http:// www.pcparch.com/#/projects/hotelresidential/the-solaire/description/.

74 Monthly rent at the Solaire: City Realty, http://www.cityrealty.com/new-york-city/apartment/rentals/for-rent/the-solaire-20-river-terrace/26573.

74 BedZED . . . demographic consists of: Interview with Shakespeare.

75 One in every hundred: Caroline Bayley, "Germany's sunny revolution," BBC Radio 4, January 10, 2008.

76 "Do you know what a heat-exchanger": Interview with Dr. Marcus A. Neu-mann, January 14, 2009.

76 retain 90 percent of its heat: Elisabeth Rosenthal, "No furnaces but heat aplenty in 'passive houses,' " *New York Times*, December 26, 2008.

76 in the United States 56 percent of all power: U.S. Department of Energy, http://www.energy.gov/heatingcooling.htm.

76 in the UK it's 58 percent: *Energy Consumption in the United Kingdom*, Department of Trade and Industry, 23, www.berr.gov.uk/files/file11250.pdf.

76 in Germany . . . closer to three-quarters: German Federal Ministry for the Environment, Nature Conservation and Nuclear Safety, http://www.bmu.de/english/energy_efficiency/household/doc/38272.php.

77 "I think when people are properly informed": Interview with Andreas Delleske, January 14, 2009.

77 Delleske recounts the early days: Interview with Delleske, January 19, 2009.

77 four barracks buildings to SUSI: Interview with Jörg Lange, January 20, 2009.

77 Forum Vauban won a sizable grant: Hannes Linck, *Quartier Freiburg Vauban: A guided tour of the district* trans. Moshe Haas and Ian Harrison (Freiburg: Stadttcilverein Vauban e.V., February 2008), 30–31.

78 the group set up an office: Interview with Lange.

78 up to between 60 and 80 percent: U.S. Environmental Protection Agency, http://www.epa.gov/CHP/basic/efficiency.html.

79 half the national average: Linck, *Quartier Freiburg Vauban*, 16–17.

79 who continue to insist more cars: Interview with Lange.

79 bureaucrats had unilaterally decided: Linck, *Quartier Freiburg Vauban*, 8–9.

80 "Minimizing the surface area": Interview with Michael Gies, January 16, 2009.

82 the most efficient buildings are made: Chris Goodall, *Ten Technologies to Save the Planet* (London: Profile, 2008), 122–33.

82 Feist's technology improved on efforts: Rosenthal, "No furnaces but heat aplenty."

82 Structures built to *Passivhaus* specifications: Goodall, *Ten Technologies*, 124.

82 energy consumption can't surpass six kilowatt-hours: Rieselfeld Projekt Group in Department 1, "The new district of Freiburg-Rieselfeld: A case study of successful, sustainable urban development," January 2009, 3, http://www.freiburg.de/servlet/PB/show/1180731/rieselfeld_en_2009.pdf.

83 it's being adopted as a standard: Walter Aussenhofer, "Carbon-neutral urban development: A German role model," PowerPoint presentation, City of Freiburg Environmental Protection Agency, 11–12.

83 the 1992 low-energy standard: Ibid., 8.

83 more than a quarter of all transport: Ibid., 30.

83 upped the low-energy rule: Ibid., 8.

84 thirty thousand people took part: Roger S. Powers, William B. Vogele, Christopher Kreugler, and Ronald M. McCarthy, *Protest, Power and Change: An encyclopedia of nonviolent action from Act-Up to women's suffrage* (New York: Garland, 1997), 104.

84 blocking the planned nuclear station: Judy Taylor, "Filming the anti-nuke movement," *Jump Cut* 24–25 (March 1981): 4–5, http://www.ejumpcut.org/archive/onlinessays/JC24-25folder/anti-nukeDocs.html.

84 similar demonstrations against nearby chemical plants: BUND (Friends of the Earth), http://vorort.bund.net/suedlicher-oberrhein/freiburg-environment-ecology.html.

84 six thousand youths lay down: Interview with Thomas Dresel, January 15, 2009.

85 more radioactive than Hiroshima: Richard Stone, "The long shadow of Chernobyl," *National Geographic,* April 2006, http://ngm.nationalgeographic.com/2006/04/inside-chernobyl/stone-text/2.

85 "really a triggering moment": Interview with Professor Eicke Weber, January 30, 2009.

85 Nuclear Exit Law: Michael Levitin, "Germany says auf Wiedersehen to nuclear power, guten Tag to renewables," *Grist,* August 12, 2005, http://www.grist.org/article/levitin-germany/.

86 14 percent of the country's electricity: Federal Ministry for the Environment, Nature Conservation and Nuclear Safety, http://www.bmu.de/english/climate/downloads/doc/40589.php.

86 on course to meet 25–30 percent: Groshschel_Geheeb_Responsible Branding GmbH, ed., *EEG—the Renewable Energy Sources Act: The success story of sustainable policies for Germany* (Federal Ministry for the Environment, Nature Conservation and Nuclear Safety, 2007), 4.

86 dearth of oil and natural gas: Frank Dohmen, Alexander Jung, Wolfgang Reuter, and Hans-Jürgen Schlamp, "Germany's energy 'wake-up call,'" *Spiegel Online,* January 10, 2006, http://www.spiegel.de/international/0,1518,394403,00.html.

86 "The real cost is": Interview with Elsa Gheziel, January 14, 2009.

88 utilities are obliged to purchase green power: Groshschel_Geheeb_Responsible Branding GmbH, ed., *EEG,* 7.

88 covers wind, solar, hydropower, biomass, geothermal: Ibid., 5.

89 renewable energy fed into Germany's grid: "Feed-in tariff for grid-connected solar systems," Energy Matters, http://www.energymatters.com.au/government-rebates/feedintariff.php.

89 "The oil companies are the most powerful": Interview with Rolf Disch, January 16, 2009.

89 In 2008 he launched a campaign: Dr. Tobias Bube, "The PlusEnergyHouse for every community," Büro Rolf Disch.

89 two hundred municipalities responded: E-mail correspondence with Dr. Tobias Bube, January 16, 2009.

90 Russia blocked gas exports to the EU: Luke Harding, "EU cautions after Putin and Ukraine PM outline gas agreement," *Guardian* (UK), January 19, 2009.

90 natural gas imported from Russia via Ukraine: Interview with Dresel. Also see Dohmen, Jung, Reuter, and Schlamp, "Germany's energy 'wake-up call.'"

90 Obama administration is showing interest: Mridul Chadha, "International renewable energy agency launched, U.S. and U.K. opt out," Red Green and

Blue, January 27, 2009, http://redgreenandblue.org/2009/01/27/interna tional-renewable-energy-agency-launched-us-and-uk-stay-out/.

90 The body is charged with spurring . . . renewable energy: Worldwatch Institute, "75 countries sign onto new clean energy agency," Environmental News Network, http://www.enn.com/climate/article/39242.

91 bombarded and leveled during World War II: Solar Region Freiburg, http://www.solarregion.freiburg.de/solarregion/freiburg_solar_city.php.

91 she . . . mentions Whyl: Interview with Hedda Jarvis, January 20, 2009.

92 73 percent of existing housing: German Federal Ministry of Transport, Building and Urban Affairs, http://www.bmvbs.de/en/artikel-,1872.983325/ The-programme-to-reduce-CO2-em.htm.

92 5 percent of all homes: *American Housing Survey for the United States: 2007* (U.S. Department of Housing and Urban Development and U.S. Department of Energy, September 2008), x, 1.

92 first multifamily *Passivhaus* structures: Wohnen und Arbeiten, http://www .passivhaus-vauban.de/passivhaus.en.html.

93 For Lange, an ecologically sane future: Interview with Lange.

93 the 2,000-Watt Society: K. John Morrow Jr. and Julie Ann Smith-Morrow, "Switzerland and the 2,000-watt society," *Sustainability* 1, no. 1 (February 2008): 32–33.

93 Current energy-consumption levels: "Earth Trends," World Resources Institute, http://earthtrends.wri.org.

93 70 percent of all economic activity: "Facts on policy: Consumer spending," Hoover Institute, http://www.hoover.org/research/factsonpolicy/ facts/4931661.html.

CHAPTER FOUR
THE FUEL OF FORESTS: BIODIESEL

97 Duta Palma Nusantara, was seizing their land: "Request for consideration of the situation of indigenous peoples in Kalimantan, Indonesia, under the United Nations Committee on the Elimination of Racial Discrimination's Urgent Action and Early Warning Procedures," Committee on the Elimination of Racial Discrimination Seventy-first Session, July 30–August 18, 2007, submitted July 6, 2007, 58–59.

97 PTLL's aim was to establish: Ibid., 58.

97 customers is Wilmar International Ltd.: Letter from Forest Peoples Programme to the Compliance Advisor/Ombudsman for the International Finance Corporation, August 12, 2008, http://www.forestpeoples.org/docu ments/ifi_igo/ifc_wilmar_fpp_cao_let_aug08_eng.pdf.

97 Archer Daniels Midland holds a 16 percent stake: Archer Daniels Midland 2007 Annual Report, 4.

97 certain rights under Indonesian law: "Customary right to land," Interna-

tional Development Law Organization, February 6, 2008, http://www.idlo
.int/docNews/Customary%20right%20to%20land.pdf.

98 Ethanol . . . emits 20 percent less carbon dioxide: U.S. Department of Energy,
http://www.afdc.energy.gov/afdc/ethanol/emissions.html.

98 Biodiesel . . . releases just a quarter the carbon: Ibid., http://www.afdc.energy
.gov/afdc/fuels/biodiesel_benefits.html.

98 half of all new automobiles and a third of the entire fleet: European Automobile Manufacturers' Association, http://www.acea.be/index.php/news/
news_detail/economic_report_passenger_car_production_stable_over_
first_quarter_2008.

98 consumption of biodiesel is set to triple: "Directive 2003/30/EC of the
European Parliament and of the Council of 8 May 2003 on the promo-
tion of the use of biofuels or other renewable fuels for transport," European
Parliament and the Council of the European Union, *Official Journal of the
European Union,* May 17, 2003, L 123/45.

99 $400 billion between 2006 and 2022: Doug Koplow, *A Boon to Bad Biofuels:
Federal tax credits and mandates underwrite environmental damage at tax-
payer expense* (Earth Track and Friends of the Earth, April 2009), 22.

99 Obama . . . aims to up the mix of biofuels: "Barack Obama and Joe Biden:
New energy for America," Obama-Biden campaign press release, August
2008, 5.

99 some biofuels may actually emit more carbon: Joseph Fargione, Jason Hill,
David Tilman, Stephen Polasky, and Peter Hawthorne, "Land Clearing and
the Biofuel Carbon Debt," *Science* 319, no. 5867 (February 29, 2008): 1235–
38.

99 Although peatlands cover just 3 percent: *Assessment on Peatlands, Biodiversity and Climate Change* (Global Environment Center, Wetlands International, 2007), v.

99 one ton of palm oil can generate thirty-three tons of carbon dioxide: Eric
Holt-Giménez and Isabella Kenfield, *When Renewable Isn't Sustainable,*
Food First Policy Brief No. 13, March 2008, 8.

100 Indonesia . . . the world's third-largest emitter of CO_2: *How the Palm Oil
Industry Is Cooking the Climate* (Greenpeace International, 2007), 1.

100 its current 16 million acres: Marcus Colchester et al., *Promised Land: Palm
oil and land acquisition in Indonesia: Implications for local communities and
indigenous peoples* (Forest Peoples Programme and Perkumpulan Sawit
Watch, November 2007), 25.

100 26 million by 2015: Evita H. Legowo, "Blueprint of biofuel development"
(PowerPoint presentation on behalf of Ministry of Energy and Mineral
Resources, Republic of Indonesia, May 15, 2007).

100 98 percent of Indonesia's forest . . . will be degraded or gone: Jack Santa Barbara, *The False Promise of Biofuels* (International Forum on Globalization
and the Institute for Policy Studies, 2007), 12.

100 "For the permit certification": Interview with Ong Kee Chao, May 5, 2008.

100 "Oil palm is one of our areas": Interview with Dr. Herry Purnomo, May 6, 2008.

101 At that time a vicious conflict erupted: Nancy Lee Peluso and Emily Harwell, "Territory, custom, and the cultural politics of ethnic war in West Kalimantan, Indonesia," in *Violent Environments,* ed. Nancy Lee Peluso and Michael Watts (Ithaca, NY: Cornell University Press, 2001), 83–84.

101 Dayaks of today deploy their warrior reputation: Nancy Lee Peluso, "Weapons of the wild: Strategic uses of violence and wildness in the rain forests of Indonesian Borneo," in *In Search of the Rain Forest,* ed. Candace Slater (Durham and London: Duke University Press, 2003), 236.

104 agreement . . . known as a plasma scheme: *Ghosts on Our Own Land: Indonesian oil palm smallholders and the Roundtable on Sustainable Palm Oil* (Forest Peoples Programme and Sawit Watch, 2006), 18.

104 One of the leaders of Muara Ilai: Interview with Asmoro, April 28, 2008.

105 require palm oil companies . . . to secure a series of permits: Eric Wakker, *Greasy Palms: The social and ecological impacts of large-scale oil palm plantation development in Southeast Asia* (Friends of the Earth, January 2005), 27.

105 devolve power to the provincial and district levels: Colchester et al., *Promised Land,* 46.

106 "No one can force communities": Interview with Tri Budiarto, May 2, 2008.

106 conglomeration of trading firms used terror and brute force: Wikipedia, http://en.wikipedia.org/wiki/Dutch_East_India_Company.

106 Dutch colonial government declared all unclaimed land: Colchester et al., *Promised Land,* 52–53.

106 Dutch control continued through the 1940s: Wikipedia, http://en.wikipedia .org/wiki/Dutch_Empire#Decolonisation_.281942.E2.80.931975.29.

106 bloody communist purge: Richard Lloyd Parry, "Suharto fears the 'Pinochet effect,'" *Independent* (UK), August 17, 1999.

106 welcoming . . . the American mining giant Freeport-McMoRan: Lisa Pease, "JFK, Indonesia, CIA & Freeport Sulphur," http://www.realhistoryarchives .com/collections/hidden/freeport-indonesia.htm.

106 direct payments for protection of the mine: Jane Perlez and Raymond Bonner, "The cost of gold, the hidden payroll," *New York Times,* December 27, 2005.

106 planet's largest gold mine: "Two wounded in Papua near Freeport's big gold mine," *Wall Street Journal,* July 16, 2009.

107 the intimidation he's experiencing began: Interview with Norman Wicaksono, April 28, 2008.

107 "The companies are not allowed": Interview with Cion Aleksander, April 28, 2008.

108 4 percent of the world's total greenhouse gas emissions: *Cooking the Climate,* 13.

108 the country's decades-old transmigration program: Wikipedia, http:// en.wikipedia.org/wiki/Transmigration_program.

109 he supposes he's fifty-five: Interview with Nazit, April 29, 2008.

109 even though he's grateful to have work: Interview with Rahmat, April 29, 2008.

109 price of crude palm oil had almost doubled: Index Mundi, http://www.indexmundi.com/commodities/?commodity=palm-oil&months=300.

110 "I've been traumatized": Interview with Marnaki, April 29, 2008.

110 higher yields per acre than any other oilseed crop: RSPO, http://www.rspo.org/About_Sustainable_Palm_Oil.aspx.

110 what he earns from his harvests isn't enough: Interview with Jhari, April 29, 2008.

111 65 percent of maintenance costs on petrochemical fertilizers: Interview with Chau, May 5, 2008.

112 among its members Wilmar, Duta Palma, Archer Daniels Midland, and Cargill: *Cooking the Climate*, 3.

112 among the biggest consumers of palm oil: Ibid.

112 played key roles in establishing the RSPO: Ibid.

112 RSPO website states its aim: RSPO, http://www.rspo.org/Our_Aspirations.aspx.

112 "No new plantings are established": "RSPO Principles and Criteria for Sustainable Palm Oil Production," Roundtable on Sustainable Palm Oil, 2006, 42.

112 Other criteria pledge to: Ibid., 33, 40, 42–43.

113 "The RSPO is a voluntary": E-mail correspondence with Sarala Aikanathan, September 24, 2009.

113 The document details illegal acts: Lely Khairnur, Claudia Theile, and Adriani Zakaria, *Policy, Practice, Pride and Prejudice: Review of legal, environmental and social practices of oil palm plantation companies of the Wilmar Group in Sambas District, West Kalimantan (Indonesia)* (KONTAK Rakyat Borneo, Lembaga Gemawan, and Milieudefensie, 2007), 5–6.

113 Wilmar's own social-responsibility policies: Wilmar International Ltd., http://www.wilmar-international.com/about_socialresponsibility.htm.

113 provided Wilmar tens of millions of dollars: International Finance Corporation, http://www.ifc.org/ifcext/spiwebsite1.nsf/0/64d0058360ce6dbc85256dd6005e35e0?opendocument; http://www.ifc.org/ifcext/spiwebsite1.nsf/f451ebbe34a9a8ca85256a550073ff10/68bdeb3d4fe3b5d38525738e0050bd85?opendocument.

113 IFC is also a member of the RSPO: *Audit Report: CAO audit of IFC,* Compliance Advisor/Ombudsman, C-I-R6-Y08-F096, June 19, 2009, 19.

113 a low-level manager who illuminated: Interview with Wilmar employee, April 28, 2008.

113 RSPO . . . gave Wilmar the all clear: E-mail correspondence with Sharon Chong, CSR Manager, Wilmar International Ltd., January 19, 2009.

113 "For more than twenty years": *Audit Report: CAO audit of IFC,* 2.

114 failed to ensure that Wilmar was in compliance: Ibid., 2–3.

114 "deal making prevailed": Ibid., 2.

114 "This is a long process": Interview with Lely Khairnur, May 2, 2008.

114 including the Sierra Club: Raya Widenoja, *Destination Iowa: Getting to a sustainable biofuels future* (Sierra Club and Worldwatch Institute, October 2007), 4.

114 Obama's own energy secretary, Steven Chu: Fiona Harvey, "Second generation biofuels—still five years away?" *Financial Times* blogs, May 29, 2009, http://blogs.ft.com/energy-source/2009/05/29/second-generation-biofuels-still-five-years-away/.

114 "a bridge to the next generation of biofuels": Timothy Gardner, "U.S. drafts rule to lower CO_2 output from biofuels," Reuters, May 5, 2009.

114 set to increase under current policy: Ibid.

114 U.S. government also committed support to automakers: Ibid.

115 over $126 billion on post-Katrina reconstruction: "Fact sheet: Rebuilding the Gulf Coast," White House, http://georgewbush-whitehouse.archives .gov/news/releases/2008/08/20080820-5.html.

115 "nowhere near what there needs to be": Interview with Purnomo.

115 displacement and clear-cutting . . . declared ecologically sustainable: REDD Monitor, http://www.redd-monitor.org/redd-an-introduction/.

CHAPTER FIVE

GREEN MACHINES: ECOLOGICAL AUTOMOBILES

117 had to join waiting lists . . . it cost about $3,000 more: Alex Taylor III, "Toyota: The birth of the Prius," *Fortune*, February 21, 2006, http://money .cnn.com/2006/02/17/news/companies/mostadmired_fortune_toyota/ index.htm. Also see "Worldwide Prius sales top 1 million mark," Toyota press release, May 15, 2008.

118 60 percent of the global Prius market: Taylor, "Toyota."

118 combined average fuel economy of 46 mpg: Environmental Protection Agency, http://www.fueleconomy.gov/feg/hybrid_sbs.shtml.

118 oil prices nearing $150 per barrel: "Oil prices fall below $65 despite OPEC's production cut; gas drops," *USA Today*, October 24, 2008.

118 nudge past General Motors: "Worldwide Prius sales top 1 million mark." Also see Chris Isidore, "GM loses sales title to Toyota," CNNmoney.com, January 21, 2009, http://money.cnn.com/2009/01/21/news/companies/gm_ toyota_sales/index.htm.

118 installing the technology in their ever-more-enormous . . . trucks and SUVs: General Motors, http://www.gm.com/vehicles/results.jsp?brand =gmc&evar10=hompage_vehicles_browsebybrand&fromHome=true.

118 "an interesting curiosity": Taylor, "Toyota."

119 Wagoner unveiled a concept car: Michelle Krebs, "General Motors' first

plug-in hybrid," Edmunds.com, January 7, 2007, http://www.edmunds.com/insideline/do/Features/articleId=119088.

119 200 mpg in the city and would sell for $40,000: Bill Vlasic and Nick Bunkley, "GM puts electric car's city mileage in triple digits," *New York Times,* August 12, 2009.

119 forty miles before any gas is needed: Scott Doggett, "Update: Range of Chevy Volt extended-range PHEV not shortened," Edmunds.com, July 9, 2008, http://blogs.edmunds.com/greencaradvisor/2008/07/update-range-of-chevy-volt-extended-range-phev-not-shortened.html.

119 eight hours for the Volt: Vlasic and Bunkley, "GM puts electric car's city mileage."

120 SUVs and light trucks accounted for half: "Americans might like these fuel-sipping cars," *BusinessWeek,* http://images.businessweek.com/ss/08/07/0731_europe_gas_sippers/index.htm?campaign_id=msn.

121 among the top advertising spenders in the United States: "TNS Media Intelligence reports U.S. advertising expenditures declined 14.2 percent first quarter 2009," TNS Media Intelligence press release, June 10, 2009, http://www.tns-mi.com/news/06102009.htm.

121 a few hundred dollars in profits: John Cloud et al., "Why the SUV is all the rage," *Time,* February 24, 2003, http://www.time.com/time/magazine/article/0,9171,1004283 -6,00.html.

121 over 80 mpg: Ford UK, http://www.ford.co.uk/Cars/NewFiesta/NewFiesta ECOnetic.

122 tax credits for plug-in hybrid purchasers: Scott Doggett, "Obama administration sparks battery gold rush as states, firms vie for $2.4 billion," Edmunds .com, May 26, 2009, http://blogs.edmunds.com/greencaradvisor/2009/05/obama-administration-sparks-battery-gold-rush-as-states-firms-vie-for-24-billion.html.

122 Obama raised fuel efficiency standards: Saqib Rahim, "White House proposes new, stricter national fuel efficiency standards," *New York Times,* May 19, 2009.

122 worldwide auto production: International Organization of Motor Vehicles, http://oica.net/category/production-statistics/.

122 more than 800 million cars and trucks . . . 1 billion by 2020: Plunkett Research Ltd., http://www.plunkettresearch.com/Industries/Automobiles Trucks/AutomobileTrends/tabid/89/Default.aspx.

123 brought in . . . William McDonough: "Ford's Rouge redesign," *Business-Week,* November 13, 2000, http://www.businessweek.com/archives/2000/b3707132.arc.htm.

123 Unveiled in 2004: "Ford overhauls historic factory to be green," MSNBC, April 27, 2004, http://www.msnbc.msn.com/id/4843708/.

123 a carpet of dense sedum: The Henry Ford, http://www.thehenryford.org/rouge/leedlivingroof.aspx.

124 "[The company] wants every owner of one of these cars": Quoted in Susan

Strasser, *Waste and Want: A social history of trash* (New York: Henry Holt, 1999), 194.

124 The average mpg for a 2008 Ford F-150 . . . is just under fifteen: *Model Year 2008 Fuel Economy Guide* (U.S. Department of Energy, Office of Energy Efficiency and Renewable Energy, U.S. Environmental Protection Agency, 2008), 15.

125 arguably worsened by the Explorer's top-heavy vehicle design: Keith Bradsher, *High and Mighty: The dangerous rise of the SUV* (New York: Public Affairs, 2002), 328.

125 $5,000 or more in pure profit: Cloud et al., "Why the SUV is all the rage."

125 American automakers had free rein: Bradsher, *High and Mighty*, 11–13.

125 SUVs qualify for a U.S. federal tax deduction: Jeff Plungis, "SUV, truck owners get a big tax break," *USA Today,* December 18, 2002.

125 Under the code the full price of an SUV: "Tax preferences for sport utility vehicles (SUVs): Current law and legislative initiatives in the 109th Congress," Congressional Research Service Report for Congress, March 21, 2005, 21.

126 the company's fantastic financial losses: Stockcharts.com, http://www.chartingstocks.net/wp-content/uploads/2009/03/ford_stock.png.

126 ecologically responsible innovations Ford is currently working on: Interview with John Viera, February 18, 2008.

126 EcoBoost technology in a few models so far: Ford website, http://media.ford.com/article_display.cfm?article_id=29681; http://media.ford.com/article_display.cfm?article_id=30663; and http://media.ford.com/article_display.cfm?article_id=29944.

126 In 2008 the company will sell almost 3 million: Ford Motor Company 2008 annual report, inside cover.

126 "Without the credits": Laura Meckler, "Fill up with ethanol? One obstacle is big oil," *Wall Street Journal,* April 2, 2007.

127 car companies receive CAFE credits regardless: Ibid.

127 1.3 gallons of corn-based ethanol can be refined: National Geographic, http://ngm.nationalgeographic.com/2007/10/biofuels/biofuels-interactive.

127 would have 250,000 hybrids on the road: Ford, http://media.ford.com/article_display.cfm?article_id=21627.

127 The goal was quietly dropped: Bryce G. Hoffman and Deb Price, "Ford bails out on hybrid promise," *Detroit News,* June 29, 2006.

127 Escape, which gets about 33 mpg: EPA, http://www.epa.gov/fueleconomy/class-high.htm.

128 GM focuses mostly on the near term: Interview with Terry Cullum, February 19, 2008.

129 hydrogen fuel supply is derived . . . from natural gas: Jeremy Rifkin, *The Hydrogen Economy: The creation of the worldwide energy web and the redistribution of power on earth* (New York: Jeremy P. Tarcher/Penguin, 2002), 186–87.

129 "We are nowhere [near] where we need to be": Edward Taylor and Mike Spector, "GM, Toyota doubtful on fuel cells' mass use," *Wall Street Journal,* March 5, 2008.

129 the article is singularly focused on the Volt: Katie Merx, "In charge of Chevy Volt," *Detroit Free Press,* February 24, 2008.

130 a veteran worker at GM: Interview with Miguel Chavarria, February 20, 2008.

131 strictly the miles racked up commuting from home to work: Bureau of Transportation Statistics, http://www.bts.gov/publications/omnistats/vol ume_03_issue_04/html/figure_02.html.

131 fuel economy of the Volt plunges to 38.3 mpg: John O'Dell, "GM's 230 mpg estimate for Volt works, or not, depending on the drive," Edmunds.com, August 11, 2009, http://blogs.edmunds.com/greencaradvisor/2009/08/gms-230-mpg-estimate-for-volt-works-or-not-depending-on-the-drive.html.

131 she indulged in more trips: E-mail correspondence with Megan Prelinger, May 2007.

132 "total crock of shit": "GM exec stands by calling global warming a crock," Reuters, February 22, 2008, http://www.reuters.com/article/latestCrisis/idUSN22372976.

132 keeping the auto industry on its highly polluting course: Bradsher, *High and Mighty,* 46–47.

132 his private helicopter . . . his own fighter jet: Di Freeze, "Bob Lutz: Guts in the sky as well," *Airport Journals,* May 2005, http://www.airportjournals.com/Display.cfm?varID=0505007.

133 10 percent of Americans owned cars: Eric Schlosser, *Fast Food Nation: The dark side of the all-American meal* (New York: Houghton Mifflin, 2002), 26.

133 created a company called National City Lines: Edwin Black, *Internal Combustion: How corporations and governments addicted the world to oil and derailed the alternatives* (New York: St. Martin's Press, 2006), 244.

133 grew by acquiring local routes everywhere: Schlosser, *Fast Food Nation,* 16.

133 paving over trolley tracks and tearing down overhead electrical cables: Ibid.

133 "In the event we maintain a 5 cent fare": Black, *Internal Combustion,* 246.

133 the companies were found guilty of conspiring: Ibid., 245.

134 routes in more than eighty U.S. towns: Jim Motavalli, *Forward Drive: The race to build "clean" cars for the future* (San Francisco: Sierra Club Books, 2001), 26.

134 88 percent of those surveyed wanted more: Ibid.

134 the Porsche hybrid: Ibid., 11–12.

134 small companies . . . turned out EVs and hybrids: Ibid., 14–15.

134 both drove Detroit Electrics: Black, *Internal Combustion,* 143.

134 Americans were buying gas-saving compact: Motavalli, *Forward Drive,* 16.

134 GM made a hybrid prototype: Ibid., 66.

135 the EV1 and its successor, the EV2: Ibid., 128–29.

135 The public-private partnership . . . entailed $1.5 billion: Bradsher, *High and Mighty,* 406.

136 GM's top lobbyist in D.C.: Ibid., 390.

136 announced that the PNGV was over: Ibid., 406.

137 focused on improved gasoline engines: Interview with Reginald Modlin, February 26, 2008.

137 scrapping of its entire hybrid program: Mike Ramsey, "Chrysler to drop first hybrids, after October debut," Bloomberg, October 28, 2008, http://www.bloomberg.com/apps/news?pid=20601087&sid=aoEM.2RDUzU8&refer=home#.

137 comprised about three-quarters of its sales: Stephen Power, Gina Chon, and Neal E. Boudette, "Daimler opens doors to Chrysler," *Wall Street Journal*, February 15, 2007.

138 For every increase of five miles per gallon: Peter Miller, "Saving energy, it starts at home," *National Geographic* 215, no. 3 (March 2009): 71.

138 U.S. carbon dioxide releases have surged by 17 percent: *Inventory of U.S. Greenhouse Gas Emissions and Sinks: 1990–2007*, U.S. Environmental Protection Agency, April 15, 2009, ES-3.

138 consumers haven't been willing: Interview with John German, February 21, 2008.

139 shows me where the tests are conducted: Interview with Jeff Alson, February 21, 2008.

140 "broad consensus for . . . fuel efficiency increases": Pew Campaign for Fuel Efficiency, http://www.pewfuelefficiency.org/pr_2007-07-23.html.

141 Rivera ended up spending almost a year: Don Gonyea, "Detroit industry: The murals of Diego Rivera," NPR, April 22, 2009, http://www.npr.org/templates/story/story.php?storyId=103337403.

141 *Economist* magazine referred to Ovshinsky: "The Edison of our age?" *Economist*, November 30, 2006, 33–34.

141 His latest innovation: Interview with Stanford R. Ovshinsky, March 13, 2008.

142 the F3DM, as it's called: Michael Graham Richard, "F3DM: The second, smaller plug-in hybrid by China's BYD," Treehugger.com, March 18, 2008, http://www.treehugger.com/files/2008/03/byd-f3dm-plug-in-electric-hybrid-china.php.

142 three years' wages to buy one: Marc Gunther, "Warren Buffett takes charge," *Fortune*, April 13, 2009, http://money.cnn.com/2009/04/13/technology/gunther_electric.fortune/index.htm.

142 Nissan with its Leaf: Green Car Congress, http://www.greencarcongress.com/2009/08/nissan-leaf-20090801.html.

143 The G-Wiz: Goingreen, http://www.goingreen.co.uk/store/pick_new.

143 Mitsubishi's i MiEV: Seth Fletcher, "Mitsubishi's i MiEV all-electric car goes on sale next month," Popsci.com, June 5, 2009, http://www.popsci.com/cars/article/2009-06/mitsubishi%E2%80%99s-electric-car-goes-production.

143 The Th!nk City: Th!nk, http://www.think.no/think/TH!NK-city/Buy-a-TH!NK/Price-info.

143 cost around US$20,000: Sebastian Blanco, "Think City coming to the U.S.,"

Autobloggreen, March 12, 2009, http://green.autoblog.com/2009/03/12/think-city-coming-to-the-u-s-info-overload/.

143   monthly battery rental fee: Sebastian Blanco, "Think City might cost $49,500 (U.S.) in Holland without leasing battery," Autobloggreen, March 30, 2009, http://www.autobloggreen.com/2009/03/30/think-city-might-cost-49-500-u-s-in-holland-withouth-leasin/.

143   ringing in at $109,000: Tesla Motors, http://www.teslamotors.com/performance/perf_specs.php.

143   planning a global rollout: Better Place, http://www.betterplace.com.

143   opened its first switching post: Ariel Schwartz, "Better Place unveils EV battery swap station in Japan," Fast Company, May 13, 2009, http://www.fastcompany.com/blog/ariel-schwartz/sustainability/better-place-takes-first-step-towards-electric-car-infrastructure.

143   Edison envisioned public charging points: Heather Rogers, "Current thinking," New York Times Magazine, June 3, 2007, 18.

144   the world's most efficient cars: Roland Jones, "U.S. 'stuck in reverse' on fuel economy," MSNBC.com, February 28, 2007, http://www.msnbc.msn.com/id/17344368/.

144   petrol taxes are about 60 percent: "Carmakers lean toward higher gas tax to fuel small-car sales," USA Today, January 13, 2009.

144   13 percent in federal and state tariffs: Energy Information Administration, http://www.eia.doe.gov/bookshelf/brochures/gasolinepricesprimer/.

144   burns 30 percent cleaner: Michael Kanellos, "Diesel: The next big thing in America?" Greentech Media, September 23, 2009, http://www.greentechmedia.com/articles/read/diesel-the-next-big-thing-in-america.

144   50 percent of all new vehicles in Europe: European Automobile Manufacturers' Association, http://www.acea.be/index.php/news/news_detail/trends_in_new_car_characteristics.

144   88 mpg on the freeway and 61 in the city: Ford UK, http://www.ford.co.uk/Cars/NewFiesta/NewFiestaECOnetic.

144   car can seat five: Ibid.

144   starts at about $17,500: "Americans might like these fuel-sipping cars," BusinessWeek, http://images.businessweek.com/ss/08/07/0731_europe_gas_sippers/11.htm.

144   fuel economy in the low 30s: Ben Mack, "Ford's ECOnetic Fiesta gets 65 mpg. You can't have one," Wired, February 10, 2009, http://www.wired.com/autopia/2009/02/ford-will-give/.

144   juicing up a plug-in electric with coal-fired energy: John Voelcker, "Consumer Reports questions plug-in practicality," Hybridcars.com, January 7, 2009, http://www.hybridcars.com/news/consumer-reports-questions-plug-practicality-25392.html.

144   three-quarters of its electricity from coal: Chi-Chu Tschang, "China looks to coal bed methane," BusinessWeek, January 3, 2008, http://www.business

week.com/globalbiz/content/jan2008/gb2008013_784582.htm?campaign_
id=rss_as.

144 more than half its voltage from the black stuff: U.S. Department of Energy,
http://www.energy.gov/energysources/coal.htm.

144 more than 40 percent of the world's electricity: World Coal Institute, http://
www.worldcoal.org/coal/uses-of-coal/coal-electricity/.

145 a quarter of the energy used in industry: Energy Information Administration, http://www.eia.doe.gov/oiaf/ieo/coal.html.

145 poised for a steep rise: Ibid.

145 deserted en masse after World War II: Interview with John Mogk, February
20, 2008.

CHAPTER SIX
THE PRICE OF AIR: CARBON OFFSETS

149 to plant ten thousand mango trees: Amrit Dhillon and Toby Harnden, "How
Coldplay's green hopes died in the arid soil of India," *Sunday Telegraph* (London), April 30, 2006. On exchange rate, see St. Louis Federal Reserve, http://
research.stlouisfed.org/fred2/data/EXUSUK.txt.

149 "You can dedicate more saplings": Dhillon and Harnden, "How Coldplay's
green hopes died." Also see The CarbonNeutral Company, http://www
.carbonneutral.com/casestudies/client.asp?id=880.

151 promising the farmers a small sum: Dhillon and Harnden, "How Coldplay's
green hopes died."

151 Only eight thousand trees were ever distributed: Ibid.

151 "I was promised two thousand rupees": Ibid. On exchange rate, see FX
Street, http://www.fxstreet.com/fundamental/economic-time-series/data/
fedstl/exinus.aspx.

151 the "Durban Declaration on Carbon Trading": "Climate Justice Now! The
Durban Declaration on Carbon Trading," signed in Durban, South Africa,
October 10, 2004.

152 made up for the loss elsewhere: TCNC, http://www.carbonneutral.com/
pages/Whatweinvestin.asp.

152 "The first step you can take": TerraPass, http://www.terrapass.com/.

152 "Reduce what you can": Carbonfund.org, http://carbonfund.org/.

152 reassuringly tenders "climate protection": Myclimate, http://www.mycli
mate.org/en.html.

152 "because it should be easier": TCNC, http://www.carbonneutral.com/pages/
whyweareinbusiness.asp.

153 worth $4 billion by 2010: Fiona Harvey and Stephen Fidler, "Industry caught
in carbon smokescreen," *Financial Times,* April 25, 2007.

153 three options that range in price: TCNC, http://www.carbonneutral.com/
cncalculators/flightcalculate.asp.

153 To do the same job, Myclimate charges: Myclimate, http://www.myclimate .org/nc/en/offsetting/co2-calculator/calculator.html?tx_myclimateiframe_ pi1[type]=flight.

154 could be one hundred years or more: "Life span of common urban trees," CBC News Online, August 11, 2005, http://www.cbc.ca/news/background/ environment/trees_lifespan.html.

154 CO_2 absorption is lower in saplings: Amelia Ravin and Teresa Raine, "Best practices for including carbon sinks in greenhouse gas inventories" (paper presented at 16th Annual International Emission Inventory Conference, May 14–17, 2007), 6, http://www.epa.gov/ttn/chief/conference/ei16/index.html.

154 TCNC uses both varieties: TCNC, http://www.carbonneutral.com/projects/ projects.asp?id=897.

154 "I can now say that producing this album": Natasha Courtenay-Smith, "Your Planet—Part 2," *Independent* (UK), September 20, 2005.

155 India is host to more than a quarter: United Nations Framework Convention on Climate Change, Clean Development Mechanism, http://cdm.unfccc.int/ Statistics/Registration/NumOfRegisteredProjByHostPartiesPieChart.html.

157 chaired by Anandi's father, Dr. K. S. Sharan: "Current Climate Issues," Anandi Sharan's blog, http://bloganandi.blogspot.com/2008/12/normal-0- false-false-false.html.

157 owned by Dr. Sharan's brother: Interview with Aklavya Sharan, November 13, 2008.

157 CER India Private Ltd.: Interview with Kaveri Uthaiah, November 13, 2008.

158 "Our grandfather was a lawyer": Interview with Sharan.

159 DESI gets 50 percent of its investments: "DESI to take EmPower project to 10 more locations," *Hindu,* March 18, 2008.

160 Karnataka Renewable Energy Development Ltd. liked the plan: Interview with V. P. Hiremath, KREDL Managing Director, November 10, 2008.

160 no such project had been developed: Interview with P. Sekhar, Director, MPPL, November 10, 2008.

161 "We are planning on building two more": Ibid.

161 MPPL has received money . . . from several other offset entities: Carbon Catalog, http://www.carboncatalog.org/projects/malavalli-biomass-power- plant/.

162 earn about US$1.50 per day: Interview with family in Chikke Gowda Halli, November 11, 2008.

162 When he started at MPPL: Interview with Sakash, November 11, 2008.

162 Neither did Amalendu: Interview with Amalendu, November 18, 2008.

162 the facility provides hard hats and goggles: E-mail correspondence with K. Krishan, September 19, 2009.

162 photos of the facility posted: Myclimate, http://www.myclimate.org/en/ carbon-offset-projects/international-projects/detail/mycproject/1/95.html.

163 a charge neither MPPL nor Myclimate disputes: E-mail correspondence with Dellantonio, September 15, 2009, and Krishan, September 19, 2009.

163 MPPL denied my request: Only after I asked for comment from MPPL on my findings, at which time I was no longer in India, did the company finally invite me to visit the factory.

163 "rural electricity distribution": Malavalli Power Plant Private Ltd., http://www.mpppl.com/.

163 "provides reliable energy": "A case study: Malavalli Power Plant, Mysore, India," brochure, Gold Standard, 3.

163 650 new jobs: Myclimate, http://www.myclimate.org/en/carbon-offset-projects/international-projects/detail/mycproject/1.html.

164 the firm has been "remiss": E-mail correspondence with K. Krishan, September 19, 2009.

164 Krishan says the company employs twenty workers: Ibid.

164 It's in the village of Heggur: E-mail correspondence with MPPL spokesperson, September 22, 2009.

164 slightly high but nevertheless realistic: Interview with Suresh and Puttaswamy, contractors who haul crop wastes, November 13, 2008.

165 people such as Manini: Interview with Manini in Heggur, November 11, 2008.

165 "not at all contribute to residents cutting": E-mail correspondence with Krishan, September 19, 2009. Myclimate also claims felling trees to sell as fuel isn't going on in Malavalli: e-mail correspondence with Dellantonio.

165 "ensure top quality projects": World Wildlife Fund, http://www.panda.org/what_we_do/how_we_work/businesses/business_industry/offsetting/gold_standard/.

165 GS has yet to issue its license to MPPL: E-mail correspondence with Jasmine Hyman, September 21, 2009.

166 "It's a load of rubbish": Interview with Harish Hande, November 10, 2008.

166 He's a little shy: Interview with Sukumar K., November 13, 2008.

167 only six months of payments left: Interview with Maranayaka, November 13, 2008.

168 According to SELCO: E-mail correspondence with Sarah Alexander, September 22, 2009.

169 Mahadevi, his wife, answers the front door: Interview with Mahadevi, November 13, 2008.

169 To Sukumar's chagrin: Interview with Suresh, November 13, 2008.

171 The reach of low-power energy: Interview with V. Santhakumar, December 23, 2008.

172 two new six-hundred-megawatt power stations: "Nod for 2 thermal power plants, 10 other projects," *Deccan Herald,* November 20, 2008.

172 NGOs that offer generous baseline interpretations: Interview with Hande.

173 "forcing investors in these projects to lie": Fiona Harvey, "Stumbling block that poses threat to Kyoto Protocol," *Financial Times,* February 15, 2005.

173 Climate Care partnered with a local energy consultancy: Trusha Reddy, "Blinded by the light," *New Internationalist,* July 2006, http://www.newint.org/features/2006/ 07/01/south-africa.

174 offsets that the company sold were not in fact offset: Graham Erion, Larry Lohmann, and Trusha Reddy, "The South African projects," in *Climate Change, Carbon Trading and Civil Society: Negative returns on South African investments,* ed. Patrick Bond, Rehana Dada, and Graham Erion (South Africa: University of KwaZulu-Natal Press, 2007), 76–78.

174 "It can also be concluded": *Validation Opinion for Crediting Period Renewal: 4.5 MW biomass (low density crop residues) based power generation unit of Malavalli Power Plant Pvt Ltd,* Det Norske Veritas, Report no. 2008-10565, January 26, 2009, 6.

174 "inflow of approximately US$5.73 billion": CDM India, http://cdmindia.nic .in/index.html.

175 increase production of the chemical to lure: Keith Bradsher, "Outsize profits, and questions, in effort to cut warming gases," *New York Times,* December 21, 2006.

175 "There are imperfections": Bruce Usher speaking at Columbia University Graduate School of Journalism International Journalism Seminar, June 9, 2008.

ASSESSMENT

183 "Turns out my dream": Text message from Morse Pitts, July 27, 2009.

184 generating electricity is the most CO_2-intensive: *Inventory of U.S. Greenhouse Gas Emissions and Sinks: 1990–2007,* Environmental Protection Agency, April 15, 2009, ES-8.

188 going green . . . will give companies an edge on their rivals: Paul Hawken, Amory Lovins, and L. Hunter Lovins, *Natural Capitalism: Creating the next industrial revolution* (New York: Little, Brown and Company, 1999), xiii.

188 "triple bottom line": "Q&A: John Elkington," *Fast Company,* February 11, 2008, http://www.fastcompany.com/social/2008/articles/john-elkington.html.

189 concept known as biomimicry: Hawken et al., *Natural Capitalism,* 10.

189 high levels of energy and hazardous chemicals: Ibid., 15.

189 When these devices break: Ibid., 134.

189 Consequently, profitability hinges . . . on delivering the needed service: Ibid., 78, 138.

189 "[industrial capitalism] neglects to assign any value": Ibid., 5.

189 the result is a gravely malfunctioning market: Ibid., 265.

189 Due to distortions: Ibid., 160, 262–66.

190 "cost/price integration": Paul Hawken, *Ecology of Commerce: A declaration of sustainability* (New York: HarperBusiness, 1993), 81–82.

190 When external costs are added into: Ibid., 81.

191 saving $6 in net costs: Hawken et al., *Natural Capitalism,* 258.

191 "America could shed $300 billion": Ibid., 243, emphasis in original.

191 the Jevons Paradox: Wikipedia, http://en.wikipedia.org/wiki/jevons_paradox.

191 "When the Wal-Marts of the world": Jesse Finfrock, "Q&A: Wes Jackson," *Mother Jones,* October 29, 2008, http://www.motherjones.com/environ ment/2008/10/qa-wes-jackson.

192 the question of resource scarcity: Wikipedia, http://en.wikipedia.org/wiki/ Malthusian_catastrophe.

192 Roosevelt . . . institutionalized resource and land conservation: Wikipedia, http://en.wikipedia.org/wiki/Theodore_Roosevelt.

192 "The question of the possible exhaustion": Cited in Heather Rogers, "Current Thinking," *New York Times Magazine,* June 3, 2007, 18.

192 "I'd put my money on the sun": Ibid.

192 "a change of spirit rather than": Quoted in Malcolm Gladwell, "The court-house ring," *New Yorker,* August 10 and 17, 2009, 32.

193 keeping money from seeking out carbon dioxide: Finfrock, "Q&A: Wes Jackson."

193 "We have to ask ourselves": Interview with Frank Ackerman, February 24, 2009.

194 top 20 percent of Americans: Who Rules America?, http://sociology.ucsc .edu/whorulesamerica/power/wealth.html.

NOTES ON THE POSSIBLE

195 "This was an important reason": Interview with Ari Munir, April 28, 2008.

195 This can take as long as fifteen years: JoAnn Kawell, "For an agriculture that doesn't get rid of farmers: An interview with Miguel Altieri," http://www .agroeco.org/doc/crp.html.

196 widespread human die-off from starvation: Paul R. Ehrlich, *The Population Bomb: Population control or race to oblivion?* (New York: Ballantine, 1968), 17.

196 "consumes around twenty times more": World Resources Institute, http:// earthtrends.wri.org/updates/node/236.

196 According to the Food Ethics Council: Adam Vaughan, "Elimination of food waste could lift 1bn out of hunger, say campaigners," *Guardian* (UK), September 8, 2009.

197 the primary reasons for food scarcity: "Reducing food insecurity via distributive access: Land, gender rights and food," *State of Food and Agriculture 2000,* Food and Agriculture Organization of the United Nations, 2000, http://www.fao.org/docrep/x4400e/x4400e00.HTM.

197 the problem isn't a shortage of food: Frederick Kaufman, "Let them eat cash," *Harper's,* June 2009, 51.

198 the connection between socially just practices: Miguel A. Altieri, "Agroecology: Principles and strategies for designing sustainable farming systems," electronic version, not dated, 2, http://www.agroeco.org/doc/new_docs/ Agroeco_principles.pdf.

198 "Agroecosystems are communities": Ibid.

198 productivity is markedly increased and sustains itself: Ibid.

198 productivity of organic crops can be doubled: Kawell, "For an agriculture that doesn't get rid of farmers."

198 ancient farming system, called Waru-Warus: Miguel A. Altieri and Clara I. Nicholls, *Agroecology and the Search for a Truly Sustainable Agriculture* (Mexico City: United Nations Environment Programme, 2005), 160. Also see Organization of American States, http://www.oas.org/dsd/publications/ Unit/oea59e/ch27.htm.

199 they began rebuilding the ancient croplands: Drew Benson, "Peru resurrects ancient ways of farming," *Los Angeles Times,* August 10, 2003.

199 a dramatic jump in yields: Miguel A. Altieri, "Applying agroecology to enhance the productivity of peasant farming systems in Latin America," *Environment, Development and Sustainability* 1 (1999): 206, http://www .agroeco.org/doc/LApeasantdev.pdf.

199 Waru-Warus consist of: Benson, "Peru resurrects ancient ways."

199 the reestablishment of Waru-Warus: Ibid.

199 increase farmers' livelihoods through greater social engagement: Altieri, "Applying agroecology to enhance productivity," 206–7.

199 Today the fields are derelict: Benson, "Peru resurrects ancient ways."

199 from about $100 to $500: Altieri, "Applying agroecology to enhance productivity," 207.

200 outmigration to urban slums reversed: Ibid., 204.

200 Brazil's southernmost states . . . began shifting: Ari Henrique Uriartt, Sonia Regina de Mello Pereira, and Xavier Simón, *Building participative processes: The case of the "Rede Ecovida de Acroecologia" in the Southern region of Brazil,* not dated, 15.

200 churches, trade unions, rural workers, and environmental groups: Ibid., 3.

200 Ecovida is a product of this movement: Ibid., 11.

200 network connecting fifteen hundred family farms: Ibid., 14.

200 Rio Grande do Sul has adopted: Ibid., 9–11.

200 But these growers must also adhere to a set of . . . principles: Ibid., 12.

201 Ecovida certification body grants its approval: Ibid., 17–18.

201 CNG was started by a group of farmers: Interview with Ron Khosla, June 26, 2009.

202 Tailored to unconventional farmers: Certified Naturally Grown, http://www .naturallygrown.org/requirements.html.

202 The co-op's network of farmers: Organic Valley, http://www.organicvalley .coop/newsroom/press-releases/details/article/california-hens-welcomed- to-organic-valley-brood.

202 management and member farmers have equal say: Organic Valley website, http://www.organicvalley.coop/our-story/our-cooperative/.

202 Organic Valley canceled shipments to Wal-Mart: Kermit Pattison, "Wal-Mart loved Organic Valley's milk, so why cut off the flow?" *Inc.,* July 1, 2007, http://www.inc.com/magazine/20070701/casestudy.html.

202 Organic Valley ditched the deal: Jim Hightower and Susan Demarco, "How to swim against the current," *Nation,* March 6, 2008, http://www.thenation.com/doc/20080324/hightower_demarco.

202 the Cornucopia Institute busted the company: "Organic Valley halts milk purchases with Texas dairy," press release, July 17, 2008, http://www.commondreams.org/news2008/0717-02.htm.

203 "The farmers who own the co-op": "Farmers at Organic Valley assert control to maintain high ethics standards at co-op," press release, June 19, 2008, http://www.commondreams.org/news2008/0619-17.htm.

204 $2 million more for a locally owned abattoir: Bonnie Azab Powell, "This little piggy goes home," *Mother Jones,* March/April 2009, 39.

206 a documentary featuring the philosopher Slavoj Zizek: *Examined Life: Philosophy is in the street,* Astra Taylor, director, 2009.

AFTERWORD

210 "explains how everyone can take part": Michael Albert and Robin Hahnel, *The Political Economy of Participatory Economics* (Princeton, NJ: Princeton University Press, 1991), 40–42, 62–71.

211 "We would make our decisions using far fuller information": Ibid., 60–61, 91.

212 "the workplace would change in other ways": Ibid., 25–31.

212 "If a worker wanted to earn more money": Ibid., 50–54.

213 "One of Ostrom's findings": Xavier Basurto and Elinor Ostrom, "Beyond the Tragedy of the Commons," *Economia Delle Fonti di Energia e dell'Ambiente,* October 1, 2009 (52: 1), 35–60.

214 "she wishes there were neighborhood governments": Interview with Elinor Ostrom, March 10, 2012.

215 "a radio interview with Hahnel": "What Is Occupy Wall Street?" *Planet Money,* NPR, October 7, 2011 http://www.npr.org/blogs/money/2011/10/07/141158199/the-friday-podcast-what-is-occupy-wall-street.

215 "Markets are sensitive only to benefits or costs": Neva Goodwin, "The Limitations of Markets: Background Essay" (Medford, MA: Global Development and Environment Institute, 2005), 3.

215 "the paper considers the cost of air pollution on a human life": Nicholas Muller, Robert Mendelsohn, and William Nordhaus, "Environmental Accounting for Pollution: Methods with an Application to the United States Economy," May 26, 2009.

216 "a radio interview with Mendelsohn": "Will Economic Growth Destroy the Planet?" *Planet Money,* NPR, October 25, 2011 http://www.npr.org/blogs/money/2011/10/25/141701559/the-tuesday-podcastwill-economic-growth-destroy-the-planet.

216 "In theory you can find these kinds of prices": Interview with Neva Goodwin, March 28, 2012.

217 "the authors outline policies, structures, and specific prescriptions": Herman
    E. Daly and John B. Cobb, Jr., *For the Common Good: Redirecting the Econ-*
    omy Toward Community, the Environment and a Sustainable Future (Boston:
    Beacon, 1989), 268.

217 "Each year we would, as a country, decide what percentage of non-renewable
    resources": Ibid., 259–60.

217 "enforced by import permits and export tariffs": Ibid., 230.

217 "The authors call for *balanced* trade as opposed to free trade": Ibid., 229–35.

218 "we should vacate much of the country's land": Ibid., 253–58.

220 "new society that shuns the market": Joel Kovel, *The Enemy of Nature: The*
    End of Capitalism or the End of the World? (London, New York: Zed Publish-
    ing, 2002, 2007), 243–45.

220 "Ecosocialist society is defined by *being*" (emphasis in original): Ibid., 270.

Index